MW01107480

SECRETS OF COMPETITIVE BIDDING

Strategies For Finding And Winning Million Dollar Contracts

GENE GAROFALO

PRENTICE HALL
Englewood Cliffs, New Jersey 07632

Prentice-Hall International (UK) Limited, *London*
Prentice-Hall of Australia Pty. Limited, *Sydney*
Prentice-Hall Canada, Inc., *Toronto*
Prentice-Hall Hispanoamericana, S.A., *Mexico*
Prentice-Hall of India Private Limited, *New Delhi*
Prentice-Hall of Japan, Inc., *Tokyo*
Simon & Schuster Asia Pte. Ltd., *Singapore*
Editora Prentice-Hall do Brasil, Ltda., *Rio de Janeiro*

© 1990 *by*

PRENTICE HALL

Englewood Cliffs, NJ

10   9   8   7   6   5   4   3   2   1

Library of Congress Cataloging-in-Publication Data

Garofalo, Gene.
    Secrets of competitive bidding : strategies for finding and
winning million dollar contracts / by Gene Garofalo.
        p.   cm.
    ISBN 0-13-797093-5 : $59.95
    1. Contracts, Letting of--United States.   I. Title.
HD2365.G37   1990
658.7'23--dc20   89-26484
                                                                        CIP

ISBN 0-13-797093-5

PRENTICE HALL
BUSINESS & PROFESSIONAL DIVISION
A division of Simon & Schuster
Englewood Cliffs, New Jersey 07632

Printed in the United States of America

To the Old Gang

Adrienne, Bryce, Kelly,
Paul, Peter and Victor

Those were the days my friends . . .

PREFACE

Competitive bidding is a turbo-charged boost to increased sales volume. It's a fast-track method for putting better numbers on the board even if your company has thin marketing and limited resources. A company can double, even triple, sales volume once it learns the strategies used by the companies which have mastered the art of competitive bidding. Six- and seven-figure contracts are often awarded by the government agencies, schools, and private companies which use the bid process to choose vendors. Even eight-figure orders are not uncommon, and an occasional nine-figure deal is landed by companies which thoroughly understand the competitive bid process.

Some of these contracts can be headed toward your company. This book can help you win big awards whether you're a newcomer who doesn't know what a bid solicitation looks like or an old pro who's been actively pursuing bid contracts for years. For the newcomer, this book will guide you through the process and show you what you need to know to go after bid business. For the experienced bidder it offers the proven tactics and strategies a few companies have used to land big contract after big contract.

Don't think you can't participate if your company is small. Bidding is a high-stakes game with huge pots for the winner, but anybody can sit in. A hole-in-the-wall outfit with few resources and no outside sales force can walk away with a million dollar contract in a single afternoon. Large size is not necessarily an advantage when bidding. In fact, smaller companies are often given an advantage when bidding against larger competitors.

This book begins by telling you exactly where to find the significant bid markets. It lists the names, addresses, phone numbers, and personal contacts for most of the largest federal, state, and local government agencies which use the bid process to award billions of dollars in contracts every year. It gives you the names and contacts at the big school districts which buy millions in goods and services through competitive bidding. It identifies the private companies who historically use competitive bidding to select vendors. Finally, this book tells you how you can find additional bidding opportunities on your own and points to other resources, such as bid information services, that you can access. This material alone is an important database for anyone interested in competitive bidding.

Knowing where the bidding opportunities are and being allowed to bid are two different things—in many instances only approved vendors are permitted to submit bids. We outline shortcuts for getting your company's name and products on acceptable vendor lists fast. You won't miss any more big bid opportunities because your company or product wasn't properly qualified. With our methods you can be receiving many bid solicitations every week. One chapter deals with the "razors" and "scissors" needed to cut through bureaucratic red tape.

Once you're on the approved vendor list and a bid solicitation is in your hands, you need to know what the bid process is all about. Bidding is a complex procedure that demands a thorough knowledge of the rules. This book not only gives you the rules, it also tells you which ones you must keep and *which are a good idea to break.*

You'll learn how to read a bid solicitation—why it's a mistake to ignore the fine print and the importance of fully understanding the specifications. This book outlines procedures for getting the specifications changed if your product can't meet them. It shows why the product you elect to bid is every bit a vital part of bid strategy as the price you quote. And the nitty-gritty details have not been overlooked. When you're ready to actually complete a bid request, a step-by-step procedure will show you how to prepare it correctly. Worksheets and checklists are included to help you submit bids that won't be rejected because the proper materials, bonds, or displays weren't included. We explain the difference between bid and performance bonds, when each is necessary and what to do if one or the other is required and you can't get it.

But this book goes far beyond the basics. It is much more than a primer for beginners. The meat of the material is devoted to proven tactics and strategies that can win million dollar contracts for your company. It tells you not only how to win big bids, but also how you can pick and choose those that are the most profitable. It shows how to develop the fine art of *specmanship*, encouraging an agency to insist on features that almost guarantee a winning bid by your company. You'll learn how to milk a bid once it's been awarded. You'll learn about "phantom discounts" and how they seem to offer a lower price when they really ensure higher profits. You'll find out how to win contracts even when your competitor has submitted a lower bid and how to successfully protest a bid awarded to another company. How to develop an intelligence system that will provide you with the product models and exact bidding price of your competitors is discussed. And, you'll learn to use an old poker trick, not allowed in many friendly games, "sandbagging," to lull your competitors into a false sense of security.

Many of these secrets are revealed through case studies of companies which are masters at competitive bidding. The examples these old pros offer provide valuable lessons about winning bid strategies. The methods they've honed and refined can be copied by others who are willing to learn. One company you'll study went from zero dollars in sales to over one hundred million dollars annually in a period of little more than twenty years. Almost all its business is obtained through competitive bidding.

You'll study the tactics used by a small business which fought off all competitors to keep a multi-million dollar state contract, awarded annually, for fourteen consecutive years. You'll learn the inside story of how one company's intelligence system assembled the information that allowed it to win a three-million–dollar contract by a single penny. We'll dissect a successful bid protest, studying the actions of the protesting company, the countertactics of the apparent successful bidder, and the viewpoint of the powerful state agency whose award was first questioned then set aside.

The strategies used in these case histories are real. They win important bids. The important points are summarized to provide guidelines for every business interested in competitive bidding.

Competitive bidding has been compared to a stud poker game where the opponent's hole cards are always concealed. *The Secrets of Competitive Bidding* turns these cards face up. Whether you're a beginner who has never submitted a competitive bid or a sophisticated contender with many years in the arena, this book has many things to offer. Your company can be the one that lands the next multi-million–dollar contract.

TABLE OF CONTENTS

CHAPTER 3   HOW TO WIN FEDERAL
GOVERNMENT CONTRACT BID CONTRACTS   37

1

WHERE TO FIND BID CONTRACT OPPORTUNITIES

SALES OPPORTUNITIES OFFERED BY COMPETITIVE BIDDING

Competitive bidding is a quick way for small companies to reach seven-figure sales revenues. The companies which go after competitive bids can get substantial orders with almost no outside sales force, limited marketing budgets, and few other resources. The market is easy to reach because the identities of the buyers which use competitive bidding to award vendor contracts are generally well known. It's simple to attack because everyone starts out on a level playing field. Contracts go to the outfit with the sharpest pencil. The size of the company doesn't matter. In fact, a small company often has a competitive advantage over a large corporation in a bidding situation.

Contracts awarded through the bid process are often worth millions to the successful bidder. You don't have to be in Washington, D.C. or a state capitol to participate in competitive bidding. There are opportunities in every state, every county, and every city in this country. Every school district uses the bid process. Even a number of commercial companies prefer to use bidding to award contracts. It's a competi-

1

tive game that is widespread, and it's a game that any company can play.

One of the most fascinating aspects of bidding is that the winners of these lucrative contracts are decided in a single afternoon when the bids are opened. One day a company might be struggling along with barely enough sales to keep the doors open; the next day they could be the holders of a contract capable of revitalizing the company.

The bid process is simple, yet many businesses and salespeople don't know much about it. They don't know how to get on bid lists, they don't know where to get information about pending bids, they're lost when it comes to preparing bids, and they're intimidated by what they regard as endless bureaucratic red tape when submitting bids.

The purpose of this book is to tell you everything you need to know about competitive bidding, to show you where the bidding opportunities are, to tell you how to get on bid lists, to teach you how to prepare bids, and to give you strategies on how to win them.

WHO USES COMPETITIVE BIDDING TO AWARD CONTRACTS

Most government agencies are required by law to use competitive bidding when they want to buy something. Unlike private companies which can purchase goods from anyone they please, government agencies must buy from the companies offering the products and services they need at the best price. The agencies write a set of specifications that must be met by bidders and may require fulfillment of additional conditions, but vendors are selected on the basis of the low bid that meets the specs. Often, both small and million-dollar contracts are awarded in this manner. Because the stakes are so high, competition is usually fierce. There are big-dollar–volume contracts to be won through competitive bidding, but these contracts don't normally carry standard profit margins. So, the first requisite for successful bidding is to carry a sharp pencil.

Competitive bidding is used by government agencies and educational institutions when the goods and services they require will exceed a certain dollar figure. The exact amount varies by locality. Organizations which traditionally use the bid process include:

- The federal government
- State governments
- County governments

- Municipal governments
- Educational institutions
- Private companies whose business is heavily involved in government sales, such as defense contractors
- Some sectors of private industry

HOW THE BID PROCESS WORKS

The various government agencies and educational institutions have different methods and procedures when requesting competitive bids. Although they often follow different regulations, the bid process itself is remarkably similar everywhere. Here's how it works:

1. The agency requiring the product or service will draw up a list of specifications. These specifications will detail equipment tolerances and features or service standards. Equipment specs usually include such things as size, weight, speed of operation, capacity, and functional features.

2. The agency's purchasing department will send out a document called a *Request For Quotation* (RFQ) to all vendors on their bid lists. In addition to the specifications the RFQ will list the quantity of product needed, the delivery dates required, installation, and warranty support materials. Several pages of boilerplate legal mumbo jumbo is also likely to be included.

3. The RFQ will contain a due date. All bids must be received by a certain date and time.

4. One minute after the due date and time, the bidding closes. The agency opens all bids and the prices quoted by each vendors is normally made public. (Sometimes this information is not released immediately. However, it is unusual for an agency to seal bid results indefinitely.)

5. The agency inspects the bids. The company bidding a product that meets all the specifications at the lowest price gets the business.

That's all there is to it. If your company has the lowest bid meeting all specifications *and can prove it can do the job,* you have a contract. (Obviously, if you're a cement contractor you're not going to get a government contract building nuclear missiles no matter what you bid.)

WHERE TO FIND BIDS

There are many ways to find out about bidding opportunities. They're all around you. Here are some of the most common.

Newspapers. Many government agencies are required by law to advertise their bidding opportunities. Look at the "Legal Notices" in the classified section of the newspaper for a list of these opportunities.

Purchasing offices of government agencies. Federal, state, and local government agencies are usually located in buildings that are open to the public. This means that access is available to anyone who wishes to enter these facilities. For example, every good size city has a federal office building, usually located downtown. Procurement officers and buyers at these agencies will see vendors during normal business hours. Of course, appointments will keep you from cooling your heels in an outer office while the procurement officer finds the time to see you. The bulletin boards of government agency purchasing offices are posted with current bidding opportunities. It's a good idea to look over these bulletin boards at least twice a month for any bids which may be of interest. When there is a bid that looks promising, get the bid number, call the purchasing office, and request a copy. Better yet, pick one up personally. At the same time ask the purchasing agent to be put on the bid list for that category of product.

Bidding information services. There are bid-alert services that put out newsletters listing hundreds of new bid opportunities every month. They deliver information on bids for the kind of product or service you sell. The cost for these services is reasonable if your company is seriously interested in entering the competitive bid arena. Here's where to get cost and other information on one such service:

BidNet
5 Choke Cherry Road
Rockville, MD 20850-4030
1-800-325-6871

Registry services. There are services that list your product or service in a directory that they send to purchasing agents. In this instance, the agency is finding out about your company when they consult the registry. Naturally, your company pays a fee to the registry service for the listing. These government buying directories are really "Yellow Pages" aimed specifically at government purchasing offices. Some government agency purchasing agents use them, others do not. Several registry services put supplier lists on microfilm, microfiche, or floppy disk to make the look-up job easier for the purchasing agents who use them. Usually these companies do not charge a fee to suppliers for listing. Instead, they charge the government offices which use the listing services. The largest of these companies are:

> Information Handling Services
> 15 Inverness Way East
> Englewood, Colorado 80150
> 1-800-525-7053

> National Standards Association, Inc.
> 5161 River Road
> Bethesda, Maryland 20816
> 301-951-1389

> Information Marketing International
> 13271 Northend Street
> Oak Park, Michigan 48237
> 313-546-6706
> (Subsidary Ziff-Davis Information Company)

HOW TO SET UP A BID INTELLIGENCE NETWORK

Using outside services to learn about pending bids can be a valuable resource, but nothing beats learning about bids first hand. When a bid-alert service tells your company about a bid, they're informing every other subscriber in their network at the same time. You learn about the opportunity, but so does everyone else. Your company has lost any chance of working with the agency requiring the product or service to help shape the specifications to your product.

The best chance to win bids comes when you've learned about the opportunity early, even before the specifications have been defined. How can you find out about bids before they're announced to the general public? It's really simple if you remember the very first rule of competitive bidding: **EVEN THOUGH A GOVERNMENT AGENCY USES THE COMPETITIVE BID PROCESS TO AWARD CONTRACTS, THE BASIC RULES OF SALESMANSHIP STILL APPLY.**

For those who need it, here's a short refresher course on the basic rules of salesmanship:

1. Call on potential users.
2. Find the need.

3. Demonstrate the product.
4. Talk about the benefits.
5. Close the sale.

That's the process most companies follow when calling on commercial accounts, and it's the process that should be used when calling on accounts which use competitive bidding to decide vendors. This process won't guarantee a sale, but it will give your company an edge. Here's the kind of specific sales effort to use with agencies that use the bid process:

THE FOUR BASIC RULES OF BID SELLING

1. Call on the agencies that may have a use for your product. These calls begin at the purchasing department. Find out the name of the buyer who specializes in purchasing what your company has to offer. You shouldn't have any trouble getting an audience. Buyers are interested in getting the product or service at the best price from a reliable supplier.

2. Prove to the buyer that you are a reliable supplier. Provide references—those companies who are buying your product and like it. If some of these users fall within the public sector, so much the better.

3. Ask to speak with the actual end users within the agency. In most cases, the end users within the agency will help the buyer write the specifications. The people using the product know what they want that product to do.

4. Show the end users a product benefit or feature that your competitors can't offer. This feature may be included in the next bid specification. Once the specs are written around your product, the bid is much easier to win.

One of the important advantages of calling on the agency buyers consistently is that they get to know you. They're more comfortable when you win bids. They won't put any roadblocks in the way of the bid award. They may also be in a position to give you small orders that aren't large enough to require the bid process. The greatest advantage is that they'll let you know when a big bid is pending. If your company has proven to be a reliable supplier, they'll want you to bid on big contracts. They may even want you to win.

Other sources for information concerning competitive bids are companies in allied, but not competitive fields. When you learn about a bid for a product your company can't supply, contact those you know who can supply it and give them the information. Ask them to reciprocate with like information when they have it. If you do this on a consistent basis, you soon will have established a bid intelligence network which consistently informs you of pending bids.

Dealers, manufacturer's reps, and distributors of your company's product are also good sources for information on pending bids. You can count on cooperation from other distribution networks if you bid through them whenever possible, allowing them to profit on successful bids. In many cases you must "educate" your dealers and the others on the advantages of calling on government agencies to solicit bids.

NINE WAYS TO LEARN ABOUT BIDDING OPPORTUNITIES

The following list summarizes where and how to learn about bidding opportunities:

• Make frequent calls on the purchasing agents for government agencies.

• Always read the bulletin boards or bid announcement sheets when in a government office.

• Check local and national newspapers for bid announcements.

• Use bid-alert services for information about pending bids.

• Buy space with government supplier registry services so the buyers know about your company.

• Get on every government bid list you can.

• Check with the actual users of your product or service to learn what their requirements are likely to be. Try to shape these requirements so they fit your product offerings.

• Establish working relationships with other companies active in the bid marketplace so there's an interchange of information about current bids.

• Use your company's dealers, manufacturer's reps, distributors, and direct salespeople to bird-dog bids for you.

HOW TO DEVELOP A "NOSE" FOR REALLY BIG BIDS BEFORE THEY BECOME COMMON KNOWLEDGE

The more advance knowledge you have about a bid, the better you're able to prepare for it. Having advance knowledge about the really big bids, the blockbusters, gives your company a better chance to win them.

How can you find out in advance whether an agency may be contemplating a big purchase of the kind of product your company offers? Here are several ways you can get a step-up on your competitors:

- With the government, everything depends on funding. Find out whether the agency has appropriated money for a project or has funds in the budget that would allow it to make a big purchase. The person heading the planned project will know whether the funds are already appropriated, or whether approval is still needed. If the grant application hasn't been completed yet, there may be a long wait.

- Learn about the various funding programs available for your company's type of product. You can obtain this information from your knowledgeable contacts in local government and pass it along to those who don't know the ropes. One resource you can use is the local Board of Education. It will usually have a Special Projects section that keeps a listing of all federal, state, and local grants. Someone there may even offer assistance on how to apply. Helping a local agency acquire funds is a great way to get an inside track on a pending bid.

- Work with friends and contacts in allied fields to exchange information related to pending bids. For example, if your company makes office equipment you're probably calling on the same buyers who send out bids for office furniture, supplies, and other items your firm doesn't carry. When you learn about a bid situation in a product category your company doesn't handle, pass it along to business associates who do. Ask them to reciprocate when they can. This kind of networking has the effect of increasing your presence in the field. Other pairs of eyes and ears will be gathering information for you.

- Discuss needs with local agencies. Some salespeople only turn up at government agencies *after* they learn about a pending bid. Those who call on a regular basis learn about any agency plans to upgrade equipment or systems. Always find out what the agency staffing plans are. An agency adding bodies often requires equipment as well. This information can be obtained in scuttlebut conversation over a cup of coffee with an agency employee. The bulletin boards are another resource. Most agencies are required by law to post new job listings on their bulletin boards.

- Maintain contact with purchasing agents and buyers. They'll be aware of pending requirements before bid requests are actually sent out to potential buyers.

WHAT A COMPETITIVE BID LOOKS LIKE

Every competitive bid has certain standard features. These features are:

- The date the bid comes out, or date of issue.
- A bid number.
- The date and time the bid is due.
- The place where the bid must be sent or delivered.
- The kind of product or service being bid.
- A list of specifications for that product or service.
- The date or dates the product must be delivered.
- The place or places where the goods or services must be delivered.
- The penalties for failure to perform.
- The quantity the agency expects to buy, the time period the contract will be in force, or both. (There will also probably be a disclaimer stating that they really don't have to buy that quantity if things don't work out.)
- The warranty requirements on the contract. (Sometimes the warranty period is left up to the individual bidder and becomes a point of consideration for the contract award.)
- Several pages of boilerplate legal paragraphs outlining the vendor's and agency's responsibilities under the contract. Usually included will be a statement to the effect that the agency can arbitrarily select any bid they choose. (They really can't. This will be discussed at length in Chapter 8.)
- Requests for product literature or other material that verifies the specification claims the vendor makes for the equipment.

Exhibits 1 and 2 show examples of a competitive bid.
The following stipulations are listed on a great many bids, but are not seen on *all* bid requests.

- Requirements for bid bonds or performance bonds.

EXHIBIT 1

WHITTIER UNION HIGH SCHOOL DISTRICT

9401 South Painter Avenue
Whittier, California 90605

698-8121

REQUEST FOR BIDS

THIS IS NOT AN ORDER

Show your firm name in this space.

BID OPENING DATE December 4, 1984   Read instructions on back before bidding.

ITEM OR CODE NO.	DESCRIPTION	UNIT	QUANTITY	BRAND OR TRADE No.	NET UNIT PRICE	NET TOTAL PRICE
	BID NO.					PAGE
	8485-509G					1
	BIDDER MUST NOT WRITE IN THESE COLUMNS			BIDDER USE THESE COLUMNS		
1.	Typewriter, electronic Facit 8001 or equal	ea	235			

Typewriter to be in accordance
with the following specifications:

General:

    Machine must be of sturdy construction.
    Must have high quality components.
    Must have component changeability versus
      board changing only.
    Must have hard wiring versus paper tape
      wiring.
    Must have good high quality power supply
      and adequate fuses and a metal heat
      sink to protect from power surge.
    Must be quiet, and easy to understand
      and to operate.
    Must be able to supply repair and
      parts manual.
    Must be able to provide repair training
      for our technicians.

Specifications:

  (a)   Paper Width, 15 3/8" or 19¼"
  (b)   Writing Line, 13" or 17"
  (c)   Keyboard Height, 56mm
        (from desk surface to middle row)
  (d)   No. of char. on print wheel, 105
        (Multi-Language)
  (e)   Pitches, 10, 12, 15, PS
  (f)   Sound Level (in decibels),
        below 60 dB
  (g)   Line Memory, 330 char.
        (more than one line)
  (h)   Multi-Format Memory (3)
  (i)   Auto. Relocate (code & tab)
  (j)   Auto. Centering

(Continued)

No. 1-4

10

EXHIBIT 1 (Continued)

REQUEST FOR BIDS

THIS IS NOT AN ORDER

Show your firm name in this space.

BID OPENING DATE December 4, 1984   Read instructions on back before bidding.

BID NO.	PAGE
8485-509G	2

ITEM OR CODE NO.	DESCRIPTION	UNIT	QUANTITY	BRAND OR TRADE No.	NET UNIT PRICE	NET TOTAL PRICE
	BIDDER MUST NOT WRITE IN THESE COLUMNS			BIDDER USE THESE COLUMNS		
	CONT:					
1.	Typewriter, electronic Facit 8001 or equal					
	Specifications:					
	(k) Auto. Bold Typing (l) Two-tone Facit colors (m) Electronic Indicator, instead of levers for various functions (n) Half-Spacing: horiz. & vert. (o) Auto. Paper Injection (p) Automatic Carrier Return (q) Auto. Decimal Tabulation (r) Auto. Underlining (s) Word-By-Word Back Space (t) Express Return					
	Warranty (Months):					
	Basic Equipment _____					
	Parts _____					
	Labor _____					
	Delivery Time:					
	Delivery time required to deliver and install after notification of successful bid.					
	District would like to know if price can be held					
	1. One year _____					
	2. Six months _____					
	3. Not at all _____					

No. 8.8

11

EXHIBIT 1 (Continued)

GENERAL INSTRUCTIONS

1. In order to preserve uniformity and to facilitate the award of contracts, no bids will be entertained or considered unless made upon forms furnished by the Whittier Union High School District.

2. Bidders must bid separately upon each item. The Board of Trustees may accept from any firm a bid on one or more items and reject the bid or bids on other items.

3. All prices or notations must be typed or written in ink. Bids written with pencil will not be accepted. Mistakes must be corrected with ink and correction inserted; correction must be initialed in ink by person signing the proposal.

4. All proposals must be signed by a responsible officer or employee. Obligations assumed by such signatures must be fulfilled.

5. Any Federal or State tax payable on articles furnished by the successful bidder hereunder which may be legally added to the price bid, and from the payment of which said Whittier Union High School District is not exempt, will be paid by the district.

6. The use of the name of a manufacturer or any special brand or make, in describing any item in the schedule, does not restrict bidders to that manufacturer or specific article, this means is used simply to indicate the quality and utility of the article desired; but the goods on which proposals are submitted must in all cases be equal in quality and utility or particular to those referred to.

7. The make and grade of the article on which a bid is submitted must be stated in the proposal and, where requested, a sample thereof shall be submitted.

8. The District reserves the right to reject any and all bids or any or all items on any bid.

9. Unless definitely specified, prices quoted herein shall not include California State sales tax or use tax.

II. PERFORMANCE

1. The successful bidder shall be required to enter into the contract resulting from call for bids and this proposal.

2. No contact awarded under this proposal shall be assigned except with the approval of the Whittier Union High School District.

3. The articles in this schedule must be delivered in quantities specified on purchase orders duly signed by the Authorized Agent, unless otherwise specified herein to the Whittier, Union High School District Warehouse, 9401 S. Painter Ave., Whittier, California 90605, or any school of the Whittier Union High School District of Los Angeles County as specified on said purchase order or orders. Vendors will quote prices F.O.B. Whittier.

4. Invoices shall be furnished in triplicate by the contractor and shall be mailed to the Accounting Office of the Whittier Union High School District, 9401 S. Painter Ave., Whittier, California 90605.

5. The contractor must save, keep, bear harmless and fully indemnify said district and any of its officers or agents from all damages or claims for damages, costs or expenses in law or equity that may at any time arise or be set up for any infringement of the patent rights whatsoever, on account of use by the manufacturer, publisher or author of any copyrighted or uncopyrighted composition, secret process, patented or unpatented invention, article or appliance to be supplied under this proposal, copyright or trademark of any person or persons in consequence of the use of said district or by any of its officers or agents of articles to be supplied under this proposal.

6. All costs for containers shall be borne by the contractor.

7. All products shall conform to the provisions set forth in the Federal, County, State and City Laws for their production, handling processing, and labeling. Packages shall be so constructed as to insure safe transportation to point of delivery.

III. PENALTIES

1. When any contractor shall deliver any aricle which does not conform to the specifications, the Whittier Union High School District may, at its option, annul and set aside the contract entered into with said contractor, either in whole or part, and make and enter into a new contract in accordance with law for furnishing such article or articles so agreed to be furnished. Any additional cost or expense incurred by the said district in the making of such contract and additional cost of supplying any articles by reason of the failure of the contractor, as above stated, shall be paid by such contractor and his sureties.

2. When a contractor fails to deliver any item on or before the date specified for delivery as established in the call for bids, this proposal and the resultant contract, the District may, at its option, cancel such items from the contract and purchase such items in an expedient manner satisfactory to the District. Any additional cost and expense incurred by the District in such purchase shall be paid by the contractor and his sureties.

3. When a sample is taken from a shipment and sent to a public testing laboratory for test, and the test shows that the sample does not comply with the specifications, the cost of such test will be borne by the contractor, and the shipment will be rejected if replacement is not made at once.

4. The Authorized Agent of the Board of Trustees shall reject any and all materials which, in his opinion, are not in strict compliance and conformity with the requirements of the specifications: and all articles so rejected shall be removed promptly from the premises of the District with cost borne by the contractor.

5. The District reserves the right to cancel any portion of this contract for cause when, in the judgment of the Whittier Union High School District Board of Trustees, such cancellation is to the benefit of the School District.

EXHIBIT 2

GENERAL CONDITIONS

1. Statement of Policy

    The bidder is advised that the District Purchasing Policy regarding Bidding and Delivery for the 1984-85 supplies is:

    A. Delivery is expected within _____3-1/2_____ weeks after receipt of Purchase Order by successful bidder.

    B. Purchase Orders will be issued on or before the _____2nd_____ working day following the bid opening date.

    C. The successful bidder, upon receipt of Purchase Order in response to his quotations as outlined in A, B, and C above, who fails to comply with these provisions is subject to conditions stated on reverse side of the REQUEST FOR BIDS form. (See III Penalties, Item 2)

2. Schedule for this bid is:

    A. Mail Bid _____November 20, 1984_____

    B. Open bid 2:00 P.M. _____December 4, 1984_____

    C. Mail Purchase Order _____December 6, 1984_____

    D. Delivery complete _____January 3, 1985_____

3. Please review General Instructions enclosed herewith and note, especially, the following:

    A. General Instructions No. 3: Reference ink and/or typing, and changes.

    B. Performance No. 3: Reference delivery, quantities, packaging, and F. O. B. Whittier.

    C. Penalties No. 1 and No. 2: Reference conformity with specifications and delivery before date specified.

4. Do not change units as specified.

5. Unit prices must reflect units as specified.

6. Each item must be packaged and/or labeled with corresponding item number as shown on the purchase order. Packing box shall show purchase order number.

7. If not bidding as specified, submit brochure or catalog describing item bid.

8. Samples shall be submitted upon request.

9. It is the District's intention to make payment only after receipt of all items listed on each purchase order. However, it is realized that it may be necessary to make a payment for some materials received prior to completion of the vendor's obligation. To this end the District may respond favorably to a vendor's request for a partial payment if the circumstances warrant such consideration.

13

EXHIBIT 2 (Continued)

BID 8485-509G

WHITTIER UNION HIGH SCHOOL DISTRICT
Whittier, California

BID AGREEMENT

Bids will be received until 2:00 p.m., on _____December 4, 1984_____ in the office of
the Director, Business Services of the Whittier Union High School District, 9401 South Painter Avenue
Whittier, California 90605. All bids must be submitted upon forms furnished by the Whittier Union High School
District.

If the bidder cannot supply the materials in accordance with the dates set below, he must so advise the
District.

Purchase Orders will be mailed _____December 6, 1984_____
and delivery of material must be complete _____January 3, 1985_____

That which follows is your official agreement with the District, and as such, must be signed and presented to
the District with your bid.

Board of Trustees
Whittier Union High School District
9401 South Painter District
Whittier, CA 90605

Gentlemen:

By the submission of this bid the bidder certifies that the bid has been arrived at by the bidder independently
and has been submitted without collusion with any other vendor of materials, supplies, or equipment of the
type described in the invitation for bids.

The bidder has checked carefully all the figures and understands that the District will not be responsible for
any errors or omissions.

The Undersigned hereby agrees that this bid may not be withdrawn for a period of thirty (30) days after the
date set for the opening thereof.

The bidder agrees to furnish _____Business Machines - Electronic Typewriters_____ as listed on the attached
pages in strict conformity with the specifications which are attached to and made a part of this document for
the following consideration:

Sub Total $ _____

                                                    _____
                                                    Vendor

Plus 6½% Sales Tax $ _____

                                                    _____
                                                    Address

Total Amount of Bid $ _____

                                                    _____
                                                    City   State   Zip Code

Terms of Sale _____

                                                    _____
                                                    Signature of Authorized Agent

_____   _____
Telephone Number   Date   _____
                                          Title

14

- Requests for spare parts and service prices that are not part of the bid itself, but a consideration in the bid award. Parts and service manuals may also be required. (Many agencies handle their own service. In this case there could a request for the cost of training service personnel.)
- Requests for references and names of users. (To avoid being guinea pigs for untested products, many agencies require a certain number of successful installations before they will accept a product.)
- Requests for the results of successful testing, such as Buyer's Laboratory reports.
- Requests for product demonstrations or samples before any final award.
- Requests for tours of vendors' facilities to determine bidders' ability to perform.

These features will be found on simple bid requests. Proposal requests for complicated systems can run to hundreds, and even thousands of pages. The responses can be longer than encyclopedias. This book won't address those kinds of bid proposals. They are for sophisticated suppliers of government-required goods and services. This text will cover the simple requests for products or services that are awarded to vendors every work day of the year.

WHAT HAPPENS TO YOUR BID

What happens after a bid is submitted? The following is a fairly standard procedure followed by the purchasing offices of most agencies.

1. The bid is date stamped. Bids must be received by the deadline specified on the request for bid. Any bid that is late, even by one minute, is disqualified. Many neophyte bidders don't fully understand this requirement. Get the bid in on time!

2. After the deadline all bids are collected. In many cases they're opened immediately. Sometimes the prices bid are announced to any bidders who care to wait in the bid room. In other instances, the prices are posted later. The point here is that competitive bidding is supposed to be public so there's no chance for favoritism or hanky-panky.

3. The bids are reviewed for completeness. If a bid bond or deposit was required, was this document included? Is the bid signed in all the right places? Many bids are disqualified only because they were not made out properly.

4. The low product bid is reviewed against the enclosed brochures to determine whether all the specification requirements are met. (The purchasing department doesn't rely entirely on a company's advertising literature to verify specifications. If they aren't familiar with a product, they'll usually call for a demonstration of features to the agency's end users. Competitors can be depended upon to protest potential bid awards to products that don't meet specifications.)

5. The company submitting the lowest bid is reviewed on its ability to perform. This could include a visit to the company's facilities, conversations with other users, and gathering information about the company's reputation.

6. If everything regarding the product and the company checks out, the lowest bidder is *usually* given the contract. (Occasionally an agency will try to circumvent its own rules in an effort to play favorites, but there are ways to fight against this.)

Does the procedure for awarding bids sound simple? That's because the bid competitive bid process really is simple. It is designed to give government agencies at all levels the benefit of the lowest possible pricing while opening opportunities for every company that wants to do business with these agencies. For those who are willing to learn some fairly basic rules, the process can be very rewarding.

2

TAKING A SEAT AT THE HIGH-STAKES BIDDING GAME

A FAST, INEXPENSIVE METHOD FOR GETTING YOUR COMPANY ON 500 (OR MORE) BID LISTS

The more bid lists your company is on, the more bid solicitations you'll receive. The more bids you respond to, the greater your chances of winning. There's a very simple way to get your company's name on the bidders' list for any number of agencies. Here's how to do it:

1. Get a list of the state, county, and local government agencies and school districts in the area you want to cover. This information is available in most public libraries. One company maintains a list of counties, municipalities, townships, special districts, and school districts on floppy disks, 83,000 addresses in all. This company is:

Melissa Data Company
32118-8A Paseo Adelanto
San Juan Capistrano, CA 92675
1-800-443-8834

Locations of local government purchasing offices can also be obtained from companies which sell mailing lists. One of the advantages of buying a list from a direct mail house is that it can be provided on adhesive labels. The listings cost about $50.00 per thousand items, but this cost is more than recouped by clerical savings since the envelopes won't have to be addressed. (Note: Most mailing houses sell their lists for one-time use only. Don't try to make copies and re-use for additional mailings. The mailing houses have included a number of dummy names and addresses, so they'll know if you try it. You'll be sent another bill.)

2. Prepare a brochure package to send to the purchasing department of the agency. The package should include the specifications and features of every product you want to receive bids for.

3. Send the agency a letter requesting to be put on its bid list. The letter should be short and to the point, like the following one:

Purchasing Agent
Lake County
Lake County Courthouse
Waukegan, Il. 11122

Dear Purchasing Agent:

Our company distributes a line of commercial vacuum cleaners, floor scrubbers, waxers, sanders, and related supplies. I've enclosed product brochures on our line. Please put us on your bid list.

    Cordially,

Bill Bidder

In many cases you've done everything that is necessary. You're on the county's bid list for the items mentioned in your letter. The next time the county puts out a bid for those kinds of products, you'll get a copy. In other cases you'll receive back a form to fill out. This form will require you to provide information about your company. (see Exhibit 3.) The kind of information the agency asks you to provide usually includes,

EXHIBIT 3

CITY OF FORT LAUDERDALE

PURCHASING DIVISION
PO DRAWER 14250
FORT LAUDERDALE, FL 33302
(305) 761-5140

BIDDER'S LIST APPLICATION
(See Instructions For Preparation On Page 3)

| | 1|33| |
(LEAVE BLANK)

1. Name of applicant. If individual, enter last name first.

| | | | | | | | | | | | | | | | | | | | | | | | | | | | | | |

| | | | | | | | | | |
(LEAVE BLANK)

2. Street or P.O. Box address to which bid requests are to be mailed.

| | | | | | | | | | | | | | | | | | | | | | | | | | | | | | |

3. City   State   Zip Code

| | | | | | | | | | | | | | | | | | | | | | | | | | | | | | | | |

4. Contact person to whom bid requests are to be mailed. Enter none if no one person should be named.

| | | | | | | | | | | | | | | | | | | | |

5a. Main telephone number   (include area code)   5b. 800 number if available

|(| | | |)| | | |-| | | | | and if available |(| | | |)| | | |-| | | |

6a. Federal Employer's I.D. number.   6b. Social Security number, if individual.

| | | | | | | | | | | | | | | | | | | | | or | | | | | | | | | | | | | | | | | | |

7. Type of ownership of business. See definitions on last page. Check appropriate box(es).

☐ Minority Business (M)   ☐ Women Business (W)   ☐ Small Business (S)
    Enterprise, MBE   Enterprise, WBE   Enterprise, SBE

8. If you checked Minority or Women Business Enterprise above check the appropriate box below.

☐ Black (B)   ☐ Hispanic (H)   ☐ Asian American (A)
☐ White (C)   ☐ Native American (N)   ☐ Other (O)

19

EXHIBIT 3 (Continued)

9. Identify the Classes of items on which you will consistently bid by referring to the Commodity Class Listing which accompanies this application. Enter the 3 Digit Classes in correct numerical sequence.

1. Class	2. Class	3. Class	4. Class
5. Class	6. Class	7. Class	8. Class
9. Class	10. Class	11. Class	12. Class
13. Class	14. Class	15. Class	16. Class

10. Address of main business office (if different from #2 & #3 on first page).

_____

_____

11. If incorporated, in which state and date _____

12. Annual gross sales   Amount $ _____ for year ending _____

13. Bank references _____

_____

14. Location of principal factory or warehouse _____

15. Other governmental entities to which you have sold in the past 2 years.

_____

16. If you currently hold any Florida State contracts list contract No.'s and expiration dates

_____

_____

17 Principal line of business _____

18. How long in present business _____

If your company has been in business less than one year, additional information concerning the experience of your personnel, financial capabilities of your firm and company affiliations should be furnished either by attached letter or in Section 19 below.

19. Bidder's comments:

- Type of company (partnership, corporation, proprietorship)
- Size of company in dollar volume
- Number of employees
- How long the company has been in business
- Whether company is owned by a member of a minority group or is classified as a small business
- Names of company officers
- Names of persons authorized to sign bids
- Products to be listed for bid

The agency may provide a booklet that provides product codes. You'll have to find the category best suited to your product and fill in the appropriate code number.

Now your company may be on the bid list, but in some cases there is still one more step to take. Some state agencies require a yearly fee to maintain bidder lists. Your company may have to send a check to cover this fee to the agency for listing.

FIVE SHORTCUTS FOR GETTING YOUR COMPANY ON APPROVED BIDDERS' LISTS FAST

Many agencies won't accept bids on items that aren't on their approved products lists. The purpose of this rule is to ensure that only products that meet certain standards will be sold to the agency. Even companies which have sold products to the agency for years must submit new models for testing.

Theoretically, anyone can submit a product for approval, but the examination process by which the agency decides that the product is "worthy" is often tedious. It frequently involves submitting the product to the agency's testing laboratory where it is put through torturous routines. Bench tests in which the product is required to run for a certain period of time without failure are very popular. Often, these agencies will only accept products at certain times of the year. If your company misses a testing period, you may be required to wait a full twelve months for another one. The testing itself is often arbitrary, focusing on the trivial while ignoring the vital. Also, agency personnel involved in the testing have been known to play favorites.

Shortcuts through the testing procedure are vital if there is a pending bid that you wish to compete for. Here are five ways to reduce the time necessary to get a product approved by an agency.

1. Show that your new model is really just an improvement on a a product that has already been tested. If the mechanism is basically the same with a few bells and whistles added, the agency may feel the new model needn't go through the testing routine.

2. Submit the results of an independent testing laboratory, such as Buyer's Laboratory, as a substitute for the agency's tests. Often, an agency will accept the testing results of a reputable testing company if they are positive.

3. Submit the results of the product testing by another agency. If the product has just been put through a testing cycle by one agency, similar agencies may accept the testing results.

4. Submit information on successful installation. Commercial success with a product is always a good indication that the product works. A long customer list is often accepted by agencies as verification of a product's reliability.

5. Pay the agency's costs for speeding up the tests. Agency personnel normally work standard eight hour days. Sometimes a testing laboratory will work a second shift if the company requesting the test will pay the additional personnel costs. There's nothing illegal or unethical about the procedure. The testing results are in no way fabricated or improperly influenced—they're just put together faster.

TWELVE KEY POINTS FOR READING A BID SOLICITATION

Certain points on a bid solicitation must be read with special care when putting together a bid response. These points are:

1. The specifications for the product or service. Bidding a product that doesn't meet specs makes no sense, because such bids are thrown out. Other vendors demand it. They too might have been able to bid a less expensive model if they hadn't adhered to the specs.

2. The date the bid is due. Bids that are submitted late, even by one minute, are thrown out. That's why incoming bids are time- and date-stamped.

3. The quantity or dollar commitment on the part of the agency. Is the bid for a specific quantity of machines, does the contract have a dollar value, or is the agency free to purchase less product than specified on the request for bid? Making quantity discount offers to agencies based on their estimated needs can be a gamble. If the agency's actual requirement falls short of its estimates, the vendor has given them a better price than is justified by the amount purchased. Of course, needs can also be underestimated. In this case, the vendor gets more business than anticipated.

4. The delivery needed and the penalty to the vendor in case of default. When does the agency need the product delivered? Is it a schedule that can be met? If there's a possibility that the company may not be able to deliver on schedule, it had better look closely at any penalties that may be incurred by tardiness. Some contracts allow the agency to purchase a similar product on the open market and bill the contract holder for any difference in price.

5. Bid or performance bond requirement. Some bids require that a bid bond be included with the actual quote. The request for bid will detail the amount of the bond. Bid bonds guarantee that the successful bidder will deliver the product at the price specified in the bid. (Some agencies will accept a certified check as a substitute. The checks are returned to the unsuccessful bidders. Bid bonds are generally not returned because they usually expire quickly.)

6. The length of warranty or guarantee required. If the request for bid calls for an unrestricted two-year warranty, obviously there will be follow-on costs that could make the contract expensive to the company. These expense exposures must be weighed before bidding.

7. Amount of training required. Does the bid call for two hours of training with each piece of equipment installed? Is service training necessary? If it is, who pays for it? Obviously, these are other cost factors that must be weighed when submitting a bid.

8. Where the equipment or product will be installed. Will the product be installed at agency offices in various locations? How will the company handle installations in offices that are several hundred miles away? How will service calls be handled?

9. Materials to be included with the bid. Are brochures sufficient? Have service or parts manuals been specified? Have parts price lists been specified? Should a list of product users be added?

10. Payment terms. Agencies have a habit of hanging on to their funds for as long as possible. What's it going to take to get paid? How long will it take to get paid?

11. Duration of commitment. Is the agency holding the company to a set price for a single order? A full year? Something in between? Long-term contracts are risky because the company is bound to a price that may not be profitable at a future date because of changing market conditions.

12. Special terms and conditions. The riders of all bid solicitations must be read carefully so that all implications are understood. There could be kickers that dramatically affect the cost or risk exposure to the company. For example, many state contracts will demand that local government agencies, counties, and municipalities, be given the opportunity to "piggy-back" orders on the state contract. This stipulation may or may not be desirable to a company wanting the state business.

The most important thing is to read each new request for bid thoroughly. Don't assume that the boilerplate is identical simply because your company has done business with that agency before. The rules do change every now and then. The change you overlook could make the difference between a profitable contract and one that is a disaster.

BID CONFERENCES

When an agency awards an important contract it will often ask vendors to attend a pre-bid conference. At these meetings, agency representatives, usually from the purchasing department, will address the vendors as to their intent on the forthcoming bid. They will discuss the general specifications of the product to be bid, the quantity that will be ordered (or the quantity taken last year if there are no quantity guarantees), the terms, requirements, and other factors that affect the bid. Usually, attendance at these conferences is not required to actually bid on the contract under discussion.

It is important to attend these pre-bid conferences whenever possible. They represent an opportunity to provide input to the agency and to suggest specification changes if those being contemplated discriminate against your company. At this point, nothing is set in concrete. The agencies are generally receptive to any ideas that will improve the quality or cost-effectiveness of the product. They're always interested in improving the competitive situation. They are not likely, however, to endorse any specification change that will give your company an advantage at the expense of others.

Another reason to attend bid conferences is that it gives you an opportunity to meet the agency officials who will be letting the contract. They'll know of your interest in getting the business. If you have a complaint about the specs, it will be difficult to register if you don't attend the bid conference.

Still another reason to attend is that it gives you an opportunity to size up the competition. You'll find out which of your competitors is interested in getting this business. Of course, they'll find out that you're interested as well.

FOUR POINTS TO COVER IN A BID CONFERENCE

When attending a bid conference you should make sure that certain points are covered. These points are:

1. The specifications of the products. You must thoroughly understand what the specs will be. In some cases, the agency will have called the conference before finally defining the specs. When this happens, be sure that you understand the parameters. If it's possible that the agency could release a bid with specs that may discriminate against your company, you'll have time to prepare a protest.

2. When the bid will be sent out. Try to find out when the bid will actually be released. This will tell you how long you have to prepare for it.

3. The kind of contract that is being released for bid. Is this a multiple award that merely gives your company a "hunting license" at agency offices, or is it a sole source contract that ensures a certain volume of business?

4. Special contract requirements. Are there any critical changes or differences in this contract as opposed to past contracts the agency has issued? A change in terms or conditions or warranty period, or the requirement for an extra period of training could materially affect the company's cost.

WHEN TO TALK AND WHEN TO KEEP QUIET

At bid conferences there is a time to speak up and a time to keep quiet. The time to speak up is when the agency is proposing specifications that your company can't meet or would find expensive to meet. There are three good arguments for getting specifications changed. They are:

1. Only one or two competitors can meet the specs. The purpose of competitive bidding is to open up the contract opportunity to as many vendors as possible. If at least three vendors can't meet the specs, the bid is considered noncompetitive. Most agencies will modify specs if this is the case.

2. The specs make the product unnecessarily expensive. Certain desirable but unnecessary features may add too much to the cost of the product. Most purchasing offices are interested in economy. If you can demonstrate that a feature adds too much to the cost of a product, you may get this spec changed.

3. There's a hidden cost attached to a particular cost. If you can prove that a certain feature could add to ongoing operating costs, for example, by higher costs for energy or supplies, you have a good argument for having that spec changed. (Agencies are particularly interested in energy efficiency.)

If the suggested specs don't favor your product and you can make one of the above arguments, the bid conference is the place to speak up.

The time to keep quiet at bid conferences is when your products meet the required specs. Don't be concerned if other vendors also comply. That's the purpose of the bid process. It's a mistake to try to get "more" by proposing additional features only available on your products. If these features aren't generally standard throughout the industry, the agency won't adopt them. If your product has exclusive features that an agency absolutely needs, there's no reason for trying to sell it through the bid process, because this would limit your profit potential.

BID WORKSHEETS: GETTING A LINE ON THE COMPETITION

The art of competitive bidding is to quote a price just low enough to win the contract. The master bidders leave just pennies or dollars on the table with their successful bids. Those who are careless or haphazard lose bids altogether or underbid their competitors by ten, twenty, or even thirty percent. How can any vendor learn what the competition is going to bid? One way is to maintain a competitive bid worksheet, a history of what your competitors have bid in the past.

The worksheet should include the following:

- Name of the competitor
- Product model
- Suggested list price
- Price bid to the agency
- Percentage of discount from list
- Quantity
- Date of bid
- Name of agency

Exhibit 4 shows what such a worksheet looks like.

After half a dozen or more bids have been accumulated, you'll have a fair idea of the competitors' bidding patterns. Keeping worksheets also helps you whenever a competitor introduces a new product. If the discounts from list are predictable, the suggested list price of the new product will give you an idea of what the bid price will be.

Where do you get all this information? Remember, most agencies allow vendors to be present when bids are opened. The prices bid by your competitors will be announced. (The prices you have bid will also be announced, so assume that your competitors are keeping a file on your bidding habits.) Just jot the prices down as they're called out. Bid prices are also usually posted somewhere in the event you can't attend the bid conference. Manufacturer's suggested list prices are generally available from a variety of sources, including the manufacturer. Call and ask.

OTHER SOURCES FOR COMPETITIVE BID INFORMATION

The competitive worksheet will help you develop a historical record of other vendors' bidding habits. However, some competitors deliberately alter their bidding patterns, bidding high on unimportant contracts and cutting prices to the cuticle on the contracts they really want. How can you determine what such a vendor is likely to bid on any given contract? There is a way to develop a "nose" for competitive interest in a contract.

1. Attend the bid conference. If the competition is there, chances are they're interested in the contract. Learn to identify the competition's surrogates who may be attending the conference on the competitor's behalf. This person could be a key dealer or distributor or even a beginning salesperson. Most bid conferences have sign-in sheets. Be sure to look it over before you leave.

2. Develop relationships with the competitor's salespeople, dealers, and distributors. Useful information can be obtained over a cup of coffee, at lunch, or at a trade show. In some industries, dealers may carry both your line and your competitor's line. One of these dual dealers might be able to let you know the competitor's plans.

3. Develop relationships with people in allied, but noncompetitive industries. One such person may know something about your competitor's intentions.

4. Ask others in your own sales organization to be alert for anything they might hear. It's really surprising how much information is available to those who are alert and receptive.

EXHIBIT 4

COMPETITIVE BID TRACKING SYSTEM

COMPETITOR _____

MODEL	DATE BID	QUANTITY BID	SUGGESTED LIST	BID PRICE	DISCOUNT FROM LIST	OUTCOME

One place *not* to go for information about the competition's pricing plans is to the bidding agency itself. It's illegal for agency personnel to give you any pricing details or other information on competitive pricing. Be suspicious of any agency employee who offers to help you out in this way. If someone is giving information to you, he or she may be giving out information about you. At worst, it's an attempt to solicit bribes in exchange for restricted information. At best, the person is trying to alter the situation from a competitive bid to an auction. If both parties know what the other is bidding, both are likely to lower prices.

CASE HISTORY OF A BID INTELLIGENCE EFFORT:
How One Company Acquired the Competitive Information it Needed to Win a Three-Million–Dollar Contract by One Cent

The guidelines we've suggested have been used by companies to exact figures on what their competitors might bid. Here's the chronological story of one such intelligence effort.

Background

The Los Angeles Unified School District, the second largest school district in the United States, announced its intention to award a three-year contract for the purchase of electronic typewriters. The bulk of these typewriters were to be used for classroom training in typing and keyboarding skills. About 15 percent would be used in school administrative offices. The total value of the contract would be as much as one million dollars a year.

Most vendors calling on the school district with any regularity knew about the pending bid months ahead of its actual release. They all tried to mold the specs to favor their particular product, but the school district opted to make the specs open, easy to meet, and therefore very competitive.

This kind of contract is extremely attractive to typewriter manufacturers because a student taught on a particular model often becomes a lifetime customer. The successful vendor gets a good volume order now while creating a demand for the future.

The actual maneuvering and intelligence gathering by the successful bidder, Brother International, took place during the thirty days between the release of the bid and the time it closed, from June 1 to June 30.

June 1

The school district sends the bid release to vendors on its bid list. It contains few surprises. The district has divided its requirement into the following three categories:

- A basic full-sized electronic typewriter suitable for classroom training
- A full-sized electronic typewriter with more features for administrative office use
- A compact basic electronic unit for locations with space constraints

Part of the specifications required that a full year's supply of supplies, ribbons, and printing elements be provided for each typewriter.

June 2

The major account representative at Brother carefully reviewed the specifications and the stipulations of the bid request. The entire contract wouldn't necessarily be awarded to a single vendor. It was possible to win one category while losing the other two. The first elementary strategy was developed: concentrate on those categories which would produce the highest sales volume and would emphasize the company's strengths. These were categories 1 and 2.

June 3

The equipment features for the twenty-five vendors of electronic typewriters were reviewed. The competitive models that met the specifications of the L.A. Unified School district bid were listed. All of the vendors, with the exception of IBM and Xerox, sold their products through office equipment dealers. IBM and Xerox were not considered serious competitors because of their pricing structures.

June 4

The competitive models that were overqualified (too fully featured and highly priced to be competitive) were dropped from the list. The list was now down to twelve different models offered by ten different manufacturers.

June 5

The companies which usually didn't compete for bid contracts were put in a separate category. The remaining six vendors were put into a primary competitor category. Their models were given special attention.

June 8

Brother dealers throughout the country who also carried the competitor models in the primary category were polled to determine whether any of them planned near-term introduction of new models that could compete for the Los Angeles contract. Two new models were uncovered, but they were too fully featured. They were not considered a factor in the forthcoming bid.

June 9

The major account team concentrated on the vendors which had been most aggressive in previous bids to the school district and in southern California generally. Two companies emerged, Panasonic and Swintec. The models they were likely to bid were scrutinized. Recent competitive bids for those models were analyzed.

June 10

The suggested list prices and dealers' discounts for the models that Panasonic and Swintec would bid were reviewed. One of the vendors, Panasonic, also offered their dealers additional discounts for orders placed by educational institutions. The discount schedules were matched to recent bids by these competitors to get a feel for their overall bidding strategy.

June 11

It was decided to use different dealers for each of the three categories on the L.A. bid. This was simply a matter of not putting all the company's eggs in one basket. Brother would handle the billing and pay the dealers for their installation and service effort so the dealers wouldn't have any accounts receivable problems.

June 12

Profit margins for dealer installations were discussed. On a contract of this size and importance, the dealers to be selected had to be willing to operate with very small margins for installing the equipment and handling any needed warranty repair. Contact was made with several dealers who knew how to work with educational accounts and could handle the volumes involved.

June 15

The three dealers were selected. They agreed to work for small margins, but the actual amounts weren't determined.

June 16

The supply-side requirement of the bid was analyzed. Very few previous bids had called for a year's supply of ribbons and extra printing elements. How would the competition react to this requirement? Would they price these items at cost or try to make a profit? It was unknown territory.

June 17

The Brother major account team went back to the rumor mill. Did any competitor have an unusually large inventory of an equipment model they might like to unload at less than cost just to get it out of the warehouse? Were any models being discontinued? If so, did these models meet the specs on the L.A. Unified bid? No evidence was discovered that indicated another vendor might be "dumping" a model.

June 18

The major account team worked on the exact company cost for the equipment and supply package required on the bid. They extracted advertising costs, overhead, and other burden to develop a true cost of the goods that would be delivered.

Winning the contract was considered to have a certain advertising and public relations value. The team noted that the winning contractor would also be creating future customers as students were trained on that contractor's products. These values were recognized, but no attempt was made to attach numbers to them.

June 19

The major account team tried to forecast what the main competitors would bid in each of the three categories. Recent past bids and known discount schedules were used to develop these numbers. The forecasters felt comfortable with their predictions regarding equipment, but were uncertain as to the tactics the competitors would use regarding supplies.

June 22

An effort was made to determine the actual supply costs for the principal competitors. The competitors' retail prices and dealer discount schedules were scrutinized. Brother International's own profit margin schedule was used to extrapolate an estimate of competitors' costs.

June 23

A visit was made to the Los Angeles Unified School District purchasing office to determine whether the district planned any last minute changes to the bid specs. No changes were contemplated.

June 24

Arrangements were made for the performance bond requirements in the event the company made one or more successful bids. Since the company planned to use more than one dealer, a separate bond was required for each.

June 25

Calls came in from non-Brother dealers requesting pricing so they could bid on the contract. These calls were considered an intelligence gathering effort by competitors.

June 26

The company's final pricing strategy was set based on the best estimate of what the principal competitors would bid. The assumption was made that they would bid equipment close to the lowest prices seen on recent previous bids and bid supplies at cost. Working backward, Brother calculated it could not match these prices unless dealers chosen to service the school district would be willing to work for substantially less than half of their already low margins. There was concern that the bid would be lost.

June 29

The dealers were contacted and briefed on the bid strategy. At first each of the dealers rejected the profit margins as being too low to sustain their effort. The dealers were not contacted earlier so the final bid prices wouldn't be known outside Brother Corporation until the last day. The dealers finally agreed to the new pricing.

June 30

The bid package was checked to make sure it was complete. One hour before the bid opening, it was delivered to the school district bid room and time-stamped. The bids were opened five minutes after the time deadline expired. The bids took some time to calculate as the school district recognizes "net" prices, the cost to the school district after discounts for prompt payment are considered. After some time the results were announced.

1. In the first and largest category (for classroom typewriters) Brother won the bid by a single penny per machine. It was the bidder's masterpiece. Not one cent of profit was left on the table.

2. In the second category (for administrative typewriters) a surprise competitor, Olivetti, entered the apparent winning bid. Brother's bid was second lowest. The self-satisfaction caused by winning the first category was quickly erased. Olivetti had not been expected to be among the finalists. However, the features on the model bid did not meet the district's standards for that category. After a month of wrangling, the Olivetti bid was thrown out. Brother was awarded category 2.

3. In the third category for compact units, Panasonic was the low bidder with Brother again in second place. This category hadn't received the attention of the other two.

The marks for the Brother bidding team were better than fair. They won the two categories they wanted the most, although they were surprised and almost bushwhacked by a competitor. There's still room for improvement. If they had paid closer attention to the third category, perhaps they could have swept the board.

A BIDDING CHECKLIST

After you have gathered all the competitive information possible, then used your sharpest pencil to prepare a bid, here's a final check list to review before sending it off to the appropriate agency:

- Is the bid number and opening date on the envelope? If a clerk at the agency opens your bid ahead of time, the bid will be rejected even though it's the clerk's error.
- Does the equipment or service you're bidding meet all the specs? It's better to bid higher-priced items that meet specs than to offer a low price on products that don't.
- Are you submitting the completed bid on time? All late bids are automatically rejected.
- Is a bid bond or cashier's check required? If so, have you included the item in your bid package?
- Have you included all necessary support materials such as product brochures, parts lists, repair locations, and support dealers. Failure to do so could cause a bid to be rejected.
- Have you offered your best prompt payment schedule? Some agencies consider discounts for prompt payment when determining net price.
- Is the bid signed in all the required places by a person authorized by your company? An unsigned bid will be thrown out.

Exhibit 5 shows a model checklist.

WHEN TO SUBMIT THE BID

Submit your bid just before the time deadline on the date specified. Hand deliver the bid to the agency whenever possible. Leave yourself enough slack in the schedule to allow for traffic jams, car failures, and the like, but bring the bid in personally. Submitting the bid on the final day and at the last hour gives you one final opportunity to check everything out and to piece together that last tidbit of competitive information. It also ensures that information about your bid hasn't been leaked to your competitors.

Submitting the bid on the date due also gives you an opportunity to stay on the premises while the bids are opened. You'll learn immediately what your competitors are bidding. The information you gather will make you better prepared for the next bid opportunity.

EXHIBIT 5

BID CHECKLIST

_____ BID NUMBER AND OPENING DATE ON ENVELOPE?

_____ DOES EQUIPMENT BID MEET THE SPECIFICATION?

_____ IS BID ON TIME?

_____ ARE NECESSARY BONDS INCLUDED?

_____ ARE BROCHURES AND OTHER SUPPORT MATERIAL
INCLUDED?

_____ ARE BEST DISCOUNTS OFFERED?

_____ IS BID SIGNED?

3

HOW TO WIN FEDERAL GOVERNMENT BID CONTRACTS

A CONDUCTED TOUR THROUGH THE BUREAUCRACY MAZE

The rules and regulations for doing business with the federal government twist and wind through more than thirty thousand printed pages. Trying to cover the same material in a single short chapter is obviously impossible. The material presented here is intended only to explain how the federal procurement process works, where the bid opportunities are, and the basic procedures of how to approach and sell to federal agencies. This chapter then is a short primer on federal government marketing.

A NOTE FOR BEGINNERS

When dealing with the federal government, patience is a needed quality. Be prepared for long selling cycles; plan for them. Quick frustration and short-term expectations work against you. Take the time to learn the regulations. One of the best ways to learn how the process works at any particular government agency is to ask the appropriate procurement officer. Most are happy to guide you through the procedure.

One of the first things to learn about federal government marketing is that form is critically important. Forget to sign a document in the proper place and a contract may be lost. Submit an invoice improperly and it may not be paid. The ponderous rules and regulations may seem to be a disadvantage, an impediment to doing business, but they can work to the benefit of those prepared to spend the time to learn the ropes. Personnel at government agencies prefer doing business with those who know how the process works. You can make their jobs easier for them if you know the way through the red tape as well as they do.

NEVER STOP SELLING

Always remember that no matter what the level of government or the size of the order, the basic rules of selling still apply. Get in front of the prospect, learn who the real decision makers are and get to them, learn what the needs are, explain the benefits of the product or service your company offers and how they meet those needs, make demonstrations when they are appropriate, and present proposals that help the agency justify a buying decision.

A GUIDE TO THE GENERAL SERVICES ADMINISTRATION (GSA)

The General Services Administration (GSA) is the primary purchasing agent for all federal government civilian agencies. Its purpose is to negotiate the lowest possible prices for the products and services used by federal agencies. Having a product on a GSA schedule is very desirable because it means that any federal agency with available funds in its budget may purchase that product if there is a demonstrated need for it. The price and terms have been set by the GSA, so there is no haggling at the agency level. The executive branch of the federal government must use GSA supply schedules. The judicial and legislative branches are not bound by these schedules, but often use them as a matter of convenience.

The GSA is an independent government agency. It buys, stores, and dispenses products that are used throughout government. Companies may negotiate yearly contracts, known as schedules, to become

GSA suppliers. Before getting a product on a GSA schedule, it's necessary to prove that the company has been commercially successful and that the product being offered has been accepted in the marketplace. This means that if you want to sell a product to the GSA, you must prove that you have sold it to someone else first. The federal government is no place to pioneer a product, except for those items that are built to spec for an agency, such as weapons for the Department of Defense.

The documentation to prove that a product has been commercially successful can be something as simple as purchase orders from customers and bills of lading showing shipment.

The GSA also demands that the government be offered the lowest price available on that product. The publicity about coffee pots costing $6,000 and toilet seats costing $10,000 notwithstanding, don't expect to sell a product for one dollar to private industry and two dollars to the federal government. In your negotiations with the GSA, they'll want to know all about your pricing and discount schedules. You will be asked to provide documentation on these points during your meetings.

Getting on a GSA schedule isn't easy. Be prepared for tough give-and-take negotiations. Don't assume that federal negotiators are easy marks because they are bureaucrats who don't understand the commercial world. This can be a fatal mistake. Of all the companies which try to get their products on a GSA schedule, only about one-third succeed.

THE DANGER OF BEING ON GSA SCHEDULES

The federal government takes its lowest price policy seriously. If it is proved that your company is selling a product on GSA schedule to other customers at lower prices under the same terms and conditions, you may be forced to rebate to that lower price level all such product sold to the federal government. That doesn't mean that your company can never sell the product at a lower price. It does mean that the conditions of sale must be different. Such conditions could include a different warranty or a large quantity order.

WHY GSA SCHEDULES DON'T ENSURE ORDERS

There's another problem with getting on GSA schedules. Some of the companies that successfully negotiate a GSA contract assume their sales job is finished and that the orders will roll in. Those who feel this way soon learn better. Just being on a schedule doesn't assure your company of making any sales. It's more of a license to hunt than a guarantee of government business, although it does help. With a GSA schedule, sales calls on government departments become much more productive. It's much easier for federal agencies to buy products that are on a GSA schedule than to purchase something on the open market. It more or less means that the product and pricing have been preapproved for purchase. However, the company still has the job of convincing the individual government agency that part of its already tight budget should be spent on this particular product.

THE TYPES OF GSA SCHEDULES

There are several kinds of GSA schedules. These are:

- *National Schedules.* Issued by both the GSA and the Veteran's Administration (VA), these schedules are mandatory procurement guides for the agencies under their control.
- *Regional Schedules.* These schedules are mandatory only for the region issued.
- *Rehabilitation Schedules.* These schedules are issued to repair or maintain commodities such as typewriters, personal computers, and air conditioners.
- *Decentralized Schedules.* These schedules are mandatory for VA purchasing offices.
- *New Item Introduction Schedule (NIIS).* These schedules contain new items from different product categories that may or may not be transferred to the permanent schedules. Essentially products in this category are temporary. The GSA often uses NIIS schedules when it wishes to test product categories.

THE IFB, OR SEALED BID PROCEDURE

The GSA also purchases products through the sealed bid procedure, known as the Item For Bid (IFB). Any procurement exceeding $25 thousand is purchased through open bid. The bid must be listed in the *Commerce Business Daily.* Interested parties must bid within forty-five days of the listing. If the requesting agency has already defined its needs with detailed specifications containing desired functions and features, the agency will issue a request for proposal (RFP). The difference between the IFB and the RFP is that the RFP provides more details of the requirements. One of the first and easiest things a vendor interested in doing business with the federal government can do to learn about bid opportunities is to subscribe to the *Commerce Business Daily*. To obtain a subscription write to:

> Commerce Business Daily
> Superintendent of Documents
> Government Printing Office
> Washington, D.C. 20402-9371
> 202-783-3238

At the time of writing the annual subscription rate was $243.00.

WHO TO SEE ABOUT GETTING YOUR PRODUCT ON GSA SCHEDULES

To discuss the possibility of getting your company's product or service on GSA schedules, contact the agency directly. It isn't necessary to go to Washington. The GSA maintains a number of business service centers which can help you with this task. The following is a list of the central and regional GSA business services offices:

> *CENTRAL OFFICE*
> GSA
> 18th & F Streets N.W., Room 6122
> Washington, DC 20405
> 202-366-1240

> *Regional Offices*
> GSA
> John McCormick Post Office & Courthouse
> Boston, MA 02109
> 617-233-2868

> GSA
> 26 Federal Plaza
> New York, NY 10278
> 212-264-1234

GSA
7th & D Streets S.W., Room 1050
Washington, DC 20407
202-472-1804

GSA
600 Arch Street
Philadelphia, PA 19106
215-597-9613

GSA
819 Taylor Street
Forth Worth, TX 76102
817-334-3284

GSA
1776 Peachtree Street, NW1 Building
Atlanta, GA 30309
404-526-5661

GSA
230 Dearborn Street
Chicago, IL 60604
312-353-5383

GSA
1500 East Bannister Road
Kansas City, MO 64131-3088
816-926-7203

GSA
Federal Office Bldg & Courthouse
515 Rusk Street
Houston, TX 77002
713-226-5787

GSA
Denver Federal Center, Building 41
Denver, CO 80255
303-234-4171

GSA
525 Market Street
San Francisco, CA 94105
415-556-0877

> GSA
> 500 North Los Angeles
> Los Angeles, CA 94105
> 213-688-3210
>
> GSA
> 440 Federal Building
> 915 Second Avenue
> Seattle, WA 98174
> 206-442-5556

When writing to the central office in Washington, D.C., address the correspondence to: Director, Business Services Management Office. When writing to one of the regional offices, address the correspondence to: Regional Director of Business Affairs. As in selling to any other market segment, a personal call to the closest office can help you obtain results much more quickly.

HOW THE PROCESS WORKS

GSA contracts start with an invitation to bid. This document includes the specs, discounts, and the commercial history of the product. At this point, the price to the government is still open. Next, the administrators review all documents to be sure they're filled out properly. Work carefully when filling out the papers—if there are too many mistakes, the document gets thrown out and you'll have to wait until next year. Once the invitation to bid passes muster, the price negotiations begin. The GSA will require a discount from the best commercial price. Expect a rough-and-tumble give-and-take in these negotiations. The federal government is no easy mark that will allow your company to make extraordinary profits, no matter what stories you may have read. The government negotiators mean it when they say that they want the best prices possible.

However, it is important not to use too sharp a pencil in your eagerness to cut a GSA deal. You must protect your distribution and servicing links. If your organization sells through dealers or distributors, you must remember to include enough margin for their installation, training, and service costs on your product. Government negotiators understand that products must be installed and serviced nation-wide

AFTER YOU'RE ON THE GSA SCHEDULE

If you're successful in getting a product on a GSA schedule, let the government agencies know about it. It may be difficult to call on the more than fifteen thousand government offices in the country no matter how your product is distributed. How do you reach all these agencies? Printing a catalog or data sheet is a good place to start. Your catalog or data sheet should contain the following basic information:

- The GSA contract number assigned to your product
- The agreed-on price
- The product's features and perhaps a picture
- The terms
- How to order

After the catalog is printed, distribute it to procurement officers at government agencies by direct mail or personal sales calls by your company's representatives.

The next thing to do is to educate your own people about the GSA schedule. If you market through direct salespeople, give them copies of the GSA schedule with instructions to deliver these copies to the procurement officers at the federal government facilities in their sales areas. Do the same if you sell through dealers and distributors.

Often, dealers and distributors may be reluctant to call on federal installations within their sales areas. This reluctance comes from lack of knowledge: they don't know how to go about it. It's often up to the equipment vendor to supply the education and encouragement necessary before dealers and distributors acquire the skill to make successful sales calls on these agencies. This education includes listing government facilities in the dealers' sales area, a primer on whom to see and how to proceed and, most important of all, a clear indication of the profit potential. One of the best ways to get an independent sales organization started in this marketplace is for the company government account sales manager to make joint calls with salespeople from dealer or distributor sales organizations.

WHAT ARE SPECIFICATIONS ANYWAY?

When dealing with any level of government, federal, state, or local, the word "specifications" always figures prominently. What, exactly, is meant by this term? Here's the definition the federal government uses. Most local government agencies use it too.

Specifications are written descriptions, drawings, prints, commercial designations, industry standards, and other descriptive references. They are primarily based on industrial and technical society standards. They are written to meet the needs of government while taking into account the ability of business to provide the needed item or service.

Exhibit 6 shows a sample specification requisition form used by the Navy.

THE SMALL BUSINESS ADMINISTRATION

Getting your company classified as a small business is an important first step in obtaining sales from federal government agencies, because they give preferential treatment of bids to firms that meet this definition. The Small Business Administration (SBA) defines a small business in a pamphlet the SBA publishes, *Doing Business with the Federal Government,* by the following criteria:

- It is individually owned and operated.
- It is not dominant in its field of operation.
- It employs fewer than 500 people.

The Small Business Administration can be your company's best friend when trying to win federal government contracts. Its purpose is to help small, minority, and woman-owned businesses and labor surplus areas locate business opportunities with federal civilian agencies and with the military. Call on an SBA office if you feel you need assistance in selling to a federal agency or just want to learn more about how to go about it. The people there can be very helpful in alerting you to selling opportunities and in working through the government procurement maze. The SBA maintains field offices in major cities. Find them in the local phone directory under "Federal Government, Small Business Administration."

SMALL BUSINESS COUNSELING FROM THE ARMED SERVICES

The armed forces have a strong interest in helping small and disadvantaged businesses obtaining a fair share of government orders. They also maintain small business offices to attract qualified companies to

EXHIBIT 6

Sample Form

NAVAL PUBLICATIONS AND FORMS CENTER
5801 TABOR AVENUE
PHILADELPHIA, PA. 19120
OFFICIAL BUSINESS
PENALTY FOR PRIVATE USE, $300

POSTAGE AND FEES PAID
DEPARTMENT OF DEFENSE
DOD-316

REQUISITION NUMBER *(For Local Convenience)*

Please self-address the above label. Forward this form to the address shown herein. A window envelope may be used. Your request submitted on this form will speed service. Reorder forms will be enclosed with each shipment.

SPECIFICATIONS AND STANDARDS REQUISITION	**IFB, RFQ OR RFP CLOSING DATE**

Send_____copies of the below listed documents which are listed in the *DOD Index of Specifications and Standards.*

STANDARDIZATION DOCUMENT SYMBOL	TITLE *(From DOD Index of Specifications and Standards)*
SIGNATURE	Fold	DATE

**TO: COMMANDING OFFICER
NAVAL PUBLICATIONS AND FORMS CENTER
5801 TABOR AVENUE
PHILADELPHIA, PA. 19120**

DD FORM **1425** 1 OCT 72   PREVIOUS EDITIONS OF THIS FORM ARE OBSOLETE. ★ U.S. GPO: 1974—540-847/9102

46

their procurement programs. These offices advise and assist interested businesspeople on matters related to government procurement, provide up-to-date information on current and proposed requirements, and sometimes even arrange appointments with buyers, engineers, and contracting officers.

WHAT THE GOVERNMENT BUYS

If you want to find out what the government buys, a list of the products and services purchased by civilian agencies of the government is contained in the booklet, *U.S. Purchasing & Sales Directory*. It can be ordered through:

> Superintendent of Documents
> U.S. Government Printing Office
> Washington, DC 20402
> (Stock # 045-000-00153-9)

Many of the source books referred to in this book can be purchased at Government Printing Bookstores which are usually located in the downtown areas of major cities. If you're in a major metropolitan area, look up the number in your local phone directory. Government publications can also be ordered by mail with the form shown as Exhibit 7.

FREE GOVERNMENT LISTING (PASS)

Want a good deal that won't cost you a penny? The SBA will list your firm in its national automated directory of small suppliers of goods and services. This directory is called the Procurement Automated Source System (PASS) and it profiles more than 150,000 companies. To get on the PASS network, just fill out the form shown in Exhibit 8 and mail it to:

> U.S. Small Business Administration
> PASS Program, Room 600
> 1441 L Street, N.W.
> Washington, DC 20416

Buyers for prime government contractors use PASS because their contracts require that a certain amount of their purchases be made

EXHIBIT 7

 U.S. Government BOOKS

Catalog Order Form

*1107
October 1989/March 1990

☎ **For faster service, phone your order!** VISA MasterCard

For faster service, charge and deposit account orders may be placed by calling (202) 783-3238 between 8:00 AM and 4:00 PM (Eastern Time) Monday-Friday (except holidays).

Customer's Name and Address	Ship To: (If other than address at left)
ZIP	ZIP

(   )
Customer's Daytime Telephone Number

Your order number _____
Date _____

All prices in this catalog include regular domestic postage and handling.

Prices are subject to change. If more than 6 months have passed since the date in the upper left hand corner of this form you may want to verify prices and stock availability by calling the Order and Information Desk at (202) 783-3238.

U.S. Industrial Outlook, 1989

1989 U.S. INDUSTRIAL OUTLOOK

Provides detailed analyses of more than 350 industries, including historical data, current trends, forecasts of future prospects, and industry statistical profiles. 1989. 652 p. il.

S/N 003-009-00547-7
$24.00

Publications

Qty.	Stock Number	Title	Price Each	Total Price
		Total for Publications		

Subscriptions

Qty.	List ID	Title	Price Each	Total Price
		Total for Subscriptions		
		Total Cost of Order		

Method of Payment

☐ Check or money order payable to Superintendent of Documents

☐ GPO Deposit Account ☐☐☐☐☐☐☐ — ☐

☐ VISA or MasterCard Account No. ☐☐☐☐☐☐☐☐☐☐☐☐☐☐☐☐☐☐☐☐

Expiration Date Month/Year ☐☐☐☐
(Signature)

Thank you for your order!

Mail to:
Superintendent of Documents
U.S. Government Printing Office
Washington, DC 20402-9325

Or to:
Your nearest
U.S. Government Bookstore
(see inside back cover for address).

EXHIBIT 7 (Continued)

To Order

1. To speed the processing of your order, please be sure to complete this special order form carefully. Photocopies of the form are acceptable.

2. Type or print your complete name and address, your order number (if any), your Superintendent of Documents deposit account number (if applicable), your VISA or MasterCard number (if applicable), and expiration date in proper places on the form. If order is to be shipped to a third party, fill in address in the box indicated. Please include your office/home telephone number.

3. When ordering non-subscriptions, type or print the stock number (the number preceded by "S/N" at the bottom of each annotation), quantity, title, price, and total payment enclosed. Allow 4 weeks for delivery (longer for international orders).

4. When ordering subscriptions, type or print the quantity, list ID, title, unit price, and total payment enclosed. Allow 4–6 weeks plus mailing time for processing. All subscriptions are for one year unless otherwise noted. Subscribers will be notified in ample time to renew.

5. Please include payment with your order. Please make check or money order payable to the Superintendent of Documents. You may charge your order by using your Superintendent of Documents deposit account, your VISA or MasterCard account. Do not send cash or stamps.

6. Shipping is by non-priority mail. United Parcel Service (UPS), first class, and airmail services are available for an additional charge. Please contact us in advance for rates if you desire this service (202) 783-3238 and indicate on your order if you desire special postage.

7. Mail this form (or a photocopy) to: Superintendent of Documents, U.S. Government Printing Office, Dept. 33, Washington, D.C. 20402–9325.

8. Please wait until at least 6 weeks have elapsed to inquire about your order. After that, to inquire about subscriptions, write to the Subscription Service Section, Stop SSOM, U.S. Government Printing Office, Washington, D.C. 20402–9371. To check on orders for non-subscriptions, write to the Publications Service Section, Stop SSOS, U.S. Government Printing Office, Washington, D.C. 20402–9325. You may also call (202) 275–3050 for non-subscription inquiries and (202) 275–3054 for subscription inquiries.

9. If our shipment is incorrect, return the shipping cards for adjustment. Please do not return books until notified to do so. All claims must be submitted within 6 months.

Bookdealers

Designated bookdealers and educational bookstores are authorized a 25-percent discount on the domestic price of any publication or subscription when delivered to the dealer's normal place of business. This rule applies to single as well as multiple copies of a publication, pamphlet, periodical, or subscription service, except on items sold at a special quantity price, on items specifically designated "no discount allowed," or on items shipped to a third party (except in single-title quantities of 100 or more). The maximum discount allowed is 25 percent, but note that GPO pays freight.

Orders for 100 or More Copies

Any customer ordering 100 or more copies of a single publication or subscription for delivery to a single destination will be allowed a 25-percent discount on the domestic price of the item, with the exception of those items specifically designated "no discount allowed." The maximum allowable discount is 25 percent, so discounts may not be "combined."

Deposit Accounts

More than 30,000 of our customers find that a prepaid Superintendent of Documents deposit account is a convenient way to do business because it permits ordering without the preparation of a purchase order. Upon receipt of an initial deposit ($50.00 minimum), an account will be established and a unique account number will be assigned. Future purchases may be charged against this deposit account number, including telephone orders as long as sufficient funds are available in the account. Order blanks are provided and monthly statements are mailed to customers with active deposit accounts. For more information, please write or call: Deposit Accounts Section, Stop SSOR, U.S. Government Printing Office, Washington, D.C. 20402 (202) 783-3238.

International Orders

In order to provide the special handling required by international mailing regulations, a surcharge of 25 percent of the domestic price will be added on all items shipped to a foreign address. Remittance in U.S. dollars must accompany every order and be in the form of a check drawn on a bank located in the U.S. or Canada, a UNESCO coupon, or an International Postal Money Order made payable to the Superintendent of Documents. NOTE: Due to Treasury Department regulations, we cannot accept checks drawn on Canadian banks for less than $4.00 (U.S. dollars). If your order totals less than $4.00 (U.S. dollars), we suggest that you use your MasterCard or VISA account. International customers may also charge their orders to a prepaid Superintendent of Documents deposit account. Please include the expiration date of your credit card with your order. Orders are sent via surface mail unless otherwise requested. Should you desire airmail service, please contact us in advance by letter, telephone (202) 783-3238, or Telex (#710–822-94113; ANSWERBACK USGPO WSH) for the total cost of your order. We cannot accept foreign currency, checks on foreign banks, and postage stamps will not be accepted. Please place all orders in English.

EXHIBIT 8

U.S. SMALL BUSINESS ADMINISTRATION
WASHINGTON, D.C. 20416

Dear Small Businessperson:

Are you taking advantage of every opportunity to sell your products or services to the Federal Government and its prime contractors?

I want to tell you about a Small Business Administration (SBA) program that can get your company's name and capabilities in front of hundreds of Government purchasing agents - at no cost to you. By filling out the form I have included with this letter, you will become part of the SBA's online computerized "directory" of small businesses - the Procurement Automated Source System (PASS).

PASS - A SOURCE OF NEW BUSINESS

Each day PASS is used by the purchasing departments of many of the large defense contractors (such as Boeing and Lockheed) as well as the procurement offices of Federal agencies such as Commerce, Agriculture, and Energy.

Since many of their contracts and purchases require them to buy from small businesses like yourself, these purchasing agents have found PASS to be a fast and effective tool to find new sources of products and services.

Many Federal agencies and prime contractors have expressed a need for small high-tech firms and small minority-owned firms. Your company has been identified as one of the aforementioned. I believe your firm can increase its contracting opportunities by listing in PASS.

For instance, the Boeing Company used PASS to locate minority and small business firms for contracting parts of the Minuteman project. They found a small high-tech firm like La Manse Industries on PASS. On another contract, a minority-owned firm, Cherokee Nation Industries, was located in PASS and was awarded a contract. Both of these firms received a multi-million dollar contract with Boeing. Many other small businesses and PASS users have the same success.

THE PASS FORM IS EASY TO FILL OUT

Filling out the PASS form is easy; the information requested is similar to the questions you are asked all the time when describing your company to a potential new client. And a full-time staff will review your form for completeness and accuracy before it is entered. We want your company to be accurately described on PASS.

Best of all, your listing on PASS is at no cost to you. Any updates you need to make to keep the information current are also free. And we even pay for the postage when you mail the form back to us. The prime contractors and Federal agencies are the ones who pay a fee when they sign-on and search PASS.

Please fill out the PASS form today and mail it back. The addition of your company will make the PASS more valuable to purchasing agents and, at the same time, could mean new opportunities for you and your company.

Sincerely,

Monika Edwards Harrison
Associate Administrator
for Procurement Assistance

Enclosure

50

from small or minority owned business. They're actively looking for small companies to supply their needs. The PASS system saves these buyers time leafing through phone books, catalogues, and brochures to find appropriate suppliers. They can simply access the on-line PASS system and get a list of profiles for companies that offer the goods and services they're looking for. There is no charge, either to suppliers or to buyers, for inclusion in the PASS system. However, buyers pay a fee for accessing the system.

PAID GOVERNMENT LISTING

Another way to get your company listed with federal buyers is to buy an ad in the *Federal Supplier Registry*, a for-profit publication that is distributed to more than fifteen thousand government buying offices. Essentially it's a directory for federal government purchasing officers. This registry is updated twice a year and indexed by specific product or service. To buy space or get more information contact:

> CAP/COM Corp.
> Computer Center
> 98-B Jones Cove Road
> Sevierville, TN 37862

Other registry publications perform a similar service.

LISTINGS ARE IMPORTANT

Less than 60 percent of the purchases made by most government offices are through GSA, VA, or Federal Service contracts. The balance is purchased on the open market. That means that the purchasing officers for these agencies simply go out and buy what they need from the most accessible source. Having your company listed on PASS or one of the commercial directories increases your exposure and chances of landing a deal.

SELLING TO THE MILITARY

The major buying sections of the military are divided into four general areas. These are:

- Department of the Army
- Department of the Navy
- Department of the Air Force
- Defense Supply Agency

Each of these agencies has a great many subdivisions. Often a service branch will be given the task of researching a product or service that will be used by all of the branches. For example, the Air Force could be given the project of researching laptop computers. Their conclusions could affect the purchase decisions of the other service branches. However, there is still interservice rivalry. Sometimes it's wise not to use referrals from one service branch when trying to sell to another.

COMPETITIVE BIDDING FOR MILITARY PURCHASES ON THE RISE

In response to demands by Congress, all branches of the military are actively seeking more suppliers. Military purchasers must now consider competitive factors when making buying decisions. The military has established standards for most items to increase competition. These standards are called *Military Specifications* (MILSPEC). This term denotes a set of specifications that a great many vendors can meet. Any procurement exceeding $25,000 must be listed in the *Commerce Business Daily*. Interested parties have forty-five days in which to bid.

CALLING ON A MILITARY BASE

Before delving into the complexities of military procurement, let's start off with something simple: One of the easiest ways to sell to the military is to call on a military base in your area. This can be an army base, naval station, air force facility, or whatever. The market potential of any given military base can be extraordinary. Many people don't recognize that bases are small cities, in some cases employing up to fifty thousand in civilian and military personnel. They need military items, but they also need all the products and services that make any city run. These bases want to be on good terms with their neighbors. They want to purchase from the local business community when they can. Some bases hold "opportunity days" for local suppliers. During these promotions local vendors have a chance to showcase their products and meet with potential users on the base. Contact the chief procurement officer at the military bases in your area to see if such an event is planned. Often it's an annual affair.

Service can be a critical factor when trying to sell to a military base, because many are in remote locations. That's why small businesses located in the vicinity of the military base have an advantage over their competitors who may be located some distance away.

One popular misconception about the military is that they buy only at certain times of the year, when budgets are approved. The fact is the military usually purchases what it needs when needed. Don't wait for a new fiscal period to make calls on this important market.

YOUR FIRST CALL AT A MILITARY BASE

The uniforms, the guards at the gate, and the atmosphere of a military base can make the first call intimidating for someone who has never done it before, but it's really quite easy. Just stop at the base gate and ask for the procurement officer. The guard will give you a pass and directions. Tell the procurement officer about the products and services your company offers. If the products are on GSA schedules, so much the better. If they're not, you can still do business. The military has a policy of buying small quantities of items from local sources. It's their way of being a good neighbor to the surrounding community. Many bases will also have a small business officer whose job it is to assist local merchants in doing business with the base.

Some bases will help local merchants arrange equipment presentations and provide facilities where demonstrations can be done. They may even provide advertising for the event in the base newspaper. Ask about this possibility when making a call on the military facility in your area. Before leaving the base, make sure you obtain the following information:

- The names and locations of all activities and commands on the base, including purchasing and supplies
- The base or agency telephone directory
- The base or agency organizational chart
- The names of the decision makers for the product or service you're selling
- The point where the decision is made: at the base, the district office, or the regional office

- The point where final approval is made: Washington, or command headquarters
- Where the purchase order is cut, at the local level, national level, or command headquarters
- What directives, regulations, or instructions govern the purchase of the kind of equipment or service you're selling
- What are the steps in the buying cycle once the decision is made: Who initiates the requisition and where does it go for approval?

PROBLEMS IN DEALING WITH THE MILITARY

There are some problems when dealing with the military. Often their ordering processes can be frustrating, and even after the order has been obtained and shipped, their payments are slow and the procedures to obtain payment are long and complicated. However, for anyone willing to put in the time, the reward can be a faithful customer who keeps on buying and buying.

DEPARTMENT OF THE ARMY MAJOR BUYING OFFICES

To sell to the army or any other Department of Defense operation, the first thing you must know is who buys what. Most of the U.S. Army's procurement function is handled by the U.S. Army Material and Readiness Command (DARCOM) in Alexandria, Virginia. Their full address is:

Headquarters, DARCOM
5001 Eisenhower Avenue
Alexandria, VA 22333
202-274-8185

Within DARCOM there are fourteen major subordinate commands. Each of these commands specializes in a particular kind of equipment, with a heavy emphasis on weaponry. The eight research and development commands are responsible for developmental contracts. The five readiness commands are responsible for most production contracts. One test and evaluation command oversees the testing of many products under consideration.

The army has a program designed to help businesses get a fix on their future requirements through a process called Advance Planning

Procurement Information (APPI). All commands have Material Information Liaison Officers (AIMILO) who release information on the command's future buying plans to the *Commerce Business Daily* and to bidders on the command's bid list. Each release contains some of the following information:

- Nomenclature of item to be purchased
- Manufacturer's part, spec, and stock numbers
- Quantity to be purchased over the next one to three years
- Past history (quantity, dollar value, testing)

To get on a command's bid list to receive this information, send standard form 129 (Exhibit 9) to the command where you'd like to do business. A complete list of Army commands and the kind of equipment they purchase can be found in the Department of Defense publication *Selling to the Military*.

SELLING TO THE NAVY

The Naval Material Command was responsible for providing materials supporting the navy's activities until it was abolished by John Lehman, who became Naval Secretary in 1981. He diminished the role of high-ranking military officers on weapons procurement and shut out the overseers in the Department of Defense. This contributed to the current scandal that is rocking the Pentagon. Insiders and consultants traded information for money and favors. As of this writing, most of the details still haven't been revealed, which means the navy will be a touchy place to sell equipment or services into the '90s. It's likely their entire procurement process will be investigated and changes made. Most of the investigation will focus on high-tech weapon systems, but there will still be a need to buy thousands of every-day items. If you want to give it a go, the place to start is:

Chief of Naval Operations
1430 South Eads Street
Arlington, VA 22202
202-692-2400

The names, addresses, and phone numbers of the other commands that buy materials can be obtained by referring to the government publication mentioned earlier, *Selling to the Military*.

EXHIBIT 9

BIDDER'S MAILING LIST APPLICATION	INITIAL APPLICATION	FORM APPROVED OMB NO.
	REVISION	29–R0069

Fill in all spaces. Insert "NA" in blocks not applicable. Type or print all entries. See reverse for instructions.

TO (*Enter name and address of Federal agency to which form is submitted. Include ZIP Code*)	DATE

1. APPLICANT'S NAME AND ADDRESS (*Include county and ZIP Code*)	2. ADDRESS (*Include county and ZIP Code*) TO WHICH SOLICITATIONS ARE TO BE MAILED (*If different from item 1*)

3.	TYPE OF ORGANIZATION (*Check one*)		4. HOW LONG IN PRESENT BUSINESS
INDIVIDUAL	PARTNERSHIP	NON-PROFIT ORGANIZATION	
CORPORATION, INCORPORATED UNDER THE LAWS OF THE STATE OF			

5. NAMES OF OFFICERS, OWNERS, OR PARTNERS

PRESIDENT	VICE PRESIDENT	SECRETARY
TREASURER	OWNERS OR PARTNERS	

6. AFFILIATES OF APPLICANT (*Names, locations and nature of affiliation. See definition on reverse*)

7. PERSONS AUTHORIZED TO SIGN BIDS, OFFERS, AND CONTRACTS IN YOUR NAME (*Indicate if agent*)

NAME	OFFICIAL CAPACITY	TEL. NO. (*Incl. area code*)

8. IDENTIFY EQUIPMENT, SUPPLIES, MATERIALS, AND/OR SERVICES ON WHICH YOU DESIRE TO BID (*See attached Federal agency's supplemental listing and instructions, if any*)

9.	TYPE OF OWNERSHIP (*See definitions on reverse*)	
MINORITY BUSINESS ENTERPRISE	OTHER THAN MINORITY BUSINESS ENTERPRISE	

10.	TYPE OF BUSINESS (*See definitions on reverse*)	
MANUFACTURER OR PRODUCER	REGULAR DEALER (*Type 1*)	REGULAR DEALER (*Type 2*)
SERVICE ESTABLISHMENT	CONSTRUCTION CONCERN	RESEARCH AND DEVELOPMENT FIRM
☐ SURPLUS DEALER (*Check this box if you are also a dealer in surplus goods*)		

11.	SIZE OF BUSINESS (*See definitions on reverse*)	
SMALL BUSINESS CONCERN*	OTHER THAN SMALL BUSINESS CONCERN	
*If you are a small business concern, fill in (a) and (b):	(a) AVERAGE NUMBER OF EMPLOYEES (Including affiliates) FOR FOUR PRECEDING CALENDAR QUARTERS	(b) AVERAGE ANNUAL SALES OR RECEIPTS FOR PRECEDING THREE FISCAL YEARS

12.	FLOOR SPACE (*Square feet*)	13.	NET WORTH	
MANUFACTURING	WAREHOUSE	DATE	AMOUNT	

14. SECURITY CLEARANCE (*If applicable, check highest clearance authorized*)

FOR	TOP SECRET	SECRET	CONFIDENTIAL	NAMES OF AGENCIES WHICH GRANTED SECURITY CLEARANCES (*Include dates*)
KEY PERSONNEL				
PLANT ONLY				

THIS SPACE FOR USE BY THE GOVERNMENT	CERTIFICATION
	I certify that information supplied herein (*Including all pages attached*) is correct and that neither the applicant nor any person (*Or concern*) in any connection with the applicant as a principal or officer, so far as is known, is now debarred or otherwise declared ineligible by any agency of the Federal Government from bidding for furnishing materials, supplies, or services to the Government or any agency thereof.
	SIGNATURE
	NAME AND TITLE OF PERSON AUTHORIZED TO SIGN (*Type or print*)

129–105

STANDARD FORM 129 (REV. 2–77)
Prescribed by GSA, FPR (41 CFR) 1–16.802

EXHIBIT 9 (Continued)

INFORMATION AND INSTRUCTIONS

Persons or concerns wishing to be added to a particular agency's bidder's mailing list for supplies or services shall file this properly completed and certified Bidder's Mailing List Application, together with such other lists as may be attached to this application form, with each procurement office of the Federal agency with which they desire to do business. If a Federal agency has attached a Supplemental Commodity List with instructions, complete the application as instructed. Otherwise, identify in item 8 the equipment, supplies and/or services on which you desire to bid. The application shall be submitted and signed by the principal as distinguished from an agent, however constituted.

After placement on the bidder's mailing list of an agency, a supplier's failure to respond (*submission of bid, or notice in writing, that you are unable to bid on that particular transaction but wish to remain on the active bidder's mailing list for that particular item*) to Invitations for Bids will be understood by the agency to indicate lack of interest and concurrence in the removal of the supplier's name from the purchasing activity's bidder's mailing list for the items concerned.

DEFINITION RELATING TO TYPE OF OWNERSHIP
(See item 9)

Minority business enterprise. A minority business enterprise is defined as a "business, at least 50 percent of which is owned by minority group members or, in case of publicly owned businesses, at least 51 percent of the stock of which is owned by minority group members." For the purpose of this definition, minority group members are Negroes, Spanish-speaking American persons, American-Orientals, American-Indians, American-Eskimos, and American-Aleuts.

TYPE OF BUSINESS DEFINITIONS
(See item 10)

a. Manufacturer or producer—means a person (or concern) owning, operating, or maintaining a store, warehouse, or other establishment that produces, on the premises, the materials, supplies, articles, or equipment of the general character of those listed in item 8, or in the Federal Agency's Supplemental Commodity List, if attached.

b. Regular dealer (Type 1)—means a person (or concern) who owns, operates, or maintains a store, warehouse, or other establishment in which the materials, supplies, articles, or equipment of the general character listed in item 8 or in the Federal Agency's Supplemental Commodity List, if attached, are bought, kept in stock, and sold to the public in the usual course of business.

c. Regular dealer (Type 2)—in the case of supplies of particular kinds (*at present, petroleum, lumber and timber products, machine tools, raw cotton, green coffee, hay, grain, feed, or straw, agricultural liming materials, tea, raw or unmanufactured cotton linters*). Regular dealer—means a person (or concern) satisfying the requirements of the regulations (Code of Federal Regulations, Title 41, 50–201.101(b)) as amended from time to time, prescribed by the Secretary of Labor under the Walsh-Healey Public Contracts Act (Title 41 U.S. Code 35–45). For coal dealers see Code of Federal Regulations, Title 41, 50–201.604(a).

d. Service establishment—means a concern (or person) which owns, operates, or maintains any type of business which is principally engaged in the furnishing of nonpersonal services, such as (*but not limited to*) repairing, cleaning, redecorating, or rental of personal property, including the furnishing of necessary repair parts or other supplies as part of the services performed.

e. Construction concern—means a concern (or person) engaged in construction, alteration or repair (including dredging, excavating, and painting) of buildings, structures, and other real property.

DEFINITIONS RELATING TO SIZE OF BUSINESS
(See item 11)

a. Small business concern—A small business concern for the purpose of Government procurement is a concern, including its affiliates, which is independently owned and operated, is not dominant in the field of operation in which it is bidding on Government contracts and can further qualify under the criteria concerning number of employees, average annual receipts, or other criteria, as prescribed by the Small Business Administration. (See Code of Federal Regulations, Title 13, Part 121, as amended, which contains detailed industry definitions and related procedures.)

b. Affiliates—Business concerns are affiliates of each other when either directly or indirectly (i) one concern controls or has the power to control the other, or (ii) a third party controls or has the power to control both. In determining whether concerns are independently owned and operated and whether or not affiliation exists, consideration is given to all appropriate factors including common ownership, common management, and contractual relationship. (*See items 6 and 11.*)

c. Number of employees—In connection with the determination of small business status, "number of employees" means the average employment of any concern, including the employees of its domestic and foreign affiliates, based on the number of persons employed on a full-time, part-time, temporary, or other basis during each of the pay periods of the preceding 12 months. If a concern has not been in existence for 12 months, "number of employees" means the average employment of such concern and its affiliates during the period that such concern has been in existence based on the number of persons employed during each of the pay periods of the period that such concern has been in business. (*See item 11.*)

● **COMMERCE BUSINESS DAILY**—The Commerce Business Daily, published by the Department of Commerce, contains information concerning proposed procurements, sales, and contract awards. For further information concerning this publication, contact your local Commerce Field Office.

STANDARD FORM 129 BACK (REV. 2–77)

The navy's purchasing policies are very similar to those in other service branches to the extent that all significant contracts are put out for bid. However, the navy has a reputation of buying what it wants from those it wishes to buy it from. The strict policies that govern all military service buying are theoretically engaged, but they aren't followed quite so closely in this branch. This attitude is terrific if your company is a favored supplier. It's not so terrific if you're on the outside trying to break in.

SELLING TO THE AIR FORCE

The air force is the Department of Defense's advance guard. Many selling opportunities exist with the air force, particularly for high-tech equipment. Besides procuring its own equipment and managing its own programs, the air force is responsible for a number of programs affecting the entire Department of Defense.

The Air Force Systems Command is responsible for the acquisition of all air force systems and the initial procurement of equipment that supports those systems. The Air Force Logistics Command is responsible for supplies and services in support of systems that are operational. All other commands are concerned with supplies and services needed to operate air force bases.

The logistical commands are a good place to start in an effort to do business with the air force because they purchase off-the-shelf supplies. The following list gives names and addresses of Air Force Logistics Centers:

Air Force Logistics Command
Wright-Patterson Air Force Base
Dayton, OH 45433
513-257-3317; 513-257-7632

Oklahoma City Air Force Logistical Command
Tinker Air Force Base
Oklahoma City, OK 73145
405-734-2601

Ogden Air Logistics Center
Hill Air Force Base
Ogden, UT 84406
801-777-4145; 801-777-4146

Sacramento Air Logistics Center
McClellan Air Force Base
Sacramento, CA 95652
916-643-2819; 916-643-6019

San Antonio Air Logistics Center
Kelly Air Force Base
San Antonio, TX 78241
512-925-6918; 512-925-6919

Warner Robins Air Logistics Center
Robins Air Force Base, GA 31098
912-926-5871

Air Force Logistics Command
Newark Air Force Station
Newark, OH 43055
614-522-7942

There are many other air force buying points. For a complete list, consult the publication *Selling to the Military.*

SELLING DIRECTLY TO THE DEPARTMENT OF DEFENSE

It is also possible to sell directly to the Department of Defense through its procurement offices. In the past, the Pentagon awarded monopolies to major suppliers through sole-source contracts. These days, more than half of the jobs are given out only after some type of competition. This new system has opened the market to many different vendors.

One location that buys everything from laundry and dry cleaning equipment to sheet music is:

Defense General Supply Center
Bellwood Petersburg Pike
Richmond, VA 23297
703-276-3617; 703-276-3287

The Department of Defense also maintains offices to assist small and minority-owned businesses in doing business with the agency. These offices are located throughout the country, with headquarters at:

Defense Logistics Agency Headquarters
Cameron Agency
Room 8B 390
Alexandria, VA 22314
202-274-7605

A list of the other procurement and small business offices is contained in the government publication *Selling to the Military.* (If you're getting the idea that this government pamphlet is invaluable to your military selling efforts, you're right on track.)

Submitting an Unsolicited Proposal

Although most contracts are awarded as a result of competitive bidding, the Department of Defense and other government agencies will accept unsolicited proposals. This kind of proposal is the way to present a new idea or product to various departments. Don't feel that this is a hopeless gesture. The Department of Defense recognizes that new technologies and ideas are emerging, not only from military laboratories, but also from the consumer sector.

A proposal made to the DOD should contain the following elements:

- A cover sheet that includes the name and address of the company, the title of the proposal, the name, address and phone number of the project manager, and the date

- A short statement of no more than a few hundred words stating the basic purpose of the proposed work

- A short narrative that discusses the relevance of the proposed work to the Department of Defense, the work plan, and the qualifications of the company making the proposal

- The cost proposal (prepared as a separate document)

Any proprietary information should be identified. A Department of Defense contract pricing proposal sheet is shown as Exhibit 10.

You can obtain more information on how to do business with the Department of Defense by sending for the government pamphlet, *Guide to the Defense Contracting Regulations for Small Business, Small Disadvantaged Business, Women-owned Small Business.* It's available from the Government Printing Office.

EXHIBIT 10

<table>
<tr><td colspan="2">

DEPARTMENT OF DEFENSE
CONTRACT PRICING PROPOSAL
</td><td>

FORM APPROVED
OMB NO 22 R0381
</td></tr>
</table>

This form is for use in procurements when submission of cost or pricing data is required (see DAR § 3-807)

NAME, ADDRESS, AND TELEPHONE NUMBER OF ORGANIZATIONAL ELEMENT RESPONSIBLE FOR SUPPORTING PROPOSAL	TYPE OF CONTRACT
	PLACE(S) AND PERIOD(S) OF PERFORMANCE

TOTAL COST	TYPE OF PROCUREMENT ACTION	
	☐ NEW PROCUREMENT	☐ OTHER *(Specify)*
PROFIT/FEE	☐ CHANGE ORDER	☐ LETTER CONTRACT
	☐ PRICE REVISION/REDETERMINATION	☐ UNPRICED ORDER
TOTAL		

LINE ITEM NO	IDENTIFICATION — NOTE: List and reference the identification, quantity and total price proposed for each contract line item. A line item cost breakdown supporting this recap is required unless otherwise specified by the Contracting Officer. *(Attach continuation page if required.)*	QUANTITY	TOTAL PRICE	REF

I. IF YOUR ACCOUNTS AND RECORDS HAVE BEEN REVIEWED IN CONNECTION WITH ANY GOVERNMENT CONTRACT (PRIME OR SUBCONTRACT) GRANT OR PROPOSAL WITHIN THE PAST 3 YEARS BY A GOVERNMENT AGENCY OTHER THAN IRS OR GAO, PROVIDE NAME, ADDRESS AND TELEPHONE NUMBER BELOW

CONTRACT ADMINISTRATION OFFICE	AUDIT OFFICE

II. WILL YOU REQUIRE THE USE OF ANY GOVERNMENT PROPERTY IN THE PERFORMANCE OF THIS WORK?
☐ YES   ☐ NO   *IF YES IDENTIFY*

III. DO YOU REQUIRE GOVERNMENT CONTRACT FINANCING TO PERFORM THIS PROPOSED CONTRACT?
☐ YES   ☐ NO   *IF YES IDENTIFY*   ☐ ADVANCE PAYMENTS   ☐ PROGRESS PAYMENTS OR   ☐ GUARANTEED LOANS

IV. HAVE YOU BEEN AWARDED ANY CONTRACTS OR SUBCONTRACTS FOR THE SAME OR SIMILAR ITEMS WITHIN THE PAST 3 YEARS?
☐ YES   ☐ NO   *IF YES IDENTIFY ITEM(S), CUSTOMER(S) AND CONTRACT NUMBER(S)*

V. IS THIS PROPOSAL CONSISTENT WITH YOUR ESTABLISHED ESTIMATING AND ACCOUNTING PRACTICES AND PROCEDURES AND DAR SECTION XV COST PRINCIPLES?
☐ YES   ☐ NO   *IF NO EXPLAIN*

VI. COST ACCOUNTING STANDARDS BOARD (CASB) DATA (PUBLIC LAW 91-379 AS AMENDED)

a. WILL THIS PROCUREMENT ACTION BE SUBJECT TO CASB REGULATIONS?
☐ YES   ☐ NO   *IF NO EXPLAIN*

b. HAVE YOU SUBMITTED A CASB DISCLOSURE STATEMENT (CASB DS 1 or 2)?
☐ YES   ☐ NO   *IF YES SPECIFY THE OFFICE TO WHICH SUBMITTED AND IF DETERMINED TO BE ADEQUATE*

c. HAVE YOU BEEN NOTIFIED THAT YOU ARE OR MAY BE IN NONCOMPLIANCE WITH YOUR DISCLOSURE STATEMENT OR COST ACCOUNTING STANDARDS?
☐ YES   ☐ NO   *IF YES EXPLAIN*

d. IS ANY ASPECT OF THIS PROPOSAL INCONSISTENT WITH YOUR DISCLOSED PRACTICES OR APPLICABLE COST ACCOUNTING STANDARDS?
☐ YES   ☐ NO   *IF YES EXPLAIN*

This proposal is submitted in response to (RFP, contract, mod, etc.) _____ and reflects our best estimates and/or actual costs as of this date, in accordance with the instructions of this form

TYPED NAME AND TITLE	SIGNATURE
NAME OF FIRM	DATE OF SUBMISSION

DD FORM 633
1 April 79

Previous edition is obsolete. Replaces DD Forms 633-1 through 3, Apr 68 and DD Form 633-4, Jun 72, which are obsolete

Pre-Award Surveys

Some readers may have gotten the impression that the company that submits a low bid on a federal government contract is home free. The only thing remaining after submitting the bid is to deliver the goods and send the invoices. This isn't true. The government wants to know if the low bidder will be a reliable supplier. Most government agencies will survey the apparent winner of a bid contract to determine whether that party has the technical and financial ability to perform according to the terms of the contract to be awarded. They try to determine the following:

- Is the prospective contractor a manufacturer or a dealer of the item to be contracted?
- Does the proposed contractor have adequate financial resources?
- Does the bidder have sufficient experience with the item or service bid to be a reliable supplier?
- Does the bidder have the equipment or facilities available to fulfill the terms and conditions of the proposed contract?
- Will the bidder be able to meet the delivery, installation, and other terms of the contract?
- Does the bidder have a good record of performance, integrity, and judgment?

Obviously, this investigation will not take place each and every time once a supplier has proven to be reliable. However, if your company is not known to the agency, expect some kind of investigation before a bid award. This process is only fair, since it eliminates irresponsible bidders.

Price Incentive Contracts

When a contract is not awarded as the result of a competitive bid, but rather because of a vendor's special expertise, the agency may try to tie profit to the contractor's ability to control costs while meeting standards of performance, reliability, quality, and delivery. This is a uniform policy throughout the armed forces.

THE SALES CALL TO A FEDERAL GOVERNMENT AGENCY

To sell to a federal government agency, your company needn't be located in Washington, D.C. There are opportunities in just about every town in the United States. We've discussed the opportunities at military bases. Similar opportunities exist at the offices of federal agencies such as the IRS, the Postal Service, VA hospitals, and Social Security Administration offices. Any good-sized city will have a federal office building somewhere.

Still, many salespeople don't know the proper procedure when calling on these government agencies. They don't know the first steps to take, much less the follow-up procedures. This lack of knowledge sometimes makes them ignore this important marketplace. But selling to the government isn't much different than selling to commercial accounts. Nothing beats planning. It works when calling on commercial accounts and it's invaluable when calling on federal agencies. The first and most important step is to learn something about the prospect in advance. The federal government offers more help with this task than does the commercial marketplace. Most government organizations have information officers whose responsibility is to help potential vendors. They can assist you with organization charts, telephone directories, maps of the facility, details on procedure, for example. Use this resource to get started. There are simple steps to follow when calling on any government military of civilian agency.

1. If you're part of an organization that has negotiated a GSA schedule, familiarize yourself with the product, pricing, and other terms of this schedule. Carry the GSA catalog and distribute it when appropriate. It is far easier to sell to a government agency when you can make its procurement job easier.

2. For most products, the initial call should be made to the administrative officer. Present information about your company, your products, and how your company can be of service. Respect this person's time. Most agencies set aside certain hours or days of the week to talk to salespeople. Find out what these hours are and schedule your appointment accordingly.

3. Obtain information as well as give it out. Here's a short list of the information you want to obtain on the first sales call to a government agency.

    a. The names and locations of all activities related to that government office, particularly including purchasing and supplies.

    b. The agency telephone directory. This book will be an invaluable tool for reaching decision makers later on.

    c. The organizational chart of the agency. Who are the decision makers?

   d. Any other information your contact will give you.

   4. If your product is tangible, always request a demonstration or trial before interested parties. Try to get others who may be involved in the decision making process to attend this demonstration.

   5. Establish a set of objectives that you want to accomplish as a result of this call. These objectives may be:

   a. Find out the chain of command of the decision makers in this organization.

   b. Find out what must be accomplished to do business with this particular agency.

   c. Determine the level of authority that is being contacted. Is the individual making decisions for the entire agency, or will purchases merely be made for the local office?

   d. Find out whether the individual has to go to a higher authority for final approval.

   e. Find out how much of your kind of product this local agency actually buys.

   f. Find out if purchase orders are cut locally, or if the national headquarters issue them.

   g. Learn something about the departmental regulations that govern the acquisition of such equipment within this particular organization.

   h. Identify the actual end users of the kind of equipment your company is trying to sell. What kind of requirements do these users have? Where are these users located?

   i. Identify the buying cycle. Once interest has been generated, who initiates the requisition? What steps are taken to issue a purchase order?

   6. Survey of the agency's needs. What is the agency using now? Are they happy with the equipment or service?

   7. Make a brief proposal to the procurement officer. Try to keep the proposal concise, one page or less, if possible. If the agency wants the equipment, the purchasing or procurement officer may take your proposal and submit it as part of the requisition request.

   8. While you want to push for demonstrations, delay them until you have established the agency's interest in your product. A demonstration before the time is ripe can kill the prospect's interest.

   9. Close carefully and without the use of overt pressure. Government procurement must go through certain procedures. Usually the

process is from the user to the user's supervisor to procurement. There's no way to rush this process. It is a serious mistake to try to rush a government order so you can meet a monthly or quarterly sales quota. Any attempt to do so may result in ill will. It can take anywhere from one day to several months to nail down an order. Just get enough potential orders in the stream, and sales quotas will take care of themselves.

10. After the sales call, follow up by mailing sales literature, providing additional information, giving other government agency references, providing details about the equipment and its applications, and so forth.

11. After the sale has been made, check on product performance. Did it live up to your promises? Are the users happy? Will they buy more of the same?

SELLING TO MILITARY EXCHANGES

The army, air force, and navy exchanges buy items for resale. They really aren't very different from traditional department stores except that they are located on military bases and their prices are usually better. They obtain the goods to stock the exchanges through procurement at regional exchanges, each one covering about twenty-five installations. The exchanges are extremely popular with service personnel, and a company with a good product can obtain excellent volume through these outlets. Naturally, consumer items are preferred. The locations of the regional exchanges are:

Alamo Exchange Region
Army & Air Force Exchange Service
Fort Sam Houston, TX 78234
512-225-5381

Capitol Exchange Service
Army & Air Force Exchange Service
Building 6
Cameron Station, VA 22314
703-751-2000

Golden Gate Exchange Region
Army & Air Force Exchange Service
Box 3553
San Francisco, CA 94119
415-556-3400

Ohio Valley Exchange Region
Army & Air Force Exchange Service
Building 2501
Indiana Army Ammunition Plant
Charlestown, Indiana 47111

Southeast Exchange Region
Army & Air Force Exchange Service
Montgomery Industrial Terminal
Building T-5
1280 Kershaw Street
Montgomery, AL 36108
205-264-7301

Purchases for overseas exchanges are handled by:

Army & Air Force Exchange Service Headquarters
Dallas, TX 75222
214-330-2763

Purchases for the navy exchanges are handled by:

Navy Resale Systems Office
29th Street and Third Avenue
Brooklyn, NY 11232

If you want to "sell it to the marines," contact:

Director, Marine Corps Exchange Service
Code LFE
Quantico, VA 22134

SELLING TO THE VETERAN'S ADMINISTRATION

Most civilians don't realize just how big the Veteran's Administration is, just as most businesspeople don't recognize the tremendous potential that this government agency represents. The Veteran's Administration employs about a quarter of a million people. It has a budget of about $28 billion and is in such lines of business as life insurance, mortgages, education, research, pensions, cemeteries, and, of course, medical care. To give you an example of the contract opportunities at the VA, in March of 1988 the administration awarded a $100 million contract to Digital Equipment Corporation for hospital computer hardware. The

VA's annual purchases of supplies, services, construction, and equipment come to about $4 billion a year.

The VA buys many items from GSA schedules, as do most other government agencies. But the VA also has special requirements for goods and services which it procures on its own. Procurement is handled centrally by the Office of Acquisition and Material Management. The address is:

Director of Acquisitions
Veteran's Administration Central
810 Vermont Avenue NW
Washington, DC 20402
202-233-3808

Procurement is also handled at regional VA headquarters and individual VA facilities. Addresses and phone numbers for these are listed in local telephone directories.

SELLING TO THE POST OFFICE

Your company can get on the Postal Service's bidding list by sending a completed Bidder's Mailing List application to:

U.S. Postal Service
Western Area Supply Center
Attn: Bidder's Mailing List
Topeka, KS 66624

Don't worry about supplying a product or service to post offices across the nation—this government agency will allow you to bid selectively for a specific geographic area. A bidder's mailing list application is shown as Exhibit 11.

CHAPTER SUMMARY

The main point of this chapter is that there are substantial opportunities for small- and medium-sized businesses to sell to the federal government. Here's a summary of the points to keep in mind.

The federal government maintains a policy of letting as many contracts as possible through the competitive bid process.

EXHIBIT 11

SUPPLIER'S MAILING LIST APPLICATION

U.S. Postal Service

1. NAME AND ADDRESS

A. COMPANY NAME:*

Address to Which Solicitations are to be Mailed

B. ATTENTION:*

C. STREET OR BOX NUMBER:*

D. CITY:* E. STATE F. ZIP + 4

G. TELEPHONE NUMBER (Include Area Code)*

2. TAX IDENTIFICATION NUMBER (Provide the appropriate numbers on the spaces provided below.)

The TIN is the offeror's Social Security Number (SSN) or other Employee Identification Number used on the offeror's Quarterly Federal Tax Return, US Treasury Form 941.

TAX IDENTIFICATION NUMBER: SSN

TIN NO.

3. PARENT COMPANY NAME & TIN (Complete if applicable; if not, enter "None" after Parent Company name.)

If your company is owned or controlled by a Parent Company enter the offeror's Parent Company TIN in Block 3. A Parent Company is one which owns or controls the basic business policies of an offeror. To own means to own more than 50% of the voting rights in the offeror. To Control means to formulate, determine, or veto basic business policy decisions of the offeror. A Parent Company need not own the offeror to control it; it may exercise control through the use of dominant minority voting rights, voting, contractual arrangements, or otherwise.

PARENT COMPANY NAME:

PARENT COMPANY TAXPAYER ID NUMBER: (TIN NO.)

4. SOCIOECONOMIC DETERMINATION.*

IS YOUR COMPANY:

A. SMALL BUSINESS? YES ___ NO ___

B. A MINORITY-OWNED BUSINESS ? YES ___ NO ___

C. A WOMAN-OWNED BUSINESS? YES ___ NO ___

D. LOCATED IN A LABOR SURPLUS AREA? YES ___ NO ___

E. A NON-PROFIT/EDUCATIONAL INSTITUTION? YES ___ NO ___

5. IDENTIFY UP TO 30 COMMODITY CODES THAT YOU WANT TO SUPPLY.*

1.	11.	21.
2.	12.	22.
3.	13.	23.
4.	14.	24.
5.	15.	25.
6.	16.	26.
7.	17.	27.
8.	18.	28.
9.	19.	29.
10.	20.	30.

6. IDENTIFY UP TO 5 ZIP CODE RANGES OF AREAS WHERE YOU DESIRE TO DO BUSINESS.*

From ___ To ___ From ___ To ___ From ___ To ___

From ___ To ___ From ___ To ___

CERTIFICATION

I CERTIFY THAT INFORMATION SUPPLIED HEREIN (including all pages attached) IS CORRECT AND THAT NEITHER THE APPLICANT NOR ANY PERSON (or concern) IN ANY CONNECTION WITH THE APPLICANT AS A PRINCIPAL OR OFFICER, SO FAR AS IS KNOWN, IS DEBARRED OR OTHERWISE DECLARED INELIGIBLE BY ANY AGENCY OF THE FEDERAL GOVERNMENT FROM BIDDING OR FURNISHING MATERIALS, SUPPLIES, OR SERVICES TO THE POSTAL SERVICE OR ANY AGENCY OF THE FEDERAL GOVERNMENT.

NAME AND TITLE OF PERSON AUTHORIZED TO SIGN (Type or print)	SIGNATURE	DATE

*SEE INSTRUCTIONS ON REVERSE

EXHIBIT 11 (Continued)

Instructions

General

This form is used by firms or individuals wishing to be added to the Postal Service active Supplier Mailing List. That list is consulted by Postal Service buyers to identify possible sources for supplies or services. The form must be properly completed and certified to be accepted.

In filling out the form, use appropriate abbreviations if the total number of characters allowed is insufficient. Do NOT exceed the total number of characters indicated.

Block 1A.: Enter the full name of your company. (Space for a Parent Company is provided below).

Block 1B.: Enter the name of the person, internal mail code, or office to be contacted by our buyer.

Block 1C.: Enter your company Street Address and/or box number.

Block 1D.: Enter your company City.

Block 1E.: Enter your company City's State abbreviation.

Block 1F.: The complete 9 digit zip code must be entered, and must be accurate. Your local post office will be able to provide you with your correct 9 digit zip code. Note: This information is a key field in our file and must be correctly entered.

Block 1G.: Enter the phone number our buyers should call. Include area code.

Block 2.: Fill in this area with *either* the Tax Identification Number (TIN) or Social Security Number (SSN) of your company, but not both. An incorrect completion of this block can result in rejection of your application.

Block 4.: If your business falls into one or more of the categories shown, check the appropriate "Yes" boxes. Check all non-applicable categories "No". For the purposes of determining which boxes best identify your company please use the following definitions.

Small Business: a "small business concern" is one which, including its affiliates, is independently owned and operated, is not dominant in the field of operations in which it is submitting an offer, and is of a size consistent with the standards set forth by SGA in 13 CFR Part 121, or if no standard has been established, of a size employing not more than 500 employees.

Minority or Woman-Owned Business: A "minority business concern" is a concern of which at least 51% is owned by, and of which the management and daily business operations are controlled by one or more members of a minority group. (The same definition applies for a woman-owned business.) For the purpose of this definition, minority group members are U.S. citizens who are Black Americans, Hispanic Americans, Native Americans, Asian-Pacific Americans, or Asian Indian Americans. The term "Native Americans" means American Indians, Eskimos, Aleuts, or Native Hawaiians. "Asian-Pacific Americans" means Americans whose origins are in Japan, China, the Philippines, Vietnam, Korea, Samoa, Guam, the U.S. trust territories of the Pacific, North Mariannas, Laos, Kampuchea, or Taiwan. "Asian-Indian Americans" means Americans whose origins are in India, Pakistan, or Bangladesh.

Labor Surplus Area: A "Labor Surplus Area" is an area of higher than average unemployment. Publication A-130, *Area Trends in Employment and Unemployment* published by the Department of Labor specifically defines this term and lists all areas of the nation categorized as labor surplus.

Block 5.: A minimum of 1 entry is mandatory. This document is the only one used to enter the Commodity Codes for those items in which you are interested in receiving solicitations. Select the appropriate Commodity Codes from the listing on Form 7429-A. Each business concern is allowed a maximum of 30 commodity codes. For example: If you would like the Postal Service to consider your company as a supplier of "BINDING MACHINES", enter "3610" as a Commodity Code. If your company is a supplier of lumber, enter "55" as a Commodity Code. NOTE: Commodity Code entries are not all the same number of characters.

Block 6.: A minimum of 1 entry is mandatory. The zip code ranges are used to identify the area(s) of the United States in which your company will be considered to supply the Commodities as identified in Block 5. See Form 7429-B for a listing of the available Zip Code Ranges. A maximum of 5 ranges are allowed.

Certification: Certify as indicated with signature and typed name and title of a person authorized to sign for your company.

After placement on the supplier mailing list of the U. S. Postal Service, failure of a firm to respond to solicitations will be understood by the Postal Service to indicate lack of interest and the firm's concurrence in removal of their name from the list. If you are unable to bid on a particular solicitation, but wish to remain on the active supplier mailing list for that particular commodity code, submit a notice, in writing, to that effect. In any event concerns not actually submitting an offer may be removed from the list after they have received five solicitations without submitting an offer. Reentry into the system at that point can only be made through a new application.

Revisions:

If you want to revise the information on this form it will be necessary for you to submit a complete new application using Form 7429. All items on file at that time will be replaced with the items shown on the subsequent application. Only the latest application will apply.

PS Form 7429, February 1989 *(Reverse)*

69

Most of the contracting for the goods and services required by federal agencies is handled through the General Services Administration.

The Small Business Administration has been specifically designated to assist small and disadvantaged businesses in obtaining a piece of the procurement pie. It is a resource that should be used by every small business that wants to do business with Uncle Sam.

The government printing office has many informative documents that contain valuable instructions on how to do business with the federal government. The GPO has outlets in most major cities.

When submitting a bid to a federal government agency, completeness counts for everything. Dot the i's and cross the t's.

Every military base in the country is a prospect for small business products and services. These facilities want to buy products from local merchants.

The military exchange system is one of the best retailing outlets in the world. It offers a great medium for products that are to be resold to consumers. The exchanges automatically get your product access to overseas markets, because they are established in U.S. military bases all over the world.

The military is our country's largest purchaser of high-tech equipment. If your company is on the cutting edge of a new technology, don't wait for the military to come to you, go to them. Almost 50 percent of new systems are purchased as the result of unsolicited proposals.

The Veteran's Administration, the Postal Service, the Internal Revenue Service, the Social Security Administration, and other federal agencies are important prospects that shouldn't be ignored.

To be successful in this marketplace you must be prepared to take the time to cultivate your prospects. Remember, the basic rules of selling still apply. The potential users must still be persuaded that they will benefit from the purchase of your product.

Federal agencies and the military market prefer doing business with companies that have taken the time to learn the system. Time spent in mastering the procedures will be rewarded in this marketplace.

4

BACK TO SCHOOL: HOW TO WIN BID CONTRACTS IN THE EDUCATIONAL MARKET

EDUCATIONAL BUSINESS CAN BE YOUR COMPANY'S MOST PROFITABLE BUSINESS

The educational market is a place where any player can hit a home run. The parks are small, and those who keep their eyes on the ball can knock one over the fence. Perhaps the metaphor is strained, but many companies that aspire to big-time sales don't even try to sell to the educational market. They assume that it's too specialized, that schools use nothing other than desks, textbooks, and blackboards. They're wrong.

Schools have gigantic appetites for products. They buy everything imaginable—from abacuses to zithers—and they buy in bulk. A good-sized college may enjoy a more liberal spending budget than many large companies. A major metropolitan school district, such as Los Angeles Unified or New York City School District, will purchase more products and services than 99 percent of all the corporations doing business in

71

those districts. Even a small elementary school buying products for a single classroom will buy them in quantities of twenty or thirty—one for every desk.

Large school districts that use centralized purchasing, and most of them do, commonly issue six-figure purchase orders. Seven-figure orders are not rare. These school districts use so many different kinds of products that almost every vendor can provide something that a school buys.

WHY THE EDUCATIONAL MARKET IS IMPORTANT

Moving a product into a classroom has the same effect as throwing a pebble into a pond: the initial splash is followed by ripples that seem to go on forever. The young students who become acquainted with your product in the classroom go on to become consumers after they graduate. You're getting first crack at their young minds before your competitors have a chance. That's why the educational market is so important. Any company that is successful in it gets the twin benefits of big orders now and a built-in customer base later.

Many major companies recognize the long-term value of school business. A few years ago, the Apple Computer Company sent a free Apple personal computer to just about every school in the country. They gave away obsolete models and obtained tax write-offs, and the "Apple to the teacher" paid off. Apple is still the number one personal computer sold to schools.

EDUCATIONAL MARKET BREAKDOWN

The educational market is broken into categories. These categories are generally based on the age of the students and the level of education taught. Each category uses different kinds of products, makes purchasing decisions in a different manner, and requires a specialized sales strategy. A dynamite marketing approach to the elementary school market could be a dud when tried at state-run universities.

The total market is large, and there are certainly enough places to call on. The following chart shows the basic education categories and the approximate number of locations for each.

- School districts   15,000
  - Elementary schools   64,000
  - High schools   27,500

- Colleges and universities 3,200
- Parochial schools 8,000
- Adult education
  and trade schools 30,000

Note that both elementary and high schools are listed under school districts, because the local school district normally controls all the public schools that fall within its geographic jurisdiction.

WHAT SCHOOLS BUY

The schools use classroom oriented products, but they also buy many other items. The following background information on each classification will help you develop a marketing plan.

Elementary Schools
The elementary (grammar or primary school), is the place where formal education begins. These schools normally teach kindergarten through grade 5 or 6. Their "customers" range from five-year-old kids facing their first class to adolescents struggling with the changes of puberty.

The elementary school buys all the products that everyone associates with a teaching institution: textbooks, pencils, paper, desks, blackboards, chalk, and so forth. The typical elementary school is also a large physical plant. It uses all the products typically associated with the maintenance and care of a large building and grounds. Primary schools need heating oil, industrial soap, floor scrubbers and wax, linoleum, bricks, and power tools. For the outside grounds the school needs grass seed, flowers, fertilizer, garden hosing, bricks, cement, mulch, lawn mowers, roofing material, and a thousand other items.

Every elementary school has a small administrative office that purchases the kind of office supplies that any paperwork-generating entity needs. The school office also buys the small, consumable items used for the grounds. Obviously, these products don't nearly cover the items used by the average primary school. The purchasing decisions are made at the school district level through the competitive bid process.

School districts will write a set of specifications for most products because they want to ensure standardization throughout the system. They buy in bulk to get the benefit of the best quantity pricing. The larger the school district, the less voice an individual teacher or school principal will have in determining what products the school purchases.

Even though principals and teachers at primary schools are not directly involved in purchasing decisions, they should not be ignored. If the product is used in the classroom, call on the teachers. If it's used in building upkeep, call on the maintenance engineers. While these individuals don't make final buying decisions, they do influence them. Their dissatisfaction with a product can prevent an order from being placed. In effect, they have veto power over products they don't like. Calling on the users is particularly important when introducing a new product into the school system. Educators at the primary and secondary school levels are not the most flexible people in the world. If your product or service will require them to do things differently than they have in the past, they'll need all the help, encouragement, and support you can provide.

Junior High School / Middle School

Junior high schools teach seventh, eighth, and ninth grades. Middle schools teach sixth, seventh, and eighth grades.

In the past several years, educators have started students on skill training at much younger ages. Courses that were formerly taught at high school levels are now being offered at the junior high or middle school. This development has created an opportunity to sell skill, trade, and technical equipment for the intermediate grades. They're now a market for lab equipment, typewriters, musical instruments, personal computers, and so forth. These products will be used for classroom training, so large quantity orders are being placed. Again, the purchasing decisions are likely to be made at the school district level. However, it's a mistake to ignore personnel at the school itself. Make sure they know you and are familiar with your products.

High School

High schools educate students from age thirteen to age eighteen. Of all segments of the educational market, high schools represent the best opportunity for obtaining the big order. Vocational training and expanded work in special skills takes place at the high school level. Many different kinds of equipment are needed to implement this training. Some of the laboratory and computer equipment required by high schools approaches the same degree of sophistication as required by colleges and universities.

Purchasing decisions are made at both the school district and the individual school level. Some small and rural school districts may contain only a single high school. In these cases, the principal and teachers at the school will have a big voice concerning the kind of products and services purchased by the school district. In very large cities, where one school district may contain more than two hundred high schools, the principal and teachers have little voice in purchasing decisions, except perhaps to veto things they don't like.

School districts

The school district is the center of administration, educational policy, and purchasing for all primary, intermediate, and high schools within a specific geographic area. This is the place to conduct your major sales effort if you wish to sell to the educational market. In a small rural area the school district may encompass only one combination grammar and high school. The district office may occupy space in this building. In large metropolitan areas, such as New York and Los Angeles, the school district administers for hundreds of schools. The Los Angeles Unified School District has about 65,000 employees, rivaling the payroll of all but one or two other employers in the city.

These large school districts buy in tremendous quantities. They set their own standards, have goods shipped into their own warehouses, and maintain their equipment when the vendors' warranties have expired. Their purchasing techniques are sophisticated. They usually use competitive bidding on orders of any size.

The purchasing department of a large school district is usually highly staffed with buyers to handle specific products. This specialization means that the purchasing agents are well informed about the products they handle. They look to vendors to keep them abreast of innovations in their fields. One of the ways to establish a close relationship with a product buyer is to become his or her conduit to your industry.

The paperwork requirements for school district orders can be horrendous. Consider these requirements as one of the costs of doing business.

You can imagine the size of an order when a large school district with thousands of students decides to put one of anything on each student's desk. The bureaucracy's paperwork itself creates the need for many different kinds of document-control equipment. School districts buy everything from buses to boilers, from air conditioners to potato chips for the lunch program.—In short, the competitive bidder's idea of heaven.

To do business with a school district it's a good idea to know something about its structure. Most districts have the following hierarchy:

1. Superintendent of schools
2. Purchasing department
3. Educational staff

You will need to contact these three departments to get your product accepted into a school district. There may be others, depending on your product. For example, if your product is a food you'll want to speak to the head of the lunchroom program.

School Superintendent

In a small school district, the superintendent of schools is the decision maker and the person you wish to see. In larger school districts, the superintendent's job is likely to be a semi-political position. He or she is more likely to be concerned about overall school policy and keeping the local politicians happy so the tax dollars keep flowing into the district coffers. These administrators are not likely to get involved in individual product decisions unless the product itself is political, such as a controversial textbook. Generally, superintendents will leave product decisions to the educators and purchasing departments. However, they should be contacted. Make sure they know about your company and your products. The superintendent's office is also a good place to register a protest if your company has not received fair treatment on a bid.

The Educators

The educators operating out of the school district office set the standards for the curricula and course material offered by the school district. Most taught classes at one time and may continue to teach occasionally, but few do much teaching while working at the district level. If your product will be used in the classroom, these are the people to see. They can help you by recommending a specification standard that favors your product. They can determine course material. Of course, you must be able to persuade them why your product specifications are necessary to train young minds.

Call on the educators at the school district level very early in the game. It's fruitless to reach a department head after a bid is out and to try to persuade him or her that a certain exclusive feature not in the specs is absolutely critical. This kind of spadework must be done well in advance.

The educational department heads are relatively easy to reach, but difficult to persuade. They usually like to see new products and hear about new ideas in their interest areas, but they're also slow to make changes. They see little reason to tinker with anything that works. The one exception is when they see a "bandwagon" rolling down the road— then they want to climb on. Most educators are reactors, not innovators. If a new program is popular with other school districts, they want it too. On the other hand, a system that hasn't been tested is hard to sell. Educators take the attitude that "If it's good, why isn't everyone else using it?" That's why success stories are so important in the school market. The most effective sales pitch you can make is to give your prospect a long list of happy customers. Obviously, a few educators are innovators, or nothing new would ever be tried. These educators are hard to find and should be treasured when they are found.

School district purchasing departments

School district purchasing departments want to buy goods and services for the fewest dollars. In that way they're no different from the purchasing department of a commercial company. However, as public agencies they are bound by rigid operating guidelines. Almost all requirements for large dollar volume purchases must be put out for competitive bid. The specifications, terms and conditions, and boilerplate on some of these bids can be longer than a Robert Ludlum novel. In most cases the school district must accept the low bid when a qualified bidder meets all the specifications. However, experienced buyers recognize that low price doesn't always mean best value. They'll work with vendors they know and trust to shape specs to favor certain products. Buyers will also place orders with favorite vendors for product quantities just under the amount necessary to trigger the bid process. It's surprisingly easy to establish this favored relationship with school district purchasing agents. This is how it can be done:

1. Call on the purchasing department often.

2. Keep your contacts abreast of new developments in your field.

3. When suggesting specifications, advance reasons for them that serve the school district's interests.

4. Whenever you win a bid, conform to all the terms and conditions on the contract.

5. Don't use the school district as a dumping ground for shoddy or obsolete equipment.

6. Respond quickly to problems.

7. Provide maintenance training for your product for school district maintenance personnel.

8. If your product is used in the classroom provide training material, such as wall charts.

Most of these actions are steps that you'd normally take to hold onto a good commercial account. However, some vendors feel that school district business doesn't deserve the same time and attention. Treat your school districts as valued customers.

In summary, selling to a school district means calling on the teachers and principals at individual schools, staff educators and superintendents at the district office, and buyers at the purchasing department. It means making a case for the specifications that favor your product or service. It means preparing a bid with a sharp pencil. It means following through on commitments so the people at the school district recognize you as a reliable supplier.

Do these steps seem like a lot of trouble? Perhaps they are, but this trouble will be rewarded with big orders that can drive up your company's sales volume in a hurry. Remember, with a school order you get business right now and you're creating additional business for the future.

COLLEGES AND UNIVERSITIES

Selling to colleges and universities is different than selling to lower grade levels. The purchasing decisions are almost always decentralized. There are few attempts at standardization even within a college or university. Individual departments and department chairs are usually autonomous. The Fine Arts Department may not use the same copy machine as used by the Physics Department. Limitations depend solely on the size of the budget. Purchasing's role is generally limited to finding the best price for the item the department head has decided to buy. The one exception to this is state-run colleges, which may be required to buy from blanket contracts negotiated by state purchasing.

This means there are fewer bid opportunities at colleges and universities, but they do exist. Some colleges are required by statute to go

EXHIBIT 12

PLEASE RETURN WITHIN 30 DAYS

CITY OF ORANGE
PURCHASING
637 W. STRUCK AVE.
ORANGE, CA 92667-5584
(714) 532-0334

Please complete and return to above address

BIDDER QUESTIONNAIRE

1. NAME OF FIRM:_____ _____

    Address_____Phone_____
                                                    (Area Code)
    City_____State_____Zip_____

    Orange Business License_____Contractors License_____
         (If Applicable)   (If Applicable)

    TERMS:_____FOB:_____Delivered_____Orange_____U.P.S._____

    Vendor Truck_____Other _____(Check Applicable Area)
                              (Specify)

    Hours Order Desk Open _____A.M.   _____P.M.
                            From   To

2. Major Commodities or Services:

    _____

    _____

    _____

    _____

3. Name of Firm Representative for City of Orange:

    _____
    (Please Print or Type)

4. Do you have repair and service facilities? YES_____NO_____

    If yes:_____Phone:_____
            (Local Address)

5. Type of Business: Manufacturer_____Distributor_____Broker___
                       Retailer____Wholesaler_____Contractor____
                       (type)_____Other (Explain)_____
                       _____

6. Number of years in business_____Present Location_____

EXHIBIT 12 (Continued)

7. List three (3) local references:

a._____

b._____

c._____
    (Name)   (Address)   (Phone No.)

I certify that the foregoing statements are correct. I understand that this information will be used as a basis for evaluating my request to receive bid invitations for purchases by the City of Orange. I also understand that being placed on the City of Orange Vendor Bid Lists does not, in any way, represent an endorsement of my firm by the City of Orange.

_____   _____   _____
 (Date)   (Signature)   (Title)

FOR PURCHASING DEPARTMENT USE ONLY

Additional Remarks:

Date sent:_____

out for bid when a purchase will exceed a certain dollar amount. Others are beginning to realize the benefits of standardization. However, for the most part, selling to a college or university means knocking on doors and calling on department heads one at a time. Start with the purchasing department to get a directory of the various departments, including the names of department heads. When you get an appointment, use your softest sell. This group has a low tolerance for traditional sales techniques. Presumptive closing and other tactics that served you well in commercial markets will get you a quick exit here.

Product knowledge is important in this market. Be prepared to field technical questions about your product. University people expect you to know what you're talking about. They'll want you to explain what your product docs and how it does it.

When you have persuaded the department head to buy your product, he or she will need to fill out a requisition for it. When this is done, hurry back to the purchasing department. Let them know that you are responsible for the department's request. While universities and colleges don't use the formal bid process too often, they use informal bidding and telephone quotes all the time. That is, they'll call several vendors and buy from the one that offers them the best price. Often, they won't take this step if they know that you're one who has done the spadework. Most university buyers will see to it that your company gets the business if your prices are in line with others in the industry.

Once you're on the books as a supplier for that particular item, the buyer may call you when another is needed. You'll also find that university and college people make for wonderful referrals when they're satisfied with a product. A happy buyer will help your selling effort with the department across the hall or the university in the next town.

That's the way most colleges and universities conduct business. Here's a review of the typical steps:

1. Introduce yourself to the purchasing department. Get a campus directory with a listing of all departments. Leave literature on your product or service with the appropriate buyer. Ask that your company be placed on the bid list for the items you carry.

2. Use legwork—call on the individual departments. Persuade one to buy your product.

3. Use the first sale as a building block to reach other departments. Tell your success story to whoever will listen.

4. Establish your company with the purchasing department as a reliable supplier.

5. Deal with all departments openly and honestly.

6. Know your product line.

7. Show the university the newest, most innovative items in your product line.

8. Trade on your success at one college or university to reach and sell others.

Time spent at universities can generate a steady flow of profitable orders. This business will be relatively safe from competition as long as you provide good service and deal openly and honestly.

ADULT EDUCATION AND TRADE SCHOOLS

Trade schools train students in basic and advanced job skills. Their purpose is to get their students into the job market as soon as possible, so the course of study tends to be shorter and more intense. The trade school owners get their incomes almost exclusively from student course fees. There are no tax dollars available to these educators.

The trade school owner is likely to be an entrepreneur struggling to get by. They need training equipment and supplies just as much as any other educational sector, but they are not as well financed to pay for it. Bargains are wanted in this market. Trade schools seldom go out for competitive bid. This is the place to sell your paint-damaged equipment, the returns, and the obsolete hardware. Trade school graduates trained on your equipment are potential customers. They come into the business world at a very fast pace.

PAROCHIAL SCHOOLS

Most of the parochial or religious schools in this country are run by the Catholic Church. Other denominations and religions also run schools. These groups offer both religious and secular instruction in an alternative to the public school system.

Parochial schools are funded through students' fees and contributions from their religious affiliations. Every time a legislator even hints about giving some kind of subsidy to parochial schools, a cry is raised about the separation between church and state and the schools come away empty. This money shortage puts the parochial school several years behind public schools in installing modern equipment. (This may or may not be a disadvantage depending on your attitude toward teaching the basics.)

The parochial school principal is almost always a member of the religious order running the school. The principal, along with teaching staff members, is also the decision maker. If the school is Catholic, the archdiocese may also play a role in any money decision, because that's where the money comes from.

Most archdioceses have purchasing offices. There is also a Catholic Archdiocese Purchasing Association made up of purchasing officers from individual archdioceses. It's possible to negotiate national buying agreements with the association. In these contracts the vendors agree to provide a certain price structure nationwide for all participating members of the association. (Not all archdioceses belong). The Association headquarters is located at:

> Diocesan Commodities Corporation
> 99 North Village Ave.
> Rockville Centre, NY 11570
> 516-764-2130

The individual school will probably have a purchasing agent as well. In many cases, it will be handled on a part-time basis by a teacher with other assignments.

Parochial schools are usually conservative in adopting anything new. Part of this conservatism is due to lack of funds, but whether it's necessity or conviction that guides them, most provide a more fundamental education. One of the first things to do when calling on a parochial school is to check to see whether there are funds available to buy what you're selling. There's little point in going beyond a product demonstration if there's no money in the till.

Parochial schools almost never go out for competitive bid. They buy products from vendors they trust. Once you have obtained this trust, you have a valuable customer you can rely on for much repeat business.

Selling to parochial schools is similar to selling to colleges and universities. It's slow, plodding work that usually requires the salesperson to go to every school. You can try the shortcut suggested of making a deal with the archdiocese, but often individual schools are not absolutely bound by these contracts. The schools must still be sold one by one.

CHAPTER SUMMARY

In summary, the educational market represents a sales potential that many companies haven't exploited. There is a requirement in this marketplace for just about any kind of product, so no company need be shut out. For products used in the classroom, suppliers get immediate business plus the opportunity to establish life-long customers. As in all markets, the basic rules of selling still apply. Schools want to do business with vendors who value that business. There's nothing more basic than that.

5

HOW TO WIN BIG CONTRACTS FROM STATE, COUNTY, AND MUNICIPAL GOVERNMENTS

DOUBLE OR TRIPLE THE VALUE OF A FEDERAL CONTRACT AWARD BY USING IT AT THE STATE AND LOCAL LEVEL

Once a company has been successful in getting its products on GSA schedule as discussed earlier, there's an easy way to increase the value of the contract: Offer the product under the same prices, terms, and conditions to state and municipal governments as to the federal government. This tactic is so successful because many local government purchasing agents buy items directly from GSA schedules. In effect, they let the federal government purchasing agents do their bargaining for them. They know the federal negotiators have forced vendors to use a sharp pencil. Buying from the GSA schedule is an easy way for these local government purchasing agents to be assured that they're getting a fair price without doing any of the work themselves. Often, local purchasing agents will use a federally established price on a product as an alternative to sending out a competitive bid.

Companies can take advantage of this local government "laziness" to put together a marketing effort to state and local government agencies that can double or triple the value of a GSA contract.

Most local government agencies' purchasing departments have access to federal buying schedules. They know what the federal government is buying, who they're buying it from, and the price that's being paid. Still, it doesn't hurt a bit to let these local agencies know about your company's specific deal with the GSA. If they're too busy to put together competitive bids, they may also not have the time to research the details of the various contracts.

The best way to inform local agencies of an existing GSA contract is simply to print extra copies of the GSA catalog you supply to the federal government. These are the catalogs that you mail or hand deliver to various federal agencies to let them know about your product and the GSA pricing schedule. This catalog is by no means restricted information. It can be released to local government agencies. Send copies, along with appropriate descriptive product literature, to state and local government agencies. Include a letter offering the agency the opportunity to buy your company's products at existing GSA schedule terms. See page 87 for an example of one such letter.

Companies using this approach are often surprised by how well it works. Many local government agencies will issue purchase orders on items they require just on the basis of the product being on GSA schedule. They know the price is fair so they needn't go to any more trouble than is necessary. The fact is, being on GSA contracts gives your company, its products and prices, legitimacy. The GSA contract by itself is enough to generate additional business.

Orders from local government agencies may not come immediately after the catalog is mailed. That beautiful four-color job your company spent so much money printing may go into the buyer's tickler file there to stand in lonely repose until pulled out when the local agency has a requirement for the kind of product your company makes. If they don't need it, they aren't going to buy it. If they do need it, being on GSA contract gives your company a better chance of obtaining the order.

A GSA contract is a sign of legitimacy. State and local agencies that don't use GSA schedules because their local statutes require them to go out for competitive bids each and every time, are still impressed

Mr. Roger Williams
Purchasing Agent
Mendocino County
County Building
Mendocino, CA 11122

Dear Mr. Williams:

Our company, Acme Shelving, is on GSA schedule for its line of adjustable steel shelves. A copy of our GSA catalog and descriptive literature is enclosed. We offer local and county government agencies the opportunity to buy our products directly from our federal price list. Delivery and terms are also per GSA schedule.

As I'm sure you know, the federal government demands the lowest available commercial prices, so the discounts offered from our list prices are substantial. Our offer gives your agency the opportunity to take advantage of the federal government's buying power without going to the time and trouble of using the competitive bid process.

If you wish to place an order, make it out directly to Acme at the address on the letterhead. If you would like more information, fill out the enclosed card or call me.

Cordially,

Bill Rankin
Sales Manager

P.S. We'd also like the opportunity to bid on the county's special requirements for shelving. Please put our company on your bid list.

by the credential of a GSA contract. As a rule, these agencies will be happy to add your company's name to their bidders' list, because being on GSA schedule is a sign of being a reliable supplier.

Any kind of direct mail program, including sending out GSA catalogs, can be more effective when followed up by some kind of personal call. Did the purchasing agent get the cover letter? Did she understand the pricing structure of the GSA contract and the products covered? Would he be interested in a personal demonstration? When might a purchase decision be made? If the products under contract don't suit, are there others in the same category that may be needed? If this office doesn't use GSA schedules when ordering, does it use the bid process? When is the next bid due? These kind of questions will help the vendor assess the path that must be taken to win business from that specific agency.

Even if the letter is not followed up by a personal call, it has performed double duty because (a) it has offered product to the agency at GSA pricing and these offers will produce some orders; and (b) it has requested that your company be placed on the agency's bid lists for larger quantity purchases.

This same tactic of offering local agencies the benefits of a large contract pricing schedule can be used by companies which have successfully negotiated a statewide contract. The company holding the state contract for a product can offer the same terms and conditions to county governments, city government agencies, and educational institutions within that state. Milking the contract in this way is an effective and low-cost way of generating additional business. Again, the key to getting additional business is letting these local government agencies know that you hold a contract, what the contract's terms are, and that "piggybacking" is not only allowed, it is encouraged.

A successful contract with a large school district can be used to pick up business with the smaller school districts in the region. The process works with many different variations because the smaller agency is reaping the benefits of large volume buying.

STATE AND LOCAL GOVERNMENTS AREN'T "LITTLE" FEDERAL GOVERNMENTS: CRITICAL DIFFERENCES YOU NEED TO KNOW TO BID SUCCESSFULLY

One of the mistakes many vendors make is to regard state and local government agencies as being miniature versions of the federal government. That isn't true. Sure, they're both bureaucracies with a delight for paperwork, a maddening slowness, and a passion for regulations. But there are also some critical differences between federal, state, and local governments. It's important that you are aware of these differences if you want to be successful at the state and local government level.

1. The bid process, particularly at the municipal level, is likely to be a good deal less formal. For example, when a product is required, a buyer at a local government agency might simply call a few vendors and ask for phone bids. This practice makes it important to be one of the companies that is called. The phone bid procedure also lends itself to abuse. In some instances, a purchasing agent will let a favored vendor know what the competition has bid, in effect giving this vendor the business, or at least the opportunity to bid a lower price.

2. Local government agencies sometimes put out "or equal" bids. In this instance, the agency has selected a specific model of one vendor's equipment, requested bids by manufacturer's model number "or equal." The unfairness of this approach is that other bidders must exactly match the specifications of the selected model. Other vendors' models can be challenged on the smallest detail. There have been instances where a lower bid has been disqualified because the color was different. The agency sending out a bid in this manner obviously favors a specific brand and is trying to discourage the bidding of alternatives. The purchasing departments that use this practice are really subverting the competitive bid process.

3. Personal relationships count for more when dealing with local government agencies. It's easier for vendors, willing to spend the time to cultivate the right people in the agency, to shape equipment specifications to fit their products. Exclusive features that make it difficult or impossible for others to bid may be specified.

4. The purchasing agents at local agencies are often less knowledgeable about the equipment they are buying. A local government purchasing agent may be responsible for purchasing hundreds of items. He or she can't know too much about any one item. There's a greater reliance on the users and the vendors to provide guidance when the agency is developing product specifications. This gives the company which is able to sell on a "specmanship" level a greater advantage.

5. Local government places more reliance on outside testing data. Local agencies often don't have the luxury of their own testing laboratories to evaluate new products and set standards. (Some states have such facilities, but very few municipalities do.) As a consequence, these agencies often rely on the test results produced by the federal government or by an independent testing laboratory such as Buyer's Laboratory. They may refuse to consider a product from a vendor unless that vendor can point to a positive test result from a recognized testing facility.

Any company selling to the local government market should submit products to independent testing laboratories on a regular basis. If your product has been tested by an independent laboratory, make the test results available to all agency buyers. (Note: An indifferent test result is better than no test at all. Obviously, if the test result is embarrassing, you may not wish to share it with potential customers.)

6. Local government agencies sometimes try to circumvent their own rules and regulations. If a bid contract has been won by a vendor they don't know or don't like, or if there was favoritism toward a specific vendor, a local agency may attempt to unfairly disqualify the low bidder. Their reasons are often nonsensical; they simply want another supplier to get the order. If your company is being subjected to this kind of discrimination, it's important to understand the protest procedure *and be willing to use it.*

7. A successful bid and contract with some agencies often isn't a guarantee of actual business. Just winning a bid contract doesn't necessarily mean that your company will be getting many orders as a result of it. Sometimes the contract holder doesn't get any business at all. Some state agencies allow their individual offices to buy products off contract whenever they please. In effect, the contract holder has given the agency the benefit of quantity pricing without obtaining quantity or exclusivity guarantees in return. To protect against this possibility, when bidding a contract to a local government agency always ask how much was actually purchased from that contract last year. That number will give you a better idea of how much volume to expect this year than will any claim by the purchasing office. A good selling job to individual offices within the agency will also help your cause. After winning the contract, arrange demonstrations and seminars on your product. Make the users comfortable with the decision of the purchasing branch.

8. Politics play a larger part when dealing with local government agencies. It is naïve to suppose that all contract awards are made strictly on the basis of merit. What you know, whom you know, past relationships, favors, "clout," the company's standing in the community, and other factors all may affect the award process. Those companies who wish to do business with local governments should develop and nurture

relationships with local political figures. I don't suggest this tactic in order to gain an unfair advantage for your company through political influence, but rather to be able to reach a sympathetic ear if it becomes necessary to protest an unfair bid award to a competitor.

If you get the idea that doing business with state and local government agencies is more rough-and-tumble than working with the federal government, you're right. The differences are substantial. However, don't consider these differences a disadvantage. It would be a serious mistake to ignore state and local governments as a potential source for new business. The mere uncertainty, the sometimes haphazard approach of state and local government agencies to contract awards, the greater reliance on personal and subjective factors, gives companies willing to expend the time and effort cultivating these agencies a greater profit opportunity.

HOW TO AVOID LOCAL POLITICS AND SELL YOUR PRODUCT OR SERVICE ON MERIT

Given the fact that local government business is entwined, if not en-snarled, with local politics, how can a company make sure that merit, value, and service are recognized and rewarded by these government agencies? Here are some steps to take that will ensure fair treatment regardless of the political climate:

 1. When approaching a local government agency, study its pattern of awarding contracts for the product or service you're trying to sell. Do one or two companies get all the business? Does the agency rely heavily on telephone bids where quotes are difficult to trace? Does the agency send out many "or equal" bids that put most vendors at a disadvantage? Do bid specs appear to be fairly written? The answer to these questions will tell you if you're likely to get a fair shake with that agency.
 2. Reach the actual user of the product or service you're trying to sell. Convince the user of the advantages your company offers. Get agreement that you have a better mousetrap. If the user can't buy anything without going through purchasing (this will be the situation in most cases), think about providing a free sample or lending a demo.
 3. When you have the user's agreement that your product offers advantages, take this information to the purchasing department. Make

sure the buyer understands that the user prefers the specific product your company offers.

4. Learn the disadvantages of the equipment or service now being purchased. What doesn't the user like about it? What extra work or expense is it creating? Make sure the purchasing department understands the extra cost or inconvenience attributed to the other product. Send a letter detailing the extra costs so there's a historical record on file.

5. Use industry studies, independent lab reports, and the experiences of other government agencies and commercial customers to dramatize the value of your product or service to the purchasing agent.

6. Point out current specification requirements that may increase the cost to the agency without adding to the value of the product. Often any agency will mindlessly reproduce the same specs year after year, even when certain features are no longer necessary. Perhaps if these features were eliminated, the cost of the product could be reduced. It's important that you get the end user's agreement that a specification feature may be superfluous. A buyer may not believe a vendor who makes an unsupported claim, but he or she will believe an end user. The buyer will appreciate supported evidence of an unnecessary specification, because lowering the specifications requirements will likely save the agency money and the buyer will look good.

If you've taken these steps, you've gone a long way toward climbing over any political barriers hindering your product from being sold on merit. Most government buyers want to act in the best interest of the agency. If they do most of their business with a few favored vendors it's because they trust these vendors to do a good job. Once you prove that your company can offer more value than a current supplier, you can achieve that favored vendor status and orders will begin to gravitate to your company. In other words, the political clout of your competitors is just another objection to be overcome, the same kind of objection salespeople have been dealing with since the first Phoenician traders were selling their wares throughout the Mediterranean.

WHY BEING ON CONTRACT ISN'T ENOUGH

Picture this: Your company has just been placed on state contract in a multiple-award state. "Multiple award" means that the price has been negotiated for any state agency office that chooses to use your product. Three other vendors have also been given awards in the same category.

The features and specifications on all four products are comparable. Your product's price is the lowest. Does your product's lower cost mean that you can just sit back and expect to receive at least 25 percent of all the state business generated for your product classification? Should you anticipate receiving more than 25 percent of the business? After all, you're the one with the best price. Relax at your own risk. You may not receive any business at all. Being on contract in a multiple-award state is nothing more than a hunting license. It gives you the opportunity to go after business, but does not guarantee that you'll actually get any business.

Some state agencies are very powerful. They exist like fiefdoms within medieval monarchies. The Department of Motor Vehicles, the Bureau Parks and Recreation, and other agencies may employ thousands of people in dozens of offices and other facilities throughout the state. The people who work in these agencies don't know anything about your product except that it is on contract at a certain price. Some of the agencies may not be thrilled and delighted with many of the past purchasing decisions made by state contract negotiators. If this is the first year you've had a product on contract, the actual users may not have even heard of your company. Why should they buy your product in place of another with which they are familiar? The answer is that they shouldn't and they won't. Companies that land a state contract and then sit back waiting for the orders to roll in are invariably disappointed. *It simply doesn't work that way.*

The way to get orders from these agencies is the same way you go about getting orders from commercial accounts. You work the territory. The only thing different about this selling situation is that the price has already been negotiated. Here are some specific suggestions on how to obtain the most business from a multiple-award contract.

1. After the award has been announced, send out a mailing to all state agencies with literature and information on your product. You can get a list of agency offices from the purchasing department. They may want to see a copy of your mail piece in advance.

2. Find out who the actual users are within each agency. Target them for demos and presentations.

3. Trials and loaners are often an effective way of acquainting agency offices with an unfamiliar product.

4. Take special care with initial installations. Often an agency will "try" one of something that's just been placed on contract. The success or failure of this trial could determine how much additional product will be sold to that agency.

5. Make special offers on peripherals and supply items that aren't part of the contract. These offers could help set you apart from the other vendors on the multiple-award contract.

CHAPTER SUMMARY

State agencies want the same attention from vendors that is paid to commercial accounts. Those companies that give it to them are the ones that succeed in getting big orders from this marketplace.

Use time-tested selling techniques. Visit agency headquarters. Talk to the decision makers. Learn the applications of the users. Talk about the advantages of your company's products. Demonstrate. Provide good and reliable after-sale service.

Don't treat state and local agencies as simply smaller versions of federal agencies. They aren't.

Use your federal GSA schedules as a means to open the doors to state and local agencies.

Keep your promises.

Build relationships with buyers and end users at state and local agencies.

Take the time to develop relationships with local political figures.

Learn how to work with the product's users to shape specifications.

Don't expect a multiple-award contract to be an automatic guarantee of business.

Use direct mail, personal contact, demonstrations, and seminars to acquaint agency personnel with your company and product.

Do all these things and the other vendors on the state contract will wonder why they aren't getting any orders while you can't keep up with the demand.

6

HOW TO PROTEST A BID

There are some vendors who never protest bid awards no matter how unfairly they've been treated. They may grumble and fume when a bid they should have won is awarded to a competitor, but they never go beyond the complaining stage. They feel that protests never get a decision reversed and only serve to anger the involved agency. "Why make waves?" is their philosophy. It's the way that losers think.

Protesting an improper bid award demonstrates to the awarding agencies that they must play by their own rules. One thing is certain when dealing with government agencies: If they have learned you'll accept being treated unfairly without a whimper, they'll do it as often as they wish. Don't be concerned about antagonizing any agency that has denied you an award that you deserved on merit. Each time you fight, no matter what the result, the next award is more likely to be given to your company.

WHEN TO PROTEST A BID

There are two occasions when an award to a competitor should be protested. These are:

1. When your offer is the lowest by a qualified bidder meeting all the specifications. If the involved agency attempts to ignore your low offer in order to give the contract to some favored vendor, *protest*. Improper awards are made to pet vendors all the time. This happens most frequently when awarding agencies are not acquainted with the company making the low bid. They prefer to trust the devil they know as opposed to the devil they don't know. That's why it's important to establish relationships with agencies requesting bids early on. Let them know something about your company and its capabilities well before the bid deadline.

2. When your competitor doesn't meet all the requirements and specifications on the request for quotation. Occasionally an agency will try to waive a specification after the results have been posted in order to take advantage of an attractive price offered by a vendor. In effect, accepting any bid that doesn't meet the specifications no matter how attractive the price, is lowering the agency's own standard. The problem is that if the standards were lowered, perhaps a number of companies could have provided lower prices on different models. By accepting a product that didn't meet its own bid specification the agency has given an unfair advantage to one bidder. If the feature wasn't necessary, why did the agency specify it in the first place?

HOW TO PROTEST A BID AWARD TO A COMPETITOR

Once you have decided a protest is necessary to protect your company's interests, there are several steps you can take to ensure that your protest is taken seriously. Here's what to do:

1. Cool down. It's normal to feel anger when a bid that rightfully belongs to your company is awarded to another. But this anger won't help you get the situation rectified. Assemble all the pertinent facts in the case and put them in sequence. A logically presented argument is worth more than hot words and unproven accusations.

2. Call the purchasing agent at the involved agency. Ask for the specific reasons your bid was rejected. If your company was the low bidder, the purchasing department must offer an explanation for rejecting your offer. Listen carefully to what you are told. The rejection you feel is unfair may be correct! Perhaps your bid wasn't filled out properly. Perhaps you interpreted the specifications incorrectly. If your bid was rejected for just cause, the call to the purchasing department will save you the trouble and embarrassment of an incorrect protest. The call will also serve to help build rapport with the purchasing department and a greater understanding on how to prepare a bid they won't reject.

3. Inform the purchasing agent of your plan to protest. If the purchasing agent's reasons for rejecting your company's bid doesn't make sense to you, tell him or her that you plan to protest the bid award. Expect a cold silence on the other end of the line. No one likes to have decisions questioned. A purchasing agent or buyer from a bureaucratic environment realizes there's trouble ahead. At this point he or she hopes that you're all bluster and won't follow through.

4. Follow up your conversation with a written letter of protest. State the reasons why you feel the bid award is unfair. Send copies of this letter to the purchasing agent, his or her immediate supervisor, and the head of the group actually using the equipment. In the letter refute the reasons the purchasing agent has given you for rejecting your low bid. For example, if the P.A. claims that your equipment doesn't meet specifications, provide evidence that it does. Offer to demonstrate any capability that is in dispute. Here's an example of a protest letter:

Chief Purchasing Agent
County Courthouse, Room 214
Sidewinder County
Devil's Dump, New Mexico 11122

Dear Purchasing Agent:

This is a formal protest of the county's intent to award bid #1289678 for sidewinder scale removers to the Hss Company. Our company, Snakes R Us, had the lowest bid by a qualified company meeting all the specifications. Your contention that our Cobra model does not meet the spec for automatic scale removal is incorrect. We are prepared to demonstrate the capability of this model in your office or ours.

Purchasing Agent, your decision to disallow our valid bid is in direct contradiction to county regulations. We have met every condition of the bid and now ask that we be awarded the contract. If the county follows through on its intent to award the contract to the Hss Company as you have indicated, we will seek other remedies.

Cordially,

Joe Hardball

This kind of letter will get the purchasing agent's attention. You've stated the case plainly and put your protest on record. You've also offered to disprove the claim that your product doesn't meet the specifications. It's now up to the agency to prove that your company wasn't the lowest qualified bidder. In "seeking other remedies" you've hinted at legal action without actually saying that you'll sue. When working with a belligerent official consider mailing the protest letter to other high-level managers within the agency.

5. Find out what the agency's plans are. When the protest letter has been received by the agency, call the person you mailed it to and ask what action the agency plans to take. You'll probably get one of the following three replies:

A. The agency will give you an opportunity to demonstrate your equipment's capability as you requested. In this instance, expect representatives from the actual user to be present. Don't expect this demonstration to be friendly. The user may prefer your competitor's equipment.

B. The agency plans to award the contract to your competitor because it feels your protest is without merit. They don't need to look at your equipment to know that it doesn't meet spec.

C. The agency will call a protest hearing during which you can present your case to a governing board.

MAKING A PROTEST AT AN AGENCY'S BOARD MEETING

Don't give up hope just because the agency has rejected your protest. You still have not lost everything. A board of directors must still approve the award. The approval is normally done at a public board meeting. You can show up at this meeting and make your case when the item comes up on the agenda. *Don't do this unless you are absolutely certain of your facts.* The board members, while interested in saving the taxpayers money, will usually try to show support for agency employees. Reinforcing their decisions is one way to demonstrate this support. Your case must be strong and clear before making this final appeal. Prepare a protest package for each board member. Keep your arguments simple and avoid accusatory statements. When you get a chance to speak, say your piece and sit down. It isn't necessary to repeat everything three times.

The board may call on the purchasing agent for a rebuttal. Be courteous. Let the agency's spokesperson complete his or her remarks. Refute anything said that is incorrect, but do so in a level-voiced manner.

If you've made a convincing presentation that the agency can't refute, expect an awkward silence. The board members had come to the meeting to conduct routine business. They hadn't anticipated controversy. Tonight someone has come along and suggested that the agency wants to spend more money than is necessary or is bending its own rules. Worse yet, a statement of the facts is in the minutes of the meeting. Something must be done.

Don't expect the board to reverse the agency's purchasing department decision on the spot. That would be too embarrassing. The best you can reasonably hope for is a decision to take the matter under advisement. What usually happens a few weeks later is a decision to rebid the entire contract. Throwing out all bids and starting over again is a tactful way of admitting that a mistake was made. You'll be surprised at how well your company will be treated on the rebid. The agency purchasing department will bend over backwards to be fair. They know that the board will be carefully monitoring the rebid process. You can be fairly sure that your bid won't be rejected a second time if it's low and meets all the specifications.

THE FORMAL PROTEST HEARING

Showing up at an agency board of directors meeting is a bit of surprise that could catch the purchasing department off guard. The formal protest hearing is no surprise to anyone. The meeting has been convened specifically for you to present your case. Both sides have time to prepare their cases.

Should You Bring an Attorney to a Formal Protest Hearing?

At the formal protest hearing the agency may have an attorney in attendance. You may feel it necessary to bring in your own legal expert to counteract. But consider going without one. Present your own case if you're at all articulate. This strategy may not put you at as much of a disadvantage as at first it might seem. Often, two opposing attorneys tend to obscure the facts with legal wrangling. The function of the agency's attorney is not to reinforce the purchasing department's decision, but rather to ensure that the agency is not leaving itself open to legal action. Sometimes an agency attorney is more on your side than any lawyer you could hire.

What to Expect at a Formal Hearing

The formal protest hearing will be an adversarial hearing. It's you against the agency with the board of directors as the judge and jury. Prepare a summary of your case for each board member. (They may ask you for advance copies. This is a fair request, because you have advance notice of the agency's reason for your bid's rejection.) When making your presentation, stick to the facts, but make certain that the agency sticks to the facts too. For example, don't allow the person presenting the agency's case to bring up feature advantages your competitor's equipment may possess that weren't listed on the bid specifications. If they were important to the operation they should have been included when the bid request was sent out. At the end of the presentation, board members may ask you questions. Answer them as completely as you can. Don't be resentful or sarcastic. When asking questions of your own, don't try to cross-examine any of the agency's people. You'll come across better as a businessman seeking legitimate redress than as a quasi-lawyer.

In all probability the hearing will end without a decision. Expect the chairman to tell you that the board will deliberate and "let you know within a week or two." They'd prefer to support the agency's recommendation, but you've forced them to take a close look at the total proposition. Your protest has made them accountable. No matter how strong your case, you're not likely to get an outright reversal. Few boards will take the action of voiding the contract to your competitor and giving it to you. If you get a notice of a rebid, you'll know that the board thinks you're in the right.

THREE STEPS NOT TO TAKE WHEN PROTESTING A BID

There are several actions that are inappropriate to a bid protest. These are:

1. Never downgrade your competitor's equipment or service. Make statements of provable fact where equipment specifications are concerned, but avoid comments concerning quality or reliability or your competitor's reputation in the industry. Don't recite horror stories about your competitor's unsatisfied customers. These kind of remarks won't help your case.

2. Never make subjective statements about your equipment. Avoid remarks like "Our equipment lasts longer," unless they're germane to the specifications *and* you have independent documentation.

3. Never accuse agency members of any impropriety. If you suspect there may have been collusion between agency members and the competition, keep your suspicions to yourself unless you can offer hard evidence. If you do come across such evidence, consult a lawyer on the best way to proceed. You're getting into the area of charges of criminal misconduct. There could be a libel suit against you if you're wrong.

SHOULD YOU EVER SUE?

If the board turns down your protest, and most are rejected, there is still one final course of action open to your company: you can sue the agency in two different ways. These are:

- Sue to have the contract given to your competitor voided and awarded it to you.
- Sue for the lost profit this contract would have brought your company.

Should you go this far? Some companies have taken this action and succeeded. Many others have failed. Success or failure, legal fees are expensive. What's more important is that a court action will take up your time and absorb your attention. There's something about a court case that crowds out other endeavors. You'll be distracted from selling, from pursuing other contracts, from paying attention to your business, and from creating other opportunities. Sue if you must, but for true sales and marketing people selling is more fun and profitable than litigating. In most cases, once the protest is lost it's time to move on to other business.

WHY PROTEST AT ALL?

Why protest a bid award? The protest action takes up valuable selling time, most are lost and a "win" usually means just another chance to bid on the contract. Why not accept the agency's decision, unfair though it may be, and move on to the next deal? The answer is that competitive bidding for large contracts is playing in the big leagues and big leaguers don't accept losses easily. A protest done without rancor does not antagonize the involved agency, but rather demonstrates that you're a determined competitor who demands to be treated fairly.

Never make a frivolous protest, but if you're right and can prove it, protests are worthwhile. You'll find the agency will respect you for it. The protest may even be the beginning of a beautiful friendship.

THE ANATOMY OF A SUCCESSFUL PROTEST

Background

The state of California awards a single-source contract for all electronic office typewriters used by state agencies. This is a highly prized, and therefore extremely competitive, contract, because the state of California is the single largest user of typewriters with the exception of the federal government. In a single year the state will normally purchase about five to seven thousand units. In addition, a number of county governments, cities, and schools within California always purchase from the state contract.

In the bid specification, the state uses a very complex formula based on the life-cycle cost of the units. Put very simply, the price of the supplies carries as much weight as the price of the typewriters when determining the successful bidder. This is the story of how the successful bidder, Brother International, developed an unorthodox bid strategy and then defended that strategy in a successful bid protest when the state sought to award the contract to another vendor.

The Bid Strategy

Brother decided to bid through a prominent Sacramento office equipment dealer, an expert at state government contracts. The dealer's size qualified for a small business "bogey" of 5 percent. That meant the dealer's bid automatically received a 5 percent edge when compared to the bid from a larger company. Because the life-cycle cost formula used by the state heavily favors low supply prices, Brother used normal discount schedules on the typewriter prices, but quoted *below cost* prices on the ribbons.

The Bid Opening

All bids were opened. After calculating the prices for both the supplies and the machines, Brother International had the lowest overall cost based on the state's complicated life-cycle cost formula.

The Purchasing Department's Decision

The state's purchasing department rejected Brother's bid. The state claimed that pricing the supplies below cost invalidated the bid. The state doesn't believe that the vendor could possibly provide the supplies at those prices. State purchasing announced its intent to award the contract to the second low bidder.

The Vendor's Protest

Brother immediately filed a formal letter of protest. In the protest letter, Brother pointed out that prices for supplies had been artificially low on past contracts. There was no requirement in the bid specification that stipulates supplies can't be priced below cost. The state was attempting to add a stipulation not in the original bid.

State Purchasing's Reaction

Brother's protest meant the state must delay the contract award. The bid and the protest were highly unusual. A hearing was scheduled, but was delayed several times. The state sent out several thirty-day bids to satisfy the immediate typewriter needs for state offices. Brother won one of these bids, and they purposely bid high on the others to confuse their competitors.

The Pot Boils

During a visit by Brother representatives to the purchasing office, a state official began to shout and use abusive language with no apparent provocation. He ordered the Brother representatives out of the building. The Brother major account representative reported the incident to several state senators and local politicians. As a California employer, Brother formally complained of the state official's behavior.

The Pot Cools

One state senator assigned a staff member to investigate the incident. Correspondence was exchanged. The state official wrote a letter of apology to the Brother personnel involved in the incident. They accepted his apology. The state senator asked to be apprised of the outcome of the protest hearing.

The Protest Hearing

Brother personnel worked with the Sacramento dealer to prepare themselves for the protest. Their principal argument was that there was no precedent for rejecting a bid on the basis that a price was too low. They developed documentation on cases in the past where the state accepted bids that appeared to be below cost.

The hearing room was packed with representatives from typewriter manufacturers, Sacramento office equipment dealers, state officials, and other spectators. The once abusive state official, also in attendance, went out of his way to be friendly and courteous.

As the hearing opened one man stood and asked to be heard. He was a member of the state attorney's office. It was his opinion that the state could be exposing itself to a lawsuit if it accepted or rejected the bid by Brother. He recommended a re-bid. The recommendation was voted on and accepted. The hearing was over a scant sixty seconds after it had begun.

The Aftermath

The state put out a new bid with different specifications placing less emphasis on the cost of supplies. The Brother representatives were treated with extreme courtesy. In preparing the bid, Brother changed the bid strategy to fit the revised specifications. They priced the type-writers much lower and the supplies higher. They won the re-bid by a few pennies. The contract belonged to them for a full year.

The Lessons

The strategy used by this vendor employed three specific suggestions presented in earlier chapters of this book. They are:

1. Brother bid through a small business dealer. They needed this dealer's small business "bogey" because the second bid was won by only a few pennies. Tacking on an extra 5 percent would have cost them the contract.

2. They took advantage of the original bid specifications to shape their proposal so their cost would appear to be lower overall.

3. They varied the pricing on different phases of the bid so the competition would have no clear idea of what their final bid price would be. When the re-bid prices were announced, the other vendors were surprised.

4. When the state announced its intention to award the contract to another vendor, Brother vigorously defended its own position with a protest.

CHAPTER SUMMARY

Protests are part and parcel of competitive bidding. They are as necessary as pricing strategies or locating bid opportunities.

Don't worry about angering an agency by making a protest. If you're right, steam ahead.

Never make frivolous protests. That will anger an agency.

Make your protest both verbally and in writing. Distribute copies of the protest to various individuals within the agency.

Show up at public board meetings if an agency rejects your rightful protest.

Avoid issues of integrity and ethics when making protests. Never make charges without hard evidence.

Don't malign your competitors during a protest hearing. It is proper to point out specification deficiencies in your competitor's equipment and improper bid procedures.

The more you fight for your rights on every bid, the more bids you will win.

7

BIDDING TO PRIVATE INDUSTRY

THE COMPANIES THAT USE COMPETITIVE BIDDING TO SELECT VENDORS

Most commercial companies don't use the competitive bid process to select equipment and service vendors. They prefer the negotiation process because it gives them greater control. Unlike government agencies, they are not required by statute to seek out the lowest price. Their supplier decisions are based on many factors including quality, delivery, reputation, reciprocity, habit, favoritism, and relationships.

However, there are some commercial companies that do use the bid process. The most prominent of these are government prime contractors. These are companies who do the bulk of their business with government agencies themselves. These companies don't always use competitive bidding, but they do so more frequently than commercial companies not involved with government contracts.

Government prime contractors use competitive bidding to select suppliers for two reasons. First, they want to tie down the costs for whatever product or service they're supplying to the government. The bid process is a good way to determine exactly the cost of the system's components. Second, they want to convince the government watchdogs overseeing the contract that they're operating in an economical manner.

HOW TO FIND GOVERNMENT PRIME CONTRACTORS

There are literally thousands of government prime contractors, commercial companies selling our bureaucracy everything under the sun. No matter where your business is located, there are some government prime contractors in your area. How do you find them? It's easy—just buy a copy of the *Government Production Prime Contractors Directory*. This publication lists every government prime contractor in the country in both alphabetical and zip code order. It is available from:

> Government Data Publications
> 1100 17th St. N.W.
> Washington, DC 20036

The publisher also puts out a list rental service on Chesire or pressure sensitive tapes. A geographical portion of the lists may be purchased. They also publish a monthly magazine, *Government Prime Contracts*, that lists prime contractors by product category. Another publication, *R & D Contracts Monthly*, concentrates on recent research and development contract awards.

HOW TO DO BUSINESS WITH GOVERNMENT PRIME CONTRACTORS

After locating a government prime contractor, the first marketing step to take is to contact its small business administrator. Most government prime contractors have a person on board who serves the same function as does the federal government SBA. His or her job is to help guide the small business through the corporate maze to land some business. If such a person does not exist in the company you solicit, try the purchasing office, identifying your company as a small or minority-owned business. You may be surprised by the cordial reception you'll receive. Many government prime contractors are required to purchase certain percentages of the goods and services they require from small or minority-owned businesses. It's in their own contracts with the government. They're actively looking for reliable small companies to act as suppliers. *They must give business to small company vendors.* Even when they go out for bid, a small or minority-owned company will receive a sizable bogey.

WHY BIDDING TO PRIVATE COMPANIES HAS DIFFERENT RULES

Not many commercial companies who aren't involved with government business use the bid process. A few do. If you receive a solicitation for bid from a private company, it's time to be wary. Here's why:

1. Government agencies are required by statute to seek out the lowest cost supplier. Private companies can negotiate any way they please. The first question you must ask is: Why has this company chosen the limiting structure of the competitive bid?

2. Government agencies are required to accept the results of the bid; private companies are not. Many a vendor has "won" a bid from a private company only to learn the company considers the low bid to be an opening offer and a beginning negotiation point.

3. Private companies sometimes put out bid solicitations as trial balloons to test the market price or the availability of a product. They don't really intend to buy anything from anyone just yet. With very few exceptions, when a government agency puts out a bid they mean to award a contract.

4. Government agencies must keep specifications broad enough to allow open bidding. Private companies may write the specs any way they please—and change them after the bid results are in.

There are other differences along the same lines, but you get the idea. The commercial company's bid request isn't binding, and this makes the process subject to abuse.

HOW TO PROTECT YOURSELF WHEN BIDDING TO A PRIVATE COMPANY

Not every commercial company that uses the competitive bid process abuses it. There are some good opportunities for volume business with these companies if you take protective measures. Here are a few of the things you can do:

1. When faced with a bid opportunity for a private company, ask about that company's reputation. Have they awarded bids based on the best price in the past? Do they send up trial balloons?

2. Ask the company sending out the bid request whether it intends to award the contract to the lowest responsible bidder. Get the company's definition of "responsible." Make sure your company qualifies.

3. Sometimes a bid request is used to narrow down the list of possible vendors. The serious negotiations begin with those remaining after the first set of numbers are delivered. This practice is ethical if you know about it in advance. You may wish to save something for the latter stage negotiations.

4. Ask the company making the bid request if your quotation will be shared with other bidders and used as a negotiating ploy. If this is the case, you may wish to walk away.

5. If specifications are not specific, but allow the respondent latitude, such as "quote the length of your warranty," ask the company requesting the bid to attach a value percentage to each variable. This will tell you where to place your emphasis.

The point is that some commercial companies use the competitive bid process to wring lower prices out of their vendors. They make up their own rules, but aren't required to abide by them.

HOW PRIVATE COMPANIES USE "BIDS" TO NEGOTIATE BETTER TERMS

One of the things that frequently happens when bidding to a private company is that you will be called into the office of the company requesting the quotation to "explain your bid." The bidder will find himself in a room faced by several people armed to the teeth with spreadsheets. At first, the person might be pleased to see that the company's bid has been thoroughly analyzed. The pleasure doesn't last long when the person discovers that the bid his company made is being compared, item by item, with the bids of his competitors. Here are some examples of the kinds of things you can expect:

- "You bid twenty dollars an hour for after warranty service, ABC Company bid sixteen dollars. Are your products more costly to repair?"
- "You're quoting sixteen weeks delivery. The Acme Company has promised us the entire lot in eight weeks. Is your production line antiquated or are we taking a back seat to other customers?"
- "You're shipping us F.O.B. your factory. Baker Company is including delivery."
- "Your terms are two percent in ten days. XYZ Company will give us a three percent cash discount with thirty days to pay."

The cost for every item, every subassembly, every step in the operation may be questioned and compared with the costs quoted by your competitors. And you can be sure that similar conversations are being held with your competitors. The idea is to hack away and hack away at each bid until there is no profit margin left for anyone.

Don't fall into this trap. Your company may already be the lowest bidder overall. When the prospect begins this carping over individual sections of the bid, line by line, demand to see everyone's bid in entirety. Your company's costs for different elements of the bid may be vastly different from those of your competitors. It's unfair to demand that you lower prices for specific line items or improve terms, particularly if you've already offered the best proposal.

When faced with this kind of negotiating strategy, stick to your guns. Don't get sucked into a line-by-line comparison of your prices against those of your competitors unless the prospect is prepared to show you the bottom line of all the bids.

THREE WAYS TO COMBAT THE LINE-BY-LINE NEGOTIATING STRATEGY

When faced with a prospect who insists on negotiating each line item on a bid consider the following strategies:

1. Insist that your bid be considered in its entirety. Some points, such as better delivery schedules, may be considered. But if you're already low bidder, why lower your prices still further?

2. Come to the negotiating table armed with your own set of spreadsheets. These spreadsheets should cover every cost item on your bid. Use them to prove that the prices you've offered can't be lowered any further.

3. Find out fast just how serious these negotiations are. When faced with a request for a better price on a line item, ask if your concession on this point will mean an order. This is a straight "if I answer this objection will you buy?" type of close applied to a competitive bid situation.

4. If forced to give ground on an item, ask for something in return. For example, if the customer wants a better lead time, ask that some of your own parts costs be prepaid, or that storage charges be accrued to items completed by you but not shipped to the customer.

*A FIVE-POINT PROGRAM FOR RENEGOTIATING A BID
CONTRACT WHEN YOUR PROFIT MARGIN ISN'T SATISFACTORY*

If the rules aren't as hard and fast for the private company requesting
a competitive bid, neither are they as restrictive to the company that
responds. If you make a mistake bidding a contract and find that you
can't live with the deal, try to renegotiate it. The company that has
accepted your bid won't be too happy, but they are business people
who may listen to reason if that reason is fairly presented. Here's the
best way to make that presentation:

1. Call the customer and state that you must have relief from the
terms of the contract. You'll get immediate attention and a hearing.

2. Come prepared to reveal your company's costs for doing the
job. Cover labor, material, burden, the whole ball of wax. Don't use
any phony padding—it will most likely be discovered. Let the facts
speak for themselves in revealing that your company can't live with the
current contract.

3. If there's a problem area such as a labor strike, material shortage,
or equipment breakdown, be prepared to discuss it in detail. *Have a
solution for the problem.* There's no point in asking for more time or
more money or more of anything unless you can prove that the problem
is now under control.

4. If you need more money to do the job, come prepared to offer
something in return. This something extra could be a better delivery
schedule, improved quality control, or warehousing some inventory for
the customer. The something extra allows the customer's management
to justify giving you more money for a contract that has already been
negotiated.

5. Come prepared to lose the contract. *Never* try to renegotiate a
contract unless you are willing to give it up entirely if you don't get
some kind of relief. Renegotiating should not be used as a ploy to
extort more money from a customer.

CHAPTER SUMMARY

Most commercial companies don't use competitive bidding to select vendors.

*The largest segment of private industry which uses competitive bidding is
that which serves government agencies. A list of these companies is available
through Government Data Publications.*

Be wary when bidding to a commercial company, because they don't operate by the same rules as do most government agencies.

Often, a bid to a commercial company is regarded by that company as nothing more than an opening offer and an opportunity to weed out some of the players. The real negotiations come later.

Commercial companies often play one bidder against another, using line items in the bid to knock down the prices.

The best defense against a company that tries to negotiate each item in a bid line by line is to insist that all bids be considered in their entirety.

If you've bid a contract too aggressively with not enough profit margin, try to renegotiate.

The following is a typical vendor questionnaire used by a defense contractor for small business sub-contractors.

EXHIBIT 13

GENERAL DYNAMICS
Electronics Division

SMALL BUSINESS/ SMALL DISADVANTAGED BUSINESS (S/SD) SUPPLIER QUESTIONNAIRE

TO:

RETURN TO: GENERAL DYNAMICS ELECTRONICS DIVISION
S/SD ADMINISTRATOR, MAIL ZONE 5205-E
P.O. BOX 85062, SAN DIEGO, CALIF. 92138

CORRECT NAME & ADDRESS IF DIFFERENT FROM ADDRESSEE

YOUR ADDRESSES	STREET ADDRESS OR P.O. BOX	CITY & COUNTY	STATE	ZIP	TELEPHONE
HEADQUARTERS ORGANIZATION					
ACCOUNTS RECEIVABLE GROUP					
SALES REP. FOR SAN DIEGO, CALIF., AREA					
FULL NAME OF PARENT COMPANY					

POINT OF SHIPMENT IF DIFFERENT THAN SHOWN ABOVE (NAME AND ADDRESS)

TYPE OF ORGANIZATION
☐ PARTNERSHIP   ☐ SUBSIDIARY   ☐ PROPRIETORSHIP   ☐ DIVISION   ☐ CORPORATION   YEARS IN BUSINESS

PRIMARY FIELD OF BUSINESS, COMMODITIES/SERVICES PROVIDED BY YOUR COMPANY	PRESENT CUSTOMERS (NAME & CITY)

TYPE OF BUSINESS (PLEASE CHECK)	
MANUFACTURER	
DISTRIBUTOR — WHOLESALE, RETAIL, WAREHOUSE	GENERAL DYNAMICS DIVISIONS WITH WHICH YOU HAVE DONE BUS.
MANUFACTURER'S REPRESENTATIVE	
PROCESSOR — PLATING, CLEANING, TESTING, ETC.	
CONSTRUCTION, INSTALLATION, ETC.	
TECHNICAL PUBLICATIONS & GRAPHICS PRODUCER	
ENGINEERING — RESEARCH, CONSULTANTS, ETC.	YOUR OFFICERS (SIGNATURE) / TITLE
LEASING AGENCY	
OTHER	PRESIDENT/PLANT MANAGER

PRESENT NET WORTH	ANNUAL GROSS SALES	% COMM.	
$	$	% GOVT.	CONTRACTS/SALES MANAGER

NO. OF EMPLOYEES IN ORGANIZATION AT THIS ADDRESS

MFG	ENGRG	QUAL. CONT	ALL OTHER	TOTAL

YES	NO		
		ARE YOU FAMILIAR WITH DEFENSE ACQUISITION REGULATIONS (DAR)?	THE FOLLOWING SUPPLEMENTAL DATA SHOULD BE SENT WITH THIS QUESTIONNAIRE FOR A BETTER EVALUATION OF YOUR COMPANY'S CAPABILITIES.
		ARE YOU A SMALL BUSINESS WITHIN DEFINITION OF DAR 1-701?	SALES BROCHURES
			ORGANIZATION CHART
		ARE YOU A WOMAN OWNED BUSINESS?	CURRENT SIGNED FINANCIAL STATEMENT
			AUTHORIZED SIGNATURE
		ARE YOU A SMALL DISADVANTAGED BUSINESS ENTERPRISE AS DEFINED IN DAR 7-104.14?	
		ARE YOU REGISTERED WITH LOCAL MINORITY BUSINESS COUNCIL?	TITLE / DATE

4-206, 11/80

114

8

STRATEGIES THAT WIN MILLION-DOLLAR CONTRACTS

THE ART OF SPECMANSHIP: THE KEY TO SUCCESSFUL BIDDING

"The person who writes the specs is the one who gets the deal." People who are familiar with the competitive bidding process have been passing along that bit of wisdom for many years, and it's absolutely true. If you can influence a government agency to write their specification requirements around your piece of hardware, you should win the contract. You certainly have a substantial edge. Few competitive products have identical features. The trick is to persuade the agency to include the prominent features offered on your equipment and to ignore the prominent features on the competitor's hardware. If the specifications match the features on one of your models closely enough, you should get the contract.

Why should a government agency want to write specs that limit competition? The purpose of the bid process is to open up government

115

buying to as many companies as possible. Still, an agency can have many reasons for "tilting" a contract toward a particular vendor. Frequently it's because a salesperson did a good job in convincing the agency that a particular piece of equipment was best suited to the kind of work the agency did. Fear of the unknown is another reason. If the agency is comfortable with a vendor, it may not want to risk doing business with anyone else. Friendship can play a part. If a vendor has developed personal relationships with the decision makers in any agency, that vendor might have an opportunity to influence specifications.

HOW TO INFLUENCE SPECIFICATION WRITING

The following tips can help a vendor influence the bid specifications on government agency contracts:

1. Learn as much as you can about the buying agency's needs. Once you understand what it wants to accomplish with the product going out for bid, you have a better chance of making recommendations on how the applications can be handled more effectively through the use of your equipment.

2. Demonstrate to the agency that you are knowledgeable in your field. Buyers and agency heads don't have enough time to learn about every piece of competitive equipment in the market. They often rely on expert vendors to help them out when it's time to put out competitive bids. You can "help" them into choosing your equipment if you're one of the experts they consult.

3. Offer suggestions on specifications that make sense to the agency. Suggesting a feature that offers money or cost-savings advantages will be looked on favorably. Suggesting something merely because it prevents your competitors from bidding is not likely to win you any friends.

4. Suggest features that other vendors can match. This may seem contradictory since the art of specmanship is developing feature requirements that will ensure your company will win the contract. However, some agencies will only write requirements that three or more vendors can meet. How does it give your company an advantage if other suppliers can match the features on the bid requirement? The trick is to push features that are only available on your competitor's higher priced models or only available from vendors who do not aggressively pursue bid business.

5. Don't suggest higher-end models with unnecessary features. While commercial companies will frequently desire products that they can "grow into," government agencies prefer to base their buying decisions on today's requirements.

6. Don't suggest obsolete models. The agencies want to buy current technology.

7. Learn the constraints faced by the agency's end user and buyer. What's the budget limitation? What is the level of training of the people using the product? What kind of service will be required? How wide is the geographical area where the equipment will be used? How critical is the application? The answers to these kinds of questions will help you formulate specification suggestions that make sense to the agency.

8. Never suggest a specification that is patently absurd or obviously unnecessary just because it gives your company a material advantage. This is the quickest way to lose the trust of agency buyers.

9. "Prove" the advantages of the features you suggest showing how costs will be reduced. Reports on your product and testimonials from other users who appreciate those particular features are often effective.

10. Demonstrate your product. If you're particularly anxious to see specific features included in the specifications, be sure to demonstrate those features to the end users. Arguments before the buyers are not sufficient.

STUDYING THE BID REQUIREMENTS: LEARNING NOT TO OVERBID

Many novice bidders make frequent mistakes in underbidding and overbidding. They bid equipment that doesn't meet the specifications, which means their bid is rejected, or they bid equipment that is overqualified, which usually means that some competitor is able to bid a lower priced product and walk away with the order.

The first step in a successful bid is to read the specifications thoroughly. Match your model features to those called for on the RFQ. Bid equipment that meets—but does not exceed—all requirements. In many cases you will not have a model available that exactly matches the specs. In these instances bid a model that is slightly overqualified. If no model you have meets specs, pass up this bid. Your bid will be rejected and you will have given your competitors valuable information on that model's bid pricing.

If you have two models that meet specs, *always bid the unit with the lower price.* Don't try to second-guess the agency. Even if you feel they need the extra speed or lower operating cost of a specific model, *don't bid it if you have a lower priced model that meets spec.* The time to point out the advantages of features is when the specifications are written. Don't expect to win arguments about equipment superiority after the bid results are in. The agency will take the product with the lowest cost that meets spec every time. *Every time.*

PRICING WITH A SHARP PENCIL. HOW TO TAKE OUT EXTRANEOUS COSTS WHEN CALCULATING BID PRICES

The bid process is designed to increase competition among vendors. Successful bidders realize they must sacrifice full margins when calculating bid pricing. Many vendors who'd like a share of the volume business that competitive bidding represents try once or twice to enter this arena, then quickly retreat because they are not successful. They feel they've gone as low as they can, cut margins to the bone and still some other bidder walked away with the deal. "They're losing money," these unsuccessful bidders mutter as they slink away. Yet, even though the successful bidders "lose" so much money, they continue to take contract after contract. How do they do it?

Some companies use different costing when calculating the prices for important bid contracts. They take out many of the costs typically associated with doing business with commercial companies. For example, advertising cost is sometimes eliminated because no advertising is needed to sell the units delivered to government agencies. Inventory maintenance cost is sometimes deducted. Here's one way they may be handling the calculations:

COST WORKSHEET
Manufacturing cost for product   _____
    Plus total overhead and burden   _____
    Less advertising costs   _____
    Less marketing costs   _____

Bid cost for product   _____
% margin needed to make job worthwhile   _____

Final bid price   _____

This simple system allows the bidder to extract certain costs from the company's normal pricing structure while leaving others intact. Product advertising doesn't apply to most competitive bidding situations. Many companies extract traditional marketing costs as well. If considerable marketing effort is required to qualify for the bid situation, these costs can easily be plugged in. Other costs that don't apply can be eliminated. The bid variable is the percentage of margin needed to make winning the contract worthwhile. This is where the soul searching comes in. No text can help you out on that one.

SANDBAGGING: HOW TO SAVE YOUR BEST SHOT FOR THAT REALLY BIG DEAL

Once you become involved with competitive bidding you'll soon discover the same few companies are pursuing all the contracts. If you're successful with a few bids, you'll find other companies with similar product lines and cost structures opposing you. They'll win some contracts and you'll win some contracts. After a while you'll become conversant with their strategies, perhaps learn something about their pricing policies, and even be able to accurately predict what they may bid in most situations. You can safely assume that the competitors have the same "book" on you. If you can predict what they'll bid, they can predict what you'll bid.

This predictability makes it difficult to win very large contracts any other way except by further trimming profit margins. The good contracts that should be the plums turn out to be the nail biters where you hope and pray you can wring out a profit. How can you resolve this dilemma? The answer is easy. *Don't aggressively pursue every bid contract.* Instead, pick and choose your spots. Bid on every contract, but save your best shot for those that represent the best opportunities for your company. In other contract situations, bid high. Use a variation of the poker sandbag strategy of passing on some bets and raising the ante on others. If you continually vary your bids, the competition can't get a fix on what you're likely to do in any specific situation. When should you bid high and when should you go for all the marbles? Use the following guidelines:

1. If the specifications favor your competitor's equipment and there is a high-priced model you can bid, you might want to bid it even higher than you have to. The competition is likely to win this deal

anyway. Another situation may favor the model you have overpriced. You can now bid it in lower and surprise the opposition.

2. If the terms and conditions indicate that a lot of unprofitable after-sale service is necessary, such as equipment installation and training over a wide geographic area, you may wish to bid high. You don't care if you lose this deal.

3. If the plant happens to be very busy and the extra business will require a second or third shift, the company might not need any more high volume, low profit business. This is another situation that may call for a high bid.

4. If the current bid is for a relatively small quantity, but there's a bigger contract opportunity a few months down the road, a high bid now may mislead your competitors when the big bid comes up.

5. If an agency has a reputation for extracting a pound of flesh from every vendor, higher bid pricing is a polite way of saying "no thank you."

If all of this sounds like competitive bidding is a game, that's because it is. The best players are those with dazzling footwork.

HOW TO USE "PHANTOM DISCOUNTS" TO BUILD EXTRA PROFITS

Many government agencies use net prices to determine contract award winners. If two bidders each quote a price of $10.00 for an item, but one bidder offers 3 percent terms for payment within ten days, that bidder's net price is considered to be $9.70 for award purposes. The reason this is important when constructing bid strategy is because many government agencies move their paperwork too slowly to take advantage of prompt payment discounts. The discount is considered when making the award, but in practice it is seldom taken. That means a few extra profit points for the contract holder. Some cagey competitive bidders use this situation to calculate their competitive bid prices this way:

Best bare-bones price	_____
Extra 5 or 10 percent margin	_____
Bid price	_____
Less 5 or 10 percent prompt payment	_____

If this bidder is awarded the contract, the company gets the bare-bones price on every invoice that's paid on time *and* an extra 5 or 10 percent profit on every invoice that gets caught in the agency paperwork snarl.

This practice has become so common that many agencies have amended the terms and conditions on their bid contracts. They limit the amount they will consider for cash discounts and disallow any prompt payment terms shorter than thirty days. Be sure to read the fine print pertaining to discount terms when bidding any contract. Use the prompt payment strategy to build extra profits.

BIDDING THROUGH THIRD PARTIES: USING SMALL OR MINORITY-OWNED BUSINESSES TO BUILD PROFITS

To encourage greater participation in the bid process, most agencies will allow small or woman- or minority-owned businesses a "bogey" when considering contract awards. This bogey is usually 5 percent. That means if a large company bids $10.00 on a contract item and a small company bids exactly the same price and the same terms, the small company's bid is considered to be $9.50 for award purposes. A few agencies, but not many, will allow a double bogey. A small woman- or minority-owned business will get a 10 percent allowance in award consideration. Some businessmen have made their wives titular owners of the company to take advantage of this situation.

In many tight competitive situations the difference of 5 percent may determine who gets the contract and who is an also-ran. That's why many large companies will use surrogates and funnel their bids through small or minority-owned dealers. There's nothing illegal about this technique. The agency understands the large company is behind the contract. They may insist on it. The dealer is paid for any effort expended. The large company gets the value of the contract.

But, there are many possible problems with this approach. If you're considering bidding a contract through a third party such as a company dealer, be sure to keep the following in mind:

1. The dealer, not your company, will be the actual holder of the contract. He or she will be responsible for meeting the terms and conditions of the award.

2. The dealer will likely be responsible for the effort to administer the contract. Purchase orders will be sent to the dealer. Invoices must come from the dealer. Complaints will first come to the dealer.

3. The agency will pay the dealer for work done or products delivered. If the contract is for a large amount and you're shipping to the dealer on open invoice, your company will inevitably have a good deal of credit exposure. When the dealer is paid by the agency, is the correct amount going to be forwarded to your company?

4. The dealer holds the contract, but your company's reputation is at stake. You're responsible for a situation that you don't completely control.

Do these four points mean that third party contracts are no good? Of course they don't. In many instances using a surrogate is the only way a lucrative contract can be obtained. However, companies that use this arrangement should realize that they're getting into a marriage-like arrangement with the selected dealer. Some marriages are heavenly bliss, others end in bitter name-calling and divorce.

WORKING WITH THE AGENCY THAT WANTS YOUR PRODUCT, BUT MUST SEND OUT A CONTRACT FOR COMPETITIVE BID

One of the problems with expending time and energy pursuing a government contract is that there is no guarantee your company will get the business no matter how hard you've worked to earn it or how much the end user wants your specific product brand. If contracts exceed a certain dollar level they must be placed for competitive bid. Once a contract is put out for bid, it is subject to the whim of the marketplace. The carefully constructed system that would reduce the user's costs by millions of dollars could be lost to another vendor who underbids by twenty-five cents.

Many vendors use this quandary as an excuse not to spend time with government agency end users. They feel that time spent with agencies that must go out for bids is useless. They're wrong. If you've done a job for the user you can, with the user's help, almost ensure that you will win the bid contract. Here's how you do it:

1. Work with the end user to shape the specifications on the product or service needed. The purchasing department will demand that the specs be broad enough to allow competition, but a careful spec writer working with a knowledge of the competitions' limitations can design a bid spec that others find difficult to meet.

2. Work with the end user to write the special training and servicing you offer into the specs. Your competitor may not be able to match the training arrangements that the end user finds so appealing.

3. If a particular competitor is extremely aggressive, work with the end user to write special terms and conditions that will disqualify this bidder. For example, if one competitor's price is better than your company can match, search for a feature or situation that this competitor can't possibly match. For example, perhaps the competitor doesn't have a local warehouse. Ask the end user to specify that the vendor must keep a local inventory. Your competitor doesn't meet this standard and is disqualified. Play it safe. Write the specs so the local warehouse must have been established for at least two years.

4. In the event a competitor has apparently won a bid when the end user would have preferred your equipment, ask the user to carefully examine the competitive model that was bid. A claim that a piece of hardware doesn't meet specs is much more effective coming from the end user than from you. An end user's complaint about the competitor's service and reputation can also be effective.

All of these steps are contingent on a compliant end user who really wants to do business with your company and likes your product better than anything else on the market. They are suggested to ensure the hard work you've done to sell an account won't be wasted.

WHEN TO SUBMIT MULTIPLE BIDS

Most agencies don't restrict a vendor to a single bid. Often, you can bid as many times as you wish. Why would anyone want to submit more than one bid? There are several interesting situations when this tactic makes sense. These are:

1. When the specifications are fuzzy and you can't get sufficient clarification from the agency soliciting the bids. If you're not absolutely sure which model to bid, you can take out some insurance by bidding more than once.

2. When there are variables in the specifications. For example, sometimes the bid request will state something to the effect that "length of warranty offered will be considered in making the award." Does the agency want the best price or the best follow-up service? Who can tell? You might bid this one at the lowest price possible with almost no warranty and at a higher price with a long-term warranty. Who knows what's in the agency's mind with this kind of vague requirement?

3. When you want to put a phony bid on record. If there's a new product model out, you might bid it into a situation at a high price knowing you don't stand a chance of winning. You hope your lower cost model will take the prize, but you've also established that the new machine won't be competitive.

4. When you want to bid through more than one entity. In these instances, you may wish directly on behalf of the company and again on behalf of a local dealer who gets a small business bogey.

THE SEVEN DEADLY SINS OF BIDDING

There are seven things a competitive bidder must *never* do when preparing a bid. These are:

1. Neglecting to read the bid solicitation thoroughly. Some bidders assume that all bids are identical just because they came from the same government agency. The terms and conditions often vary from bid to bid. The bid you had put away in the win column may be lost because the terms or conditions had changed.

2. Neglecting to include the required materials with the bid package. If product features, a list of company dealers, or a Buyer's Lab report is required, then be sure this material is in the bid envelope before it is sealed. Wouldn't you feel silly about losing a bid because you didn't insert a product brochure?

3. Neglecting to sign the bid in the designated space. Government agencies know that a bid must be signed by an authorized person before it is considered a valid offer. If it isn't a valid offer, it's thrown out.

4. Neglecting to include bid or performance bonds if required. The bid is considered nonresponsive if the proper indemnification isn't included.

5. Bidding at full profit margins. Yes, we all know that healthy margins are necessary to sustain a business. The government bid business is a place to build volume, not profit.

6. Submitting a late bid. This is perhaps the greatest sin of all because it is so unnecessary. Get the bid in on time or get it disqualified.

7. Ignoring a bid that you don't think you can win. It's okay to sandbag if you don't think you have a shot at the contract, but keep your hand in even if you feel the price is too high. Sometimes several vendors may be disqualified and you could be awarded a particularly lucrative contract.

AFTER THE BID: THE SPADEWORK NECESSARY TO ENSURE THE CONTRACT AWARD

What happens after the bid has been opened and your company is announced as low bidder? Is your work over? Can you expect the contract in the next day's mail? Don't bet on it. The mere act of submitting a low bid doesn't ensure the contract award. The following suggested actions will help you bring home that bacon:

1. Call or visit the purchasing agent's office. Speak to the buyer responsible for the bid. Ask the following questions: Does the buyer agree that your company's bid is the lowest? Does the buyer agree that the product meets all the bid specifications? Are there any perceived irregularities with the bid? When will the bid award be made? What are the procedures at this agency? If the buyer requests, bring the product into the buyer's office for demonstration.

2. Visit the end user who requested the equipment. This step is particularly important if you and your company are not known to the bidding agency. Show the end user the product you have bid. *Go over the feature specifications one by one.* Get agreement that your product meets all of these specifications.

3. Speak to your industry peers. Are there rumors of a bid protest? If so, on what basis? If there are likely to be objections, prepare to answer them.

4. Arrange a tour of your facility for buyer or end user, or both. Let the agency people see that your company can support the contract that is about to be awarded.

5. Keep a record of all contacts with the agency. Put any agency requests in writing. Maintain a log of activities related to the bid. You'll be in much better shape if a false protest is made.

Here are a few things not to do when trying to pry a contract out of an agency.

1. While demonstrations are fine, don't leave sample equipment at the using agency unless the specifications require a trial. The samples may be used by an agency reluctant to risk purchasing equipment from an unknown vendor to "prove" that your equipment isn't reliable or doesn't meet specifications.

2. If a buyer or end user falsely claims that your product doesn't meet feature specs, don't lose your temper. Point out where and how the equipment does meet spec, and request any claim that your equipment doesn't meet spec be put in writing. Put your answer in writing as well.

3. If you're disqualified legitimately because your equipment doesn't meet specs, take your medicine. Save the fighting for just causes.

4. Don't pester the buyer every day about the bid award. However, if the award is late, find out why and how long the delay will be.

Taking these steps will facilitate bid awards. They will also help develop cordial relations with the bidding agency and establish your company as a reliable, trustworthy supplier.

CHAPTER SUMMARY

The key to successful bidding is influencing the specifications so they favor your company's products.

It's important to thoroughly study each new bid before completing it.

Don't expect to win big dollar volume contracts unless you're prepared to lower your normal profit margins.

Organizing a bid worksheet is one way to ensure that you've included all elements in your bid preparation.

Sandbagging, saving your best price for a really big opportunity, is one way to catch your competitors at unawares.

You can make extra profits on bids through the judicious use of prompt payment discounts.

Bidding through third parties, small business owners, and minorities can often give your company a better chance at the contract.

"Selling" a product to an agency can often eliminate the competition's chances for winning a contract.

Just because you've submitted the lowest price, doesn't automatically mean you'll get the award. There's still work to be done.

Doing a good job for a government agency is the best way to secure favored vendor status.

9

THE LEGAL SIDE OF COMPETITIVE BIDDING

Some companies are so concerned about the legalities involved in competitive bidding that they shy away from this market opportunity. Their concerns are misplaced. Certainly there are legal considerations, but you don't need a staff of lawyers to engage in the bid process. In most cases, no lawyer is needed at all. The contracts offered by the agencies to successful bidders are generally standard boilerplate with few surprises. Most agencies won't accept alterations so the vendor has the options of signing the contract offered or walking away from the deal. Of course, a lawyer can explain what is at risk to a company on the brink of a contract with a government agency, and this advice is often valuable.

Do obtain legal advice if you feel uncomfortable before entering into an agreement. Penalties for late delivery and nonperformance should be understood before entering into any agreement. However, it's extremely unlikely that a lawyer would be able to amend a standard government agency contract.

Special contracts for tailor-made products or services are another matter. In these cases it is always wise to consult legal counsel.

INSURANCE BONDS

An agency putting out a request for a competitive bid for a product or service will often require that an insurance bond or other form of indemnification be included with the bid or provided later by the successful bidder. Failure to include such a bond when required is always grounds for disqualification. When a bond isn't included when one is specified, the bid will be thrown out. The problem is the bonds cost the bidder money up front at the time the bid is entered and well before it's known who the successful bidder is. That makes the cost for bonds like ante money in a poker game: you never know if you'll get it back.

Bid bonds, performance bonds, and other forms of guarantees are just another cost of doing business through the competitive bid process. The expense of these bonds should be included when calculating costs in your bid proposals.

The most common type of bonds required with bid proposals are bid bonds, performance bonds, product liability bonds, and employee bonds.

Bid Bonds

Agencies sometimes require that bid bonds be included with bids to ensure that the vendor will actually deliver the goods or services specified in that bid at the bid price. The agencies don't want reneging on the part of vendors who perhaps regret a low price after it has been bid. (A vendor who feels too much money has been left on the table after the bids were opened may prefer to default on a bid. Another company may regret its initial enthusiasm.) If a vendor who is the apparent winner of a contract attempts to walk away from its bid, the agency must engage in the bid process all over again. It incurs additional costs and time is lost. Bid bonds are a way of making certain that vendors stand behind their bids.

Often, the estimated value of a contract determines whether bid bonds are required. Agencies may not require them for small contracts, but insist on them for bids when there's a good deal of money involved.

WHERE BONDS ARE OBTAINED

Vendors obtain *bid bonds* from insurance companies. Usually, an insurance broker is the actual point of contact. The insurance company will provide a bonding certificate showing that the proper coverage has been obtained by the bidder. This bonding certificate is included in the bid package submitted by the vendor.

The amount of the bond usually is for 10 percent of the total dollar value of the contract to be awarded. If the bid request is for one million dollars worth of equipment, the bid bond required may be for one hundred thousand dollars. If the successful bidder for any reason fails to deliver per the stated schedule, the amount of the bond is forfeited. (There's normally quite a fudge factor in the delivery schedule or the performance requirement. These bonds are required to prevent frivolous bids. They're not designed to penalize the vendor who runs a few days late on delivery because of unforeseen circumstances.)

Some state agencies will accept a cashier's check, usually for 10 percent of the contract award, in lieu of a bid bond, but few experienced bidders use this alternative. Even though the check is eventually returned, the vendor's money is tied up during the period it is held. It's less expensive to pay the cost of a bond to the insurance company.

Most commercial insurance carriers can provide bid bonds. Their cost is based on the total value of the contract being bid and the length of time the bond is in effect (from the time the bid is submitted to the time the product is delivered). Most bid bonds are for a very short term and therefore are not very costly. When requesting a bid bond from an insurance broker be prepared to give the following information:

- The total dollar value of the contract you're bidding on
- The amount of the bond required
- When the bid is due
- The name of the agency requiring the bond
- The kind and amount of product required
- The number of the bid

It's a good idea for companies that plan to become involved in much competitive bidding to establish a working relationship with an insurance agency that understands and can supply bid bonds on short notice. Sometimes a company will get wind of a competitive bid opportunity only a day or two before the bid deadline. Getting the bid bond delivered in that short a time can be a scramble. If the procedure is already in place, you can get emergency service.

Performance Bonds

Performance bonds differ from bid bonds to the extent that they are in force throughout the entire duration of the contract. Agencies sometimes require them for contracts that will be in effect for a long period of time. For example, the agency may be awarding a sole-source contract for office desks for a one-year period. They want the price and delivery for a specified model desk guaranteed by the vendor. In return, they're guaranteeing the vendor all their desk business for the next twelve months. The performance bond provides the guarantee the agency requires. If the vendor fails to make delivery, or if product or service is substandard, the performance bond provides recourse.

Performance bonds are more expensive than bid bonds because they are in force for longer periods and expose the insurance company to greater risk. They are usually not required as part of the initial bid, but only required of the apparent winner. If the low bidder fails to obtain a performance bond, the contract is often awarded to the next low bidder if that company is successful in obtaining a bond.

Many state agencies will demand that the performance bond be on file in a compliance office at the agency's headquarters. In some cases the agency will require that the bond be issued by a carrier licensed to do business in that state *and with a current balance sheet on file with the state agency.* If this is the case with your customer, be sure the insurance broker selling you the policy is obtaining it from a carrier not only licensed in the state, but one familiar with the requirements of that specific agency.

Be sure that your insurance agent knows the difference between a bid bond and a performance bond. Also make sure that the carrier providing the actual coverage is recognized and licensed by the state.

Product Liability Insurance

Not very many agencies currently require product liability insurance on items they buy, but as consumer advocates become more vocal, expect to see more demand for this kind of coverage. Essentially, product liability insurance protects the user against any product defect that could prove harmful. This kind of coverage can be expensive indeed. It's usually beyond the scope of dealers and distributors of a product. Product liability insurance is almost always the responsibility of the equipment manufacturer. If you're a dealer or distributor bidding to an agency that requires product liability insurance, contact the actual

EXHIBIT 14

<u>BOND</u> <u>OF</u> <u>FAITHFUL</u> <u>PERFORMANCE</u>

WHEREAS, LOS ANGELES UNIFIED SCHOOL DISTRICT OF LOS ANGELES COUNTY

hereinafter called the District, and BROTHER INTERNATIONAL

hereinafter called the Contractor, have entered into a contract

dated . . . . NOVEMBER 17, 1986

for . . . . ELECTRONIC TYPEWRITERS   C-431   11/1/88 THROUGH 10/31/89
                                                        (EXTENSION)

Amount
of Bond . . . THIRTY ONE THOUSAND TWO HUNDRED FIFTY AND NO/100 DOLLARS
                     ($31,250.00)
NOW, THEREFORE, the Contractor, as Principal, and the following named Surety,

---

are held and firmly bound to the District jointly and severally in the penal sum of this Bond
set forth above as Amount of Bond for which payment, well and truly to be made, the Principal
and Surety bind themselves, their heirs, executors, administrators, successors and assigns,
jointly and severally, firmly by these presents.

The conditions of this obligation is that if the Contractor shall promptly and faithfully perform all the conditions of the contract in strict conformity with the terms and conditions
set forth in the Contract, then this obligation shall be null and void, otherwise it shall
remain in full force and effect.

The Surety, for value received, hereby stipulates and agrees that notwithstanding California
Civil Code Sections 2819 and 2849, no change, alteration or addition or extension of time in
the terms of the contract or in the goods, supplies or service to be furnished thereunder shall
in any wise affect its obligations on this bond; and it does hereby waive notice of any such
change.

Signed, sealed, and dated _____, 19___.

       <u>Contractor/Principal</u>   <u>Surety</u>

   BROTHER INTERNATIONAL   By_____

By_____   Address_____

Title_____   Bond No._____

* *

The District will obtain the following certification:

<u>CERTIFICATION</u> <u>BY</u> <u>LOS</u> <u>ANGELES</u> <u>COUNTY</u> <u>CLERK'S</u> <u>OFFICE</u>

I hereby certify:
1. That the Surety named above has been certified by the State Insurance Commissioner as an
   admitted Surety Insurer and that such authority is in full force and effect.
2. That the person executing this bond on behalf of the Surety is authorized to do so under
   a power of attorney on file in this office.
3. That there is on file in this office the financial statement of the Surety for the period
   ending_____ showing capital and surplus not less than ten times the
   amount of this bond.

                                          Frank S. Zolin, County Clerk

Date_____   By_____
                                             #875493   Deputy

Form 82.4
Rev. 6-82

manufacturer. If the insurance is not available, this may be a deal to walk away from. (Or it may be a good time to submit an artificially high bid as explained in the chapter on bid strategy.)

Employee Bonds

Some agencies require that service contracts be performed by a company whose employees are bonded. That means that the company performing the service or the bonding company must pay if the employee steals something, or maliciously destroys property, or injures someone while working at the agency. The bonding company may make a careful scrutiny and background check of company employees before approving them for bonding. What they turn up can be surprising. If the bonding company turns down someone, that doesn't mean the person must be dismissed from the company. But it does mean that he or she can't work on the project that requires employee bonding. Employee bonds are expensive and their cost must be considered and factored in when bidding on service contracts.

YOUR COMPANY'S LEGAL EXPOSURE THROUGH NONPERFORMANCE OF A CONTRACT

What if you've made a bad deal? What if you've grossly underestimated the cost for a product or service, or forgotten an important element, and just can't perform without incurring heavy losses? What if those losses could put your company out of business? What can you do to get out of a situation when you discover a bidding error after you've actually contracted to do business with a government agency?

If the loss is small, the best action might be to bite the bullet and perform as best you can. Chalk it up to experience or seek your profit in goodwill. Reneging on a bid that the agency accepted in good faith is not likely to endear you to that agency and it could cost your company dearly.

Any relief you might have depends on the terms and conditions of the bid solicitation and the time when you first discovered that the company can't turn a profit on the deal. If you've discovered a mistake in the bid price before the contract is awarded, you might be able to walk away without further harm. Here's a simple course of action:

1. Have your lawyer look over the original bid solicitation and the contract, if one has been signed. Exactly what exposure do you have?

What did you agree to? What penalties can be exacted for nonper-formance? Are there escape clauses? What are the provisions for a price increase?

2. Understand your legal alternatives, but before rushing to court, visit the agency and explain your problem. If the mistake is obvious, such as incorrect addition, confusion over a model number, or trans-posed figures, the agency might let you off the hook, cancel the contract and simply go out for another bid. Simple cancellation is what will happen most of the time if you're forthright about your problem. Most agencies recognize that honest mistakes are sometimes made.

3. If the agency is adamant about enforcing the terms of the contract, file a formal protest. At the very least this is a stalling tactic that means you won't have to deliver anything until the protest has been heard and a judgment rendered. If the agency needs the product right now, they may decide to drop the issue.

If a bid bond was required with the contract, the agency will probably seek to enforce it. The insurance company will pay and then come after your company for compensation of their loss.

The existence of a performance bond is another problem. If you decline to perform, the agency can go after the insurance company that issued the bond. The insurance company pays, but then they'll come after you for reimbursement.

SIX STEPS FOR RENEGOTIATING CONTRACT PRICES

Sometimes a vendor's costs rise uncontrollably during a contract period. Perhaps the vendor's suppliers have raised costs. Perhaps currency fluctuations have created cost increases. Perhaps the product under contract is in short supply and the vendor can't obtain the quantity needed to service the contract. These reasons, and others, are sufficient cause to try to get an unprofitable contract renegotiated. Here's a simple six-step process on how to conduct this renegotiation with an agency if a contract is causing heavy losses:

1. Don't seek relief unless you're really suffering. You may not get much sympathy from an agency that gave you a contract in good faith just because your profit margins are a bit slimmer these days.

2. Document all the facts. Show your original costs when you bid the contract and exactly how and when your costs have risen. Be as complete as you can. Don't try to bend the facts, you'll certainly get

no relief if discovered. Most agency negotiators realize that their suppliers must turn a profit to stay in business. If you can prove you're losing heavily on a contract, you stand a good chance of obtaining relief.

3. Know what you want out of the renegotiation. Do you want a price increase? Would you prefer that the contract be canceled? Could you live with the current contract if some of the conditions were changed? If you have alternatives already in mind, you can help the agency come to a decision on how best to provide relief for your situation.

4. Be prepared to compromise. The agency may have some ideas for providing your company relief that you have not considered.

5. Document any agency specifications that have changed during the term of the contract. This is a good offensive tactic because agency personnel frequently make demands on vendors which weren't part of the original specifications. For example, the specs may call for an hour of training with each equipment installation. In practice, the training time may take three hours. You may not have made a point of it before in the interests of harmony and a well-running system, but your people are taking extra time for each unit installed. This is cause for a price increase, and when your own costs have risen is a good time to bring up the matter. At the very least, you will have demonstrated that you can only provide the service and training spelled out in the contract.

6. Be sure that you're talking with the real movers and shakers within the agency. A request for a price increase to an assistant buyer is not likely to get the attention of the people who count.

WHAT HAPPENS WHEN YOU CAN'T DELIVER PRODUCT

Long-term set price contracts always involve some degree of risk on the part of the vendor. The vendor's own prices or costs can rise while the prices charged to the agency are fixed. Another problem with the long-term fixed price contract is that the product promised to the agency may not be available through the entire term of the contract. If the vendor is a dealer, the manufacturer may cancel the model. Even for manufacturers there are problems such as strikes, parts unavailability, production glitches, and damage to the plant.

Exactly what happens when the vendor can't deliver? It isn't good. There's usually a stipulation in most bid contracts of any size that states "If the vendor cannot deliver within X days, the agency is free to seek an equal quality product on the open market. *The vendor will be charged the difference between the contract price and purchase price on the open market.*" The message may be written in legalese, but the meaning is clear. If you can't deliver within a specified period of time, the agency is free to buy a similar product wherever it can and charge your company anything extra it is forced to pay. The agency buyers don't have to worry about negotiating a good deal when they go into the open market, because your company is footing the bill.

There are usually stipulations covering mitigating circumstances such as acts of God, war, and so forth. However, it's important to read all the fine print when signing a long-term contract at a fixed price to a government agency. Understand what your obligations are, and make sure that you have a reliable source of supply *and that your costs during the contract period are also fixed by contract.*

When delivery is impossible, the best policy is to visit the decision makers at the contracting agency as soon as possible. Outline the situation to them and the reasons why your company can't make delivery. You may be allowed to provide a substitute. Most agencies will accept an equal or better product if the one on the contract can't be provided.

HOW TO MAKE MODEL CHANGES IN MID-CONTRACT

What happens when the factory changes the model on you and the contract still has six months to run? This is not as much of a problem as it might appear, because industry is constantly changing and improving products. Agencies recognize that models may change. If you can offer a new model with the same or more features, you can usually substitute. *What you can't change is the price.* In other words, the agency will allow you to deliver a superior product for the same money during the remainder of the contract. This may seem unfair, but look at it from the agency's point of view. If vendors were allowed to raise prices with the introduction of new products, the bid process would become a gigantic bait and switch operation.

The way to proceed with a new model you wish to substitute is to bring it in for evaluation. If it's simply an upgrade on the model currently on contract, the approval is usually quick and painless. You could have a problem getting fast approval if the agency has a testing laboratory that must approve products or if the new model operates in a radically different manner.

CHAPTER SUMMARY

Many agencies require bid or performance bonds from vendors who wish to compete for their business.

The bid and performance bonds indemnify agencies from vendors who fail to deliver after a successful bid or perform according to the terms of a contract.

Nonperformance of a contract exposes a company to the risk of damages.

If a vendor's costs rise dramatically during the term of a contract that vendor may seek relief from the contracting agency in the form of higher prices or reduced services.

Failure to deliver a contracted product to an agency can be costly to the vendor because the agency can buy a like product on the open market and charge the vendor for any difference in price.

The best course to follow when losing money on a contract or when the product under contract becomes unavailable is to explain the situation to the contracting agency as soon as possible.

Switching models in mid-contract is generally not too difficult providing the new model meets all the specifications and is delivered for the same price.

Finally, this chapter is not intended to be a substitute for legal counsel. Rules, regulations, and practices vary from state to state and even from county to county within a state. When necessary, use an attorney to interpret the rules and contract fine print.

10

LIFE AFTER THE CONTRACT IS AWARDED

HOW TO WRING EXTRA PROFITS OUT OF A BID CONTRACT

Some vendors wonder how their competitors can sometimes offer such low prices on competitive bid contracts. In some instances the bid seems to be taken with no profit at all, and a few appear to be bid at prices that will ensure the bidder suffers a loss. How can they do it?

The bidders who offer these special low prices are not philanthropic organizations out to save the taxpayers a few dollars by supplying goods and services to government agencies at a loss. They are clever business people who realize there is more than one way to make a profit.

Here are four ways vendors can increase profits on bid contracts sold at low margins:

1. By selling supplies. Is yours a razor blade business? Does the cost of the supplies eventually add up to more than the cost of the equipment? (Gillette can give away the razor as long as you'll only buy the blades from them.) As the product vendor you have an inside track on the agency's requirement for the supplies chewed up by that product.

Often, these supplies can be sold for full list price. Even if the supplies contract goes out for bid, as the equipment vendor you can still ensure some supply business. Most agencies will allow their individual offices to purchase items up to a certain dollar level, say $100, from their petty cash fund. When delivering equipment to the agency, always bring along a supply package order form that totals a few pennies less than the dollar amount the agency is authorized to buy locally. If the cap is $100, have an order form with a supply package that totals $99.50. The agency local office will order this package because they'll be able to get delivery faster than if they bought through central purchasing.

2. By servicing the equipment. The warranty on your product will eventually run out. After-warranty service presents a good profit opportunity for many companies. Even if the agency has its own service personnel there is still the opportunity to sell the spare parts needed to fix the equipment at full margins.

3. By selling training. Most contracts will call for a specific number of training hours on the equipment to be installed. If additional time is needed, that time can be charged. Even if the time specified on the contract is adequate to train agency personnel, there's still the matter of turnover and replacement. New people on the job must be trained, and fees for this training are legitimate charges.

4. By selling the agency items not under contract at better profit margins. Once your company and products have established a reputation at an agency there's always a chance that you can sell them additional products in quantities small enough so no bid is required. Perhaps a new office needs an enhanced version of the product under contract. A telephone quote at full list price may be enough to get you the order.

HOW TO INCREASE THE DOLLAR VOLUME OF A CONTRACT THROUGH PIGGYBACKING

What is piggybacking? It is using one successful contract to obtain orders from other agencies. The way it works is very simple. Let's say that your company has been successful in winning a bid for erasers to the Pittsburgh Unified School District. This is a big contract for erasers and you're very proud of it. You can increase the value of the contract by offering the contract price to other school districts in the immediate area. In effect, you're letting those other school districts piggyback on the Pittsburgh school order. For small school districts whose eraser requirements don't nearly equal Pittsburgh's volume, the price might be very attractive. Other school districts are saved the trouble of going through the bid process. Here's how you might make other school districts aware of the offer:

Purchasing Agent
ABC School District
Elm and Maple Streets
Altoona, Pa. 11122

Dear Purchasing Agent:

Our company, the Chalkless Eraser Company, is proud to announce that we have just been awarded a contract by the Pittsburgh Unified School District to supply them with one thousand dozen of our model 432 erasers for the next school year. These are our finest felt erasers, rated "best buy" by *Buyer's Laboratory* in their August 1989 issue.

The regular list price for these erasers is $100.00 per dozen. The contract price for the Pittsburgh School District is $60.00 per dozen, a saving of 40 percent.

For the next semester we will permit other school districts in Pennsylvania to purchase our model 432 eraser at the Pittsburgh Unified School District contract price. This is a wonderful opportunity for your school district to take advantage of Pittsburgh's tremendous buying power. I've enclosed an order form that reflects the contract price. To take advantage of our offer, simply complete the enclosed order form with the name of your school district, the quantity required, and mail the form to my attention at the above address.

Cordially,

Johnny Eraserhead

Why sell other customers at a very low bid contract price when their volume requirements don't normally justify the kind of discount you're offering? *Because piggybacking orders often circumvents the bid process.*

The purchasing departments at the other agencies know the price is okay, so they just go ahead and buy. Often, there's a stipulation in agency regulations that allows one agency to piggyback on another's contract even when dollar volumes normally dictate putting an item out for bid. Whenever an item is put out for bid there's an opportunity for the competition to win the business. The competition doesn't get a shot at piggybacked business.

HOW TO GET REPEAT CONTRACTS FROM AGENCIES WITHOUT GOING THROUGH THE UNCERTAINTY OF THE BID PROCESS

Trauma time is when a lucrative contract has run its course and is almost up for a new bid. Your company has gotten used to the volume of business a bid contract provides. All that sales volume is at risk now because the agency is going out for bid again. Their regulations require it. Every new bid represents an opportunity for the competition to unseat the current contract holder. Opportunity for the competition means jeopardy for the existing contract holder.

Still, there are ways that contracts can be extended for months, and occasionally for several years. If you have a contract you'd like to keep without risking another bid here are several ways contracts can sometimes be extended.

1. Every method suggested here will require some degree of support and cooperation by the agency which is your current customer. So, the first rule in extending an existing contract beyond its stated term is to service that contract to the best of your ability. Make agency personnel trust you by being trustworthy. Make the equipment, system, or service reliable. Become so much a part of the agency operation that they can't conceive of life without you. They'll want to work with you in extending the contract because they won't want to risk doing business with a new, unknown vendor.

2. When agency contracts are written ask that the specifications include options for additional years. These options normally give either party, the contracting agency and the vendor, the choice of extending the contract for an additional term of one or two years. Price increases can be tied to something like the Consumer Price Index. If you win the contract, work on the agency to exercise the option. If one of your competitors wins, work on the agency to go out for a new bid at the end of the term. With this system you can keep a lucrative bid contract for as many as three years.

3. Suggest specification changes near the end of the contract term. One way to hold up a new bid is to make sensible suggestions regarding the specifications near the end of the contract. Seeing a possible change in the specs, other interested vendors will demand a chance to make their own recommendations. They won't want you to be dictating the specs. (The person who writes the specs is the one who gets the deal, remember?) Different vendors making diverse recommendations may confuse the agency to the point where the new bid is delayed for thirty to sixty days. Meanwhile, your existing contract is extended by that same period of time so agency offices are not without the product.

4. Announce a new model shortly before the contract is scheduled to be put out for bid. If the model seems perfect for the agency requirements, they may delay the bid for a few weeks to take a look at it. (This tactic will seldom buy you more than a few weeks).

5. Protest a bid that is won by your competitor. The protest process usually takes several weeks, perhaps a month. Meanwhile, as the current contract holder you continue to supply product to the agency.

HOW TO USE A CONTRACT TO SELL MORE PROFITABLE ITEMS

Often a bid contract only calls for the major item required by the agency. The agency can also be sold supplies, spare parts, and training to improve profit margins. Auxiliary equipment, add-ons and peripherals, and other products that enhance and expand the use of the contract item can also be sold to the agency at normal profit margins.

Let's say your contract is for computer printers. Every agency office that orders one of your printers is also a prospect for printer stands, cut sheet and continuous form paper feeders, forms bursters, decollaters, sound shields, font styles, computer ribbons, and so on. The best way to sell these products is not through the purchasing department, but rather by offering them to the office that actually took delivery on the printer. They know what kind of auxiliary equipment would be useful in their operation. To take advantage of the opportunity to sell additional products to an agency where a contract is already in place, do the following:

1. Always include a catalog of your company's other products and a price sheet when delivering the items under contract.

2. Put a decal with your company's name, address, and phone number on the product so the agency office will know how to get in touch with you.

3. Keep a list of delivery points and the name of a person at that office. Every so often conduct a direct mail campaign to these offices, offering some peripheral product not under contract at a special price.

HOW TO WIN GOVERNMENT AGENCY BUSINESS WHILE AVOIDING THE BID PROCESS ENTIRELY

If the theme of this book is how to win competitive bids, why is there a section on how to avoid bidding? This material is included because while bids are profit opportunities for your company, they are also present opportunities for your competitors. If an agency is absolutely convinced that your product, and only your product, will serve its needs, then the bid process should be circumvented if possible. There are perfectly legal ways this can be accomplished, including the following:

1. Have the agency order in quantities under the dollar limit that automatically triggers the bid process. If the agency must go out for bid on any order exceeding ten thousand dollars, ask it to place orders with your company totaling nine thousand dollars and under.

2. Some agencies treat lease payments as monthly expenditures. If the agency you're working with operates in this manner, an item that can't be purchased without going out for bid can be leased. Work with leasing companies willing to handle leases from government agencies. Not all lessors are willing to do this because government agencies can and will suspend payments when their budgets are reduced.

3. Sell agencies special products, systems, and services that aren't standardized and therefore don't adapt to the bid process. The key to getting business in this manner is writing a strong proposal. The art of government proposal writing is a book-length subject in itself.

CHAPTER SUMMARY

You can wring extra profits from a government contract by selling the agency supplies, training, extra services, and items not on the contract.

Piggybacking is a way to increase the number of products sold on a government contract. Piggybacking means allowing other agencies to obtain the item on contract on the same terms and conditions.

There are ways to get repeat contracts without risking another competitive bid situation. These ways include asking the agency to write option clauses into the specifications, announcing a new model, delaying getting specifications or testing data to the agency, and protesting an apparent winning bid by a competitor.

Additional and more profitable business can be obtained from a contract by selling the agency other systems, auxiliary equipment, and peripherals.

When an agency likes your product and company you can avoid the bid process entirely by writing orders for just under the amount that automatically triggers the bid process, by leasing, and by writing special proposals.

11

SELLING TO MAJOR COMMERCIAL ACCOUNTS

Companies seeking bid business from major commercial customers should consider taking the next step: soliciting sales through normal channels from these corporate giants. It's a natural progression from competitive bidding. If products can be sold through the bid process to Fortune 500 companies, why not seek regular orders at normal profit margins from these same customers?

Every company, every sales professional, gets the idea sometime. After all, major accounts are the big leagues of the business world. Sales to Fortune 500 companies mean bigger orders, juicier commission checks, and a more prestigious customer list. Even the credit manager likes major accounts because these customers usually pay their bills. Getting a good share of major account business can be the difference between a company struggling for success and one that serves champagne and caviar at the company's annual stockholders' meeting. For the individual salesperson, the ability to bring in that blockbuster order will place him or her at the top of the profession with the ability for almost unlimited earnings.

But it's not easy to knock over major accounts. The Fortune 500 definitely are not easy pickings. There's a decided difference between competing in a bid situation where your company may get an edge because of its small or minority business status and going up against large and resourceful competitors for non-bid orders from corporate heavyweights. Superior products don't guarantee success, a better pricing structure won't necessarily bring your company the business, quality service won't bring corporate purchasing agents pounding at your door, and a "gift of gab" can get a salesperson sent back to the bench before the bat is off the shoulder.

The rules are different when dealing with the corporate elite. The approach is different, the selling cycle is different, the intensity level is different, and the closing strategies are different. The sales techniques used on smaller customers may actually hinder your efforts when dealing with big business. Those clever little closing tricks that capture the order at the five-person shop down the block may get the unwary salesperson shown the door when dealing with a major corporation. That's because big companies recognize their buying clout. They are sophisticated buyers who play in a high-stakes game and they don't have time for anyone or any company who doesn't know the rules. You've got to learn the rules before you can play the game, but even before the rules, there are some things you should know about the opponent.

HOW MAJOR ACCOUNTS VIEW THE WORLD: SIX THINGS YOU SHOULD KNOW

1. When calling on a small company, you'll often be talking to the head man. When calling on major accounts, you'll be talking to and trying to sell middle managers. It's very unlikely that you'll ever get an opportunity to reach the president of the Ford Motor Company or any of his peers. Middle managers have two basic objectives. They are:

• To take credit for things that go right
• To avoid blame for things that go wrong

These objectives make it difficult to convince major account prospects to make a change unless they have a perceived problem. Given his or her druthers, a middle manager from a corporate powerhouse would much prefer doing business with another company in its own class. Why is that so? Because if things go wrong, a big company supplier will be assessed much of the blame. If a small company is used and there are problems, the person who opted to use that company receives the blame. His or her judgment is questioned. The money saved from lower costs will long be forgotten if delivery is late or the product doesn't perform as promised.

2. Corporate customers place a greater value on service and reliability than they do on price. A corporate prospect with offices all over the country will raise the question (and a proper question it is, too), "If I give you the order for the entire company, how are you going to service my office in Altoona, PA?"

3. Purchasing decisions often impact several divisions within a large organization. Because they're involved, they all want a voice in how the decision is made. For example, a petroleum company's apparently simple decision to use a different printer to manufacture a credit card receipt would impact marketing, data processing, gas station operations, and purchasing. They'd all want their say in selecting the vendor.

4. If a major corporation has a satisfactory relationship with a vendor, they're reluctant to change. They like no-problem relationships. This is great if you're in and terribly vexing if you're out.

5. Large corporations have their own agendas. They know the projects they wish to address. It's difficult to get them to pay attention to anything else. The cost-saving idea you have may not be exciting for them because their minds are elsewhere.

6. Some corporations only wish to do business with their corporate peers. GM feels comfortable doing business with United States Steel. In effect, they want designer labels on the equipment they buy. Their corporate egos demand it.

If after reading these caveats you're still interested in doing business with major accounts, you'll need to know some basic rules if you hope to get some orders.

HOW TO DEVELOP A BIG-LEAGUE ATTITUDE TOWARD MAJOR ACCOUNTS AND WHY ONE IS NEEDED

The first lesson of major account marketing is to forget what all traditional sales manuals tell you about selling. Of course basic sales technique still works. There are no substitutes for persistence, finding and solving problems, demonstrating, effective proposals, and strong closes. However, the rhythms are different. The beginner is better off with no technique at all than using a method that is bound to fail. Once the old rules are forgotten the next step is to develop a big-league attitude toward major accounts.

HOW ONE COMPANY'S MAJOR ACCOUNT PROGRAM FAILED

Several years ago a major computer company proudly announced a major account program. This was the outfit that spearheaded the personal computer revolution, making multi-millionaires of its two founders. During the company's phenomenal growth it established a national network of dealers who did an excellent job in reaching independent computer users and small business owners, but who couldn't reach many major corporate customers.

Selling to big business was considered vital to the company's continued growth. The company decided to bypass their dealers and pursue this market with its own sales staff. After a flurry of planning, the company unveiled the program designed to capture the hearts, minds, and purchase orders of corporate America. They began by recruiting fifty of the best major account salespeople available. The company wanted top performers and paid to get them. The assembled crew all had excellent histories of selling to major accounts. The company felt confident that the quality and quantity of their new major account staff would ensure a quick capture of corporate market share.

The company developed attractive pricing schedules for their products with volume discounts designed to make corporate purchasing agents salivate. These end user prices were often lower than those available to their dealers. The company wanted the business, and it was prepared to slice profit margins to get it.

They understood the value of name recognition when dealing with Fortune 500 companies, so they took out full page ads in the *Wall Street Journal, Business Week, Forbes,* and other trade publications. They designed a blitz campaign guaranteed to put one of their golden-throated major account hotshots before large company decision makers.

The fifty major account representatives marched off with their attaché cases crammed with blank purchase orders and their special prices tucked away where the company's dealers couldn't see them. They were going to cut the same kind of path through corporate America that Sherman did on his march to the sea. They couldn't miss. They had the right product, sexy pricing, the best marketing talent money could buy, and the advertising campaign was beginning to get them the needed name identification.

They missed by light years. The campaign was a dismal failure. Ten sad months later the fifty super-achievers had managed to sign up only a handful of major accounts. The accounts that did sign up purchased only a fraction of the units that had been projected. The company was light years away from achieving any of its major account objectives. The campaign's only real achievement was to alienate the company's dealer organization, which viewed the major account program as a blatant effort to steal customers. Some dealers gave up the product or lost their enthusiasm for it. The company was forced to retreat. The program that began with so much fanfare was terminated. The miserable results shook up the corporate suite. For this and a host of other reasons, the two founders left. It took the company some time to win back the full confidence of its dealer organization.

What went wrong? The computer company appeared to have mixed all the ingredients of success into a sweet, rich batter. Why didn't the cake turn out? This chapter is not intended to be a case study of a major account program gone awry, but noting some of the mistakes made can help in developing the right attitude, a big-league attitude toward major account selling. It was attitude, as much as any specifics of the plan, that caused the program to fail. Here are the four basic mistakes they made.

1. They expected and counted on quick results. The company's biggest attitude problem, and it was a fatal blunder, was in its expectation of quick results. It had captured the consumer computer market in a few short years and didn't see why things wouldn't move even faster when selling to major corporations. But the consumer market and the major corporation market are different. Fortune 500 companies are the big leagues. Most ballplayers don't reach the big leagues overnight. They spend years in the minors honing and polishing their skills. The analogy isn't quite appropriate because it won't take years to make significant sales to major corporations. But the job can't be done overnight either. The Ford Motor Company or General Electric isn't going to change a reliable supplier because a fast-talking pitchman makes a brilliant fifteen-minute presentation.

Corporate clients carefully weigh potential new suppliers. Whether it's a complicated system that requires the client to change the way things are done, or a commodity that's used every day, large corporation

purchasers want to know everything about a vendor. Here are some
of the things they look at:

a. The credibility of the person calling on them. Does the person
   seem reliable, truthful? Does he or she tell the truth when
   facing the user?

b. What is the vendor's reputation? Are their users generally
   satisfied? Do they deliver on time? Do they follow through?
   What's their record on service?

c. What's the history of the product? Is it reliable? Are others
   using it for similar applications? Does it hold up? Is it competitive with others like it on the market? What is the cost
   of maintenance? What are the cost of supplies?

2. They used too much pressure in trying to close orders and tried
to close before the prospect was ready to buy. The major account
salespeople for the computer company had large quotas to justify their
big salaries and short-term timetables, and that put pressure on them
to make sales fast. That pressure was transferred to the corporate
clients. Large corporations won't be forced into premature action by
sales pressure or so-called closing techniques. They have their own
timetables, their own agendas and couldn't care less about their vendors'
priorities. The attempt to speed up the evaluation process was coun-
terproductive because it caused the corporate prospects to withdraw.

When the computer company put out a cattle call for fifty major
account hotshots, all brought on board at approximately the same time,
they set up expectations, a *demand*, for short term results. The size and
cost of the program accentuated that need. There was pressure to
product sales, to knock over the corporate account *right now*. Spending
a day with one of these people was probably better than going to a
clinic on trial closing. The more pressure the sales people applied, the
more prospects deferred decisions. The more delay in getting agreements signed, the more frantic and hysterical the salespeople became.
As delays became defeats, management grew more impatient. They
demanded results, adding still more pressure. The program disinte-
grated. When the computer company signed up an army of major
account representatives and assigned them short-term goals, it virtually
guaranteed the failure of the program. This leads to another important
rule: *In major account selling, blitzkrieg doesn't work.* Throwing money and
people at a program won't shortcut the time needed to get results.

3. They circumvented their company's normal sales channels. Another crucial mistake made by the computer company was in circumventing its dealer organization and going after the large corporate customer with its own direct sales staff. Even if a dealer had never made a call on a large corporate prospect in the immediate geographic area, there was a feeling that anyone within range was "their" prospect. The major account program was viewed by the dealers as branding strays on another man's range. The efforts of the major account crew were regarded as attempts to "rustle" these accounts. Special pricing not available to the dealer organization only heightened the resentment. The result was that many of the dealers, who were sometimes necessary for follow-up service and training and who were invaluable in making introductions, not only didn't support the program, but they actively worked against it. A major account representative making a call on a corporate prospect often found that a local dealer in the area had been sabotaging his or her efforts. The computer company's experience gives us another important rule of major account selling. *A major account program that circumvents the company's normal sales channels is doomed to fail.*

4. They succumbed to the prima donna syndrome. Still another mistake made by the computer company was in hiring an entire crew of hotshots at inflated salaries. This sales crew was separated from the normal sales force that called on the dealer network. They differed in temperament, objectives, and the size of the compensation checks cashed every two weeks. In many cases the dealer sales reps worked at cross-purposes, because every major account signed meant one less prospect the local dealer could call on and sell. As such, the major accounts represented lost opportunities for the dealer salespeople. These were the salespeople who had built the company. Now, they saw higher paid people coming in and, in effect, ruining their work. They sided with the dealers who were their customers. Few worked to support the major account program, and some worked to defeat it.

FIVE PREREQUISITES TO A POWERFUL MAJOR ACCOUNT PROGRAM

The computer company's example provides good insight on what not to do. However, negatives never built a positive program. Here are the steps that can lead to a successful major account program. (Incidentally, the computer company learned by its mistakes. A year or so later it launched another major account program. This time it proved to be a success.)

1. The most important ingredient in a major account program is **patience.** Don't expect too much too soon. This patience should be built into the program and reflected by everyone from the executives on top to the people on the firing line. Take the time necessary to develop big-league selling skills. Demonstrate this patience by taking the following actions:

    a. Plan the major account program carefully before implementation. Set up the structure first and make sure that it is a structure that can work within your company's organizational structure.

    b. Build the major account team slowly. Start with one person to help with initial planning and setting of the company's major account policies. Add staff only when it is apparent that the program is becoming successful.

       One of the problems with many major account programs is high overhead. Good major account salespeople command respectable salaries. Often, it takes time for them to produce because of the nature of major account sales. Moving forward slowly keeps overhead at a minimum. New people are added only as prior major account hires become productive.

    c. Set modest goals for the first year. This is the time to cultivate and fertilize. The harvest will be gathered later.

    d. Develop a major account compensation plan that isn't heavily dependent on commission income for the first year. Give your people time to properly develop major corporate accounts.

    e. At the beginning, set quotas based on the number of negotiations in progress rather than orders closed. In the early stages of a program if the major account representative has significant dialogues going with a number of large companies, he or she is doing the job. The orders will come later.

If these steps are taken, you will have demonstrated to company personnel and the major account prospects that your company is committed to be in the game for the long haul.

Psychologists claim that one of the principal factors that separates mature from immature behavior is that the mature person is willing to *wait for gratification*. That must be your position when setting up a major account program. The work begins now. The gratification comes later.

2. Involve everyone within the sales organization in the major account program. There are enough books on the importance of team play and team spirit, so that subject doesn't have to be addressed here. The best spirit, and the closest cooperation is based on self-interest. You won't persuade the people in your current sales network that the major account program is good for everyone by simply circulating a memo to that effect. The benefits must be patently clear.

3. Make the major account team part of the regular sales organization. Don't set the major account salespeople apart or treat them differently; otherwise; the existing sales staff will view them as an elitist group.

4. Use the skills and contacts of the current sales group to promote major account activity. If the company markets on a direct basis, use the territory sales people as bird dogs, sniffing out accounts, setting up initial appointments, making contacts when the major account representative isn't available, and just keeping the pot boiling when necessary. If the company sells through dealers, use them as well. A dealer organization can be valuable for customer installations, warranty repairs, bird-dogging, and handling complaints. Dealers, particularly in small towns, can be powerful marketing factors within their own arenas. Don't ignore them. The better national coverage that can be demonstrated to a major account, the more likely the chance of getting and keeping the business.

5. Develop a compensation plan that allows the people in the company's normal selling channels to profit from major account sales. This step is critical to a successful major account operation. Why should a dealer or a direct salesperson tell the home office about a potential major account if that prospect will be snatched away and declared off limits? Cooperation comes when commissions are paid, dealers are given finders' fees, sales volume is credited toward quota, and so forth.

These five points will help develop the *structure* of a successful major account selling organization. But structure by itself never sold anything to anyone. The following thirteen-point program will help make a major account program a success.

A THIRTEEN-POINT PROGRAM FOR MAJOR ACCOUNT SUCCESS

1. Learn everything you can about the target account. If the target is a publicly traded stock company, there is much information available in public domain. The *Thomas Registry* will have a list of company officers. The company's own annual report will contain data on sales volumes, divisional operations, products made, profits, and long-term debt. A *Standard & Poor* report will go into more detail about the company's operation. A visit to the purchasing office may yield a handbook on purchasing policies. Sales literature may contain a list of branch offices. An internal newspaper may have a story about an important project. There is much that can be learned before a single sales call is made.

2. Find out the names of the individuals who are normally involved in the purchasing decisions for the kind of product your company makes. Where do you get this information? The simplest way is to ask. Visit the purchasing office (with an appointment), tell the appropriate buyer about your company's product, and ask him or her to tell you the names of the actual users. These people are often the real decision makers at large corporations. In many large companies the buyer's function is limited to price negotiation. Asking the purchasing department is the simplest way, but it doesn't always work. Buyers sometimes want to shield the end users from pesky vendors. If you encounter a tight-lipped buyer who won't give out any information, use the job title approach. In other companies of a similar nature what are the job titles of the people who actually use the kind of product your company makes? If the Head of Field Service at company A made the buying decision for your company's innovative tool carrying case, chances are he's the person you want to see at company B. Once you have the job title, the company phone operator or receptionist can give you the actual name. (In some cases, the phone operator won't know. In that event, try the personnel department.)

3. After the name of the user has been discovered, learn the prospect's reporting structure. Who's the next person up the ladder? Who maintains control of the purse strings? You want to be sure this person, or group of individuals, will be present at your closing presentation.

4. Find out the name of the prospect's current supplier. How can you do this? Ask and look. Call up the buyer and ask him or her what company's product is currently being used. Look about when walking through the prospect's office. What typewriter is on the desk? Who makes that desk? Call up one of the prospect's branch offices and ask someone there what brand of product is used. Ask the prospect's competitors. They usually have a handle on what others in the industry are doing. When you learn who your competition is, analyze the product being bought and the company behind it. Is the company well regarded? Are they the price leader? Do they enjoy a good reputation for quality? Do they own the industry? Is your prospect's application for the product unique?

5. Develop a plan of attack. Forgetting personalities and personal relationships and past history, why should the prospect stop buying from their current supplier and begin buying from you? Look at the problem as objectively as you can. Remember, when the prospect tries something new he is at risk. Why should the prospect gamble on you and your company? What overriding benefit can you offer?

6. Take stock of what you've learned. You know something about the target prospect, the names of the individuals who may participate in the buying decision, the current supplier, and you think you know why they should buy from you. You've done all this homework and still have not made a call, except for a courtesy visit to the purchasing department. However, now you're ready to begin the campaign in earnest.

7. Make an appointment with the actual product user. This is easier written than done. The user's first reaction will be to shuffle you off to purchasing. "They issue all the orders." Sure they do, but in most big companies they don't write the requisitions that result in those orders being placed, and it isn't their budget money being spent. You'll have to come up with a good reason why the person should see you. Here are short lists of reasons that work and reasons that may fail.

WHAT WORKS

- Something absolutely brand spanking new that no one else in the industry has. The prospect will be interested in being the first to see it.
- A success story in a similar industry: "ABC industries used this stuff and saved $47,000 the first month. Call them and see."
- Obvious expertise. People like to talk to experts knowledgeable in their area of endeavor. If your phone pitch indicates you know what you're talking about, you may get an appointment just so

the person can pick your brain. (Encourage brain picking, but always suggest there's still more crop to be harvested.)

- Industry information. This almost goes in the expertise category, but they're really two different things. The industry expert knows the gossip. He or she is active at the trade shows, knows the names of the players, and so forth. Dropping a tidbit about the business is a good way to get an appointment.

- Verifiable claims about time saving. Prove you cut the time of an operation and getting an audience is no problem.

WHAT DOESN'T WORK.

- Claims about lower prices. There are too many peddlers on the street telling the same story for a lower-price claim to have any effect on a major commercial customer. Even if the claim is believed, the prospect will likely equate lower cost to lower quality.

- Claims about labor savings. Again, these claims have been over-done. Too many systems and products have been installed with no resultant reduction in personnel for this claim to have much meaning. Besides, many managers in large companies are compensated on the basis of the number of people who report to them. They don't want to reduce their staffs.

- Claims about superior quality. This is almost a Catch-22 situation. Claims about lower pricing don't work because the prospect fears the quality is lower. Claims about higher quality don't work because the prospect automatically assumes the price will be higher.

There are, of course, exceptions to all of these rules. A prospect experiencing a product quality problem is likely to be receptive to a salesperson who calls and offers to demonstrate the superior features of his like product. Low price can work when tied to a number of product success stories that allay fears about product quality. A prospect who is truly satisfied with the current supplier may not respond to any of the "will work" strategies.

What to do When the Prospect Won't Even Answer the Phone

Some prospects have guard-dog secretaries who protect them against all intruders. The secretary insists that all callers state their names and business. The boss is never immediately available. The secretary doesn't know when the boss will be able to take calls. No, she can't make appointments for the boss. One glimmer of hope is tossed across the phone line. The boss will call you back. Don't be deceived. The call back seldom comes.

Persistence sometimes works in these cases. The boss may be intrigued by the sheer volume of your calls and return one to find out what you wanted to say. A great many calls staggered at different times may catch the secretary out for a coffee break or lunch. If the boss picks up the phone, you've got the rascal.

Another possibility is a short letter asking for an appointment. Use the letter to state the case you wanted to make on the phone. Here's an example of such a letter:

Mr. William Frankel
Lamp Industries
3456 Main Street
Gilpin, Ohio 11122

Dear Mr. Frankel:

Our company, Sockets Unlimited, makes a product that is used by the majority of companies within your industry. It is our Model 444 anodized socket, which comes in a variety of sizes. The Model 444 has a unique design that significantly reduces assembly time over like competitive models. One company, Acme Lamps, benefited by a 30 percent reduction in the line assembly time for their table lamp line when they switched to the Model 444.

Mr. Frankel, I'd like to meet with you, to show you the unique design of the Model 444. This product can bring your company some manufacturing economies. I'll call you next Monday to arrange a time that is mutually convenient.

Cordially,

Bill Persistent

This letter is short enough so the receiver is likely to read it. Very long letters often get tossed in the circular file unread. It dangles the carrot of reduced production time and cites a reference to prove it. Note that the sender will follow up with a phone call. *Never* wait for the prospect to call you. Few do it. When the appointment call is made, don't offer much additional information over the phone. You've already fired one shot with the letter, don't waste any more ammunition until you're face to face with the major account prospect.

When To Go To The Top

What's the best action to take when the prospect *still* won't see you? If you've tried persistent calling, written letters stating your business, and still can't get an appointment with a likely prospect, go up the ladder to the next level of authority. Tell your story via phone or letter to the person's superior. If the boss is interested, he'll ask the person to investigate your proposition. The next time you call, you'll get that appointment.

Many sales experts prefer starting at the highest level they can reach and working down. There's nothing wrong with this approach. If it works for you, use it. However, many executives resent an effort to bypass them. If higher authority has paved the way, you may find yourself making a presentation before a hostile audience. That's why I recommend going after the exact level of authority necessary to make a decision on your product. If there is no other choice, go higher.

8. Set sales calls objectives. You're now ready to make that first personal call on the major account prospect. Well, you're *almost* ready. There's still one bit of planning that needs to be done. You must determine what you want to accomplish, what result you want from this call. Major accounts are not one-call closes. In some cases they are not even five- or six-call closes. Many so-called sales professionals give up in frustration when calling on major account prospects. They aren't willing to spend all the time it takes to get the job done. They've made many calls with no apparent result. That's why setting intermediate goals is so important. You're not only inching the prospect closer to a decision on your company's product, you're seeing your achievement as you climb the ladder toward the sale.

A reasonable set of objectives for a first sales call might be as follows:

a. Establish your credibility. This comes before all other objec-
    tives because credibility determines whether the other ob-
    jectives can be reached. *Does the prospect believe what you're
    telling him or her?* We live in an age where people are skeptical
    of salespeople's claims. The brilliant fifteen-minute sales pitch
    doesn't mean much if the person at whom it is aimed doesn't
    believe a word of it.

    How is credibility established? First, do everything you
    say you're going to do. If you promise to send literature the
    next day, send it. If you say you'll phone the next day about
    two in the afternoon, be on that horn at 1:59. Next, never
    lie. Don't sacrifice the truth in order to obtain a temporary
    advantage. That advantage won't last long. Third, be candid.
    Tell your prospect things they way they really are. Don't
    conceal by omission. There is so little candor in the business
    world today that its use is almost always disarming. The
    process of establishing credibility may take some time, but it
    can begin on the very first call.

b. Establish the credentials of your company. Tell the prospect
    something about the outfit you work for, its place in the
    industry, its capabilities, and its success stories.

c. Establish your own credentials. This is different than estab-
    lishing your credibility. In the first instance, you're trying to
    show that you're reliable and trustworthy. In the second,
    you're trying to establish that you're familiar with the pros-
    pect's industry or know a good deal about your product. If
    you're a beginner, don't try to fake industry or product
    knowledge. Ask the prospect for guidance. This tactic often
    works if the salesperson is *candid* about his or her shortcom-
    ings.

d. Find out something about the prospect's operation. This step
    is much more important than telling the prospect what your
    company has to offer. If you let the prospect talk first, you
    have a better chance of tailoring your product, or at the
    very least tailoring your sales pitch, to the prospect's require-
    ments.

e. Find out something about the person with whom you're
    dealing. What's the size of his or her office? Is this really the
    decision maker? What's your assessment of his or her per-

sonality? Is the person likely to move on this project if you can make a convincing case for change? Is this person a mover and shaker? What reinforcement will you have to provide?

f. What other factors will influence a buying decision? Are there long term contracts in place? Is there a sweetheart relationship with the current vendor? Does the prospect have a big enough budget for the project? Are other departments involved who must be consulted? Who are the players? What internal movement is going on within the company?

g. Finally, whet the prospect's appetite. You want to get sufficient interest from the prospect to go on to the next step. This next step might be a survey, a demonstration, a visit to a friendly installation, a chance to make a presentation before a larger group, or in some cases, even a proposal. *It is critical that the first appointment end with some definite future action planned and agreed upon by both parties.* It bodes better for a future sale if this action is the responsibility of the prospect. For example, the prospect agrees to research the files or access the computer to review how much product of the kind you're trying to sell was used by the company in each of the last twelve months.

9. Draw up a sales "ladder" with the top rung being the sales close. The call you've made to the account should have provided you with enough information to do this. Here's what a typical ladder might look like:

Rung 10   Close the sale
Rung 9   Formal presentation before prospect's full panel of decision makers
Rung 8   Polish proposal based on prospect's input
Rung 7   Informal proposal to sympathetic prospect decision makers
Rung 6   Visit by prospect to site currently using product or system
Rung 5   Demonstration of equipment
Rung 4   Agreement on objectives to be accomplished
Rung 3   Survey of prospect's current operation
Rung 2   Meet all interested departments and parties
Rung 1   Initial sales call

Some of these steps can be mere inches forward, others can be giant leaps. But this ladder approach helps keep morale high during the long selling cycle that many major accounts require.

10. Find a "rabbi" within the prospect company. The seventh rung in the sales "ladder" suggests making an informal proposal to employees at the prospect company who are sympathetic to your cause. That's so the proposal can be polished and honed with hopefully many of the objections eliminated before it comes up for formal consideration. The tactic presumes that the salesperson has found a person or group within the prospect company who will act as advocate for the system or product the salesperson is trying to sell. This is important because the salesperson can't always be there when his or her proposition is discussed. Someone is needed inside the company who will act as a surrogate during these times. Why should someone be willing to do this? For career reasons mostly. Some managers want to be associated with internal change, particularly if those changes will improve the company's operation or bottom line.

11. Don't try to close too soon. Premature closing can be fatal when working with major accounts. There's little point in asking for the order when the prospect tells you there won't be money in the budget for this project until the next fiscal year. The relationship with an in-house "rabbi" can be ruined if you ask for the order when the decision comes from the next level up. (You can ask for help in obtaining the order.) Listen carefully to the problems the prospect poses when you make the first few calls. Some may be designed merely to put you off. Others are genuine obstacles to the sale that must be overcome.

The biggest mistake that can be made in dealing with major accounts is trying to close an order just because the sales volume is needed to meet short-term objectives. Many a major account salesperson has lost all the effort made with a big company prospect by applying pressure so that an order could be entered before the end of the month or quarter or to win a sales contest. Of course it's appropriate to send out trial closing signals. Sometimes it's possible to go directly from rung five or six directly to the top of the ladder. In other instances things must be done by the numbers.

12. Agree to tests and trials. Major accounts are wary when considering new suppliers. Often, just when you think a contract is in the bag, the account will request a test or a trial. In most cases, these requests should be granted with one important stipulation. *The prospect must have a financial stake in the test.* If the potential customer won't allocate any funds to support the test, little attention will be paid to the results. The tests should be limited in scope and time, with prior agreement on specific objectives and commitments to place orders if those objectives are reached.

13. Don't close before it's time to close, but do close. It's important not to ask for the order before the prospect is in a position to buy, but it's also important to seek the business you've earned. Some salespeople are so intimidated by the prestige of a major account that they never ask for the business even though the prospect may have indicated a willingness to go forward.

Putting these thirteen steps into practice will help you attain major account business. Of course, you must have an attractive proposition. If your company can't offer an attractive product at an attractive price, a five-hundred-step program won't be of much use. In the final analysis major accounts buy value, service, and vendor reliability. Isn't that what we all want from our suppliers?

CHAPTER SUMMARY

A small company can do business with corporate giants if this company learns how the game is played. The selling rules are different.

Corporate customers, and particularly the managers who run them, are more concerned about making mistakes than they are about saving their organization's money. That's why they want to do business with companies and individuals they trust.

When setting up a major account program, don't expect quick results.

Large corporations are often reluctant to change suppliers unless they become concerned about that supplier's reliability.

Persistence is usually required in getting to the decision maker at large accounts.

Changing vendors can impact many different departments within a large organization. Be sure to touch bases with all involved departments.

All sales calls to major accounts should have specific objectives.

Progress in reaching a sales objective to a major account should be measured in terms of a "sales ladder." The higher the rung you're on, the closer you are to the sale.

A "rabbi" within the company you're trying to sell can provide invaluable assistance in reaching your sales objective.

Attempting to close an order prematurely can ruin many weeks of hard work when calling on major accounts. Timing is everything in this marketplace.

Don't object to trials and tests at major accounts, but set up specific objectives with purchase commitments if the tests are successful.

Make sure the major account prospect has a substantial financial stake in a test before you agree to it. If not, the test results won't mean much.

12

SETTING UP A NATIONWIDE MAJOR ACCOUNT SALES TEAM

WHY THE REGULAR SALES TEAM ISN'T THE ANSWER IN MAJOR ACCOUNT SALES

A small company seeking competitive bid and major account business in its own backyard can handle this effort very nicely with current members of the executive team. The owner or the sales manager solicits the bid requests, talks about the features, and demonstrates the equipment or service to the proper individuals at the using agency. The same individual also handles the strategy and does the necessary pencil work to prepare the actual bid. There are few communication problems because everything is localized and under direct control of the company's senior management.

Expansion to a national program requires more thought and organization. But the United States is one big smorgasbord groaning with competitive bid and major account opportunities. A seat at the local feast often isn't enough to satisfy some companies. They want to expand into the national arena. However, the company that wishes to pursue competitive bid, federal government sales, and commercial account business from the Fortune 1000 on a national basis finds itself with a different set of marketing problems.

One of the first ideas that occurs to many companies that wish to enter the national bid and major account arena is to delegate this activity to their regular sales force. After all, these fellows and gals are already in place, they know the product line, no additional recruitment or salaries are needed and, if their call reports are any indication, heaven knows they have plenty of time on their hands. Simple? No, but unfortunately it is simplistic. Using the regular crew to cover major account and bid opportunities doesn't often work. In fact, *one of the ways to wreck a direct sales force is to give it responsibility for major account and bid business sales activity.*

"That's crazy," you're mumbling as you read this, "Most of my crew would love to go after the biggies. They would be darned good at it too."

But they are not good at it. Turning a territory-oriented salesperson loose on the competitive bid or major commercial account marketplace is often a disaster. Even if your sales crews are the hottest things on this planet when they work through normal selling channels, that doesn't mean they can be successful in understanding winning bid strategies or in selling to Fortune 500 commercial customers. The selling styles in these markets are different, the sales cycles are longer, the needed skills are different and the payoffs, while often bigger, can take forever.

There are specific reasons why using the regular sales team is a mistake when trying to increase competitive bid or commercial major account business.

1. The salesperson accustomed to running a territory and a monthly quota responsibility is often not prepared for the different rhythms associated with competitive bid situations. Under pressure of producing sales *today*, the salesperson may not pay proper attention to an opportunity that is six months, perhaps even a year away. The salesperson may also react to the slower pace by trying to force something to happen. Pressure improperly applied is a deal killer in the major account arena.

2. Some salespeople are seduced by the big number possibilities of some bid and commercial major account situations. They ignore their normal business to spend every minute trying to land a "bluebird." If they're successful, they enjoy a wonderful year. If the bluebird isn't netted, the person's performance looks awful, perhaps so bad, that he or she is forced out of the company or leaves voluntarily.

3. A successful major bid may artificially inflate the territory's sales figures for a period. This year the salesperson wears the crown at the company's star club. Next year the quota is increased to reflect this year's performance, the big bid isn't retained and the salesperson appears to be a crashed meteor.

4. Bid business is often taken at vastly reduced profit margins. Companies are not able to pay normal commissions on these kind of sales. The salesperson who is forced to accept these reduced commissions feels the company has not played fairly. This leads to resentment and ill feeling. On the other end of the spectrum, the salesperson may bid too high, at profit margins calculated to give him or her full commissions, and lose the deal.

5. The sales techniques used to close normal business are often a handicap when used in the competitive bid or commercial major account arena. Closing patterns are very different.

6. Competitive bidding is a complex activity that involves much more than submitting the lowest price. Specmanship is important, attention to detail is important, an intuition that often borders on ESP about the competition's intent is important, follow-through is important, patience is vital.

7. Accurate sales projections are almost impossible to make for a sales territory because competitive bids are all-or-nothing situations. The difference between exceeding quota by 200 percent or running less than 50 percent of projection can be the matter of a few cents miscalculation on a single contract.

THE DEDICATED MAJOR ACCOUNT TEAM

The preferred way to attack major account and bid business on a national basis is to set up a dedicated major account team to go after it. Give this team exclusive responsibility for obtaining major commercial accounts and winning bids. Obviously, the first person on the team should be the national major account manager. A summary of the NMAM's job description is as follows:

Job Description for the National Major Account Manager

- Establish major account objectives and goals
- Establish and implement major account policy
- Develop the major account marketing plan

- Set major account sales targets
- Develop job descriptions of the regional or district major account managers
- Hire the regional or district major account managers
- Direct the activity of the regional or district major account managers
- Develop the bid strategy on major bid opportunities
- Maintain a national database on competitive bid activity

In many instances, the national major account manager will directly handle the company's marketing effort to the federal government. Other companies will employ a federal government marketing specialist located in Washington who reports to the major account sales manager. Still other companies, particularly defense contractors, have entire federal marketing teams whose entire activity is dedicated to winning business from federal government agencies. The largest employ lobbyists, often ex-congressmen, whose jobs are to present these companies in the best possible light to the inhabitants of that strange and mysterious swamp some call "Foggy Bottom."

National Major Account Manager's Profile: What To Look For

What specifically should you look for when seeking a paragon who can handle the tasks outlined in the national major account manager's job description? Here are some of the traits, characteristics, and experience that indicate a winner:

1. You want a warrior with visible scars gained in the pit, one who has had experience in the major account arena. This experience should include handling competitive bids, working with the federal or state government on proposals, both solicited and unsolicited, knowledge of the ins and outs of GSA schedules, and general knowledge of how government procurement works. The salesperson who is a commercial hotshot, but whose background doesn't include "hard" time in major account sales, just won't do to head up and run the major account program. That doesn't mean you can't take a quality person who has successfully handled the major account activity in a region or district and move the person up to head a national program.

2. A plodding and detail-oriented personality is okay, even desirable. A stereotype still exists of the salesperson as flashy, personable, and extroverted. However, patience, dogged determination, and the ability to sift through the specifications on a bid requirement looking for an edge will usually produce better results in the competitive bid marketplace than will a line of persuasive patter.

3. Intelligence never hurts. Getting someone who is a quick study and generally bright will never handicap your company's major account selling effort.

4. A flexible attitude is another important attribute. The rigid person, the one who feels strongly that certain profit margins must always be maintained, that deals must always be constructed in certain ways, and that the price book was passed down from Moses on stone tablets, won't do well in competitive bid situations. For one thing, the competition will be able to predict what this manager will bid. For another, bid requests are sometimes limited. They are windows of opportunity, open only for brief periods. Many government agencies let out exclusive contracts for a time period of two or three years. Losing an agency contract for this term means being deprived of a business opportunity for a very long time. Given these circumstances, the person developing the bid strategy for your company cannot be bound by set formulas, but must develop a strategy based on the facts of the specific situation at hand.

5. Refined selling skills and a pattern of success in selling to major commercial customers is another big plus. Selling to Fortune 1000 companies is different than selling to smaller industry. The national major account manager should know just how different it is from personal experience. (Some companies separate their marketing team with both competitive bid managers and commercial major account managers.)

6. The major account manager should also possess the standard laundry list of desirable sales management characteristics. These include the ability to lead, the ability to motivate, the ability to persuade, the ability to organize, the ability to write and speak well, and the important ability to sell the program internally.

SETTING UP THE PROGRAM: WHAT THE NEW NATIONAL MAJOR ACCOUNT MANAGER DOES FIRST

The first task of the newly appointed national major account sales manager is to set up the parameters of the major account program. A series of self-directed questions can help establish these parameters. The following are basic questions that must be answered:

1. What are the specific goals and objectives of the program?

2. What marketplaces will the company attack? Federal government? State government? Municipalities? Educational institutions? Major commercial accounts?

3. What company products does the company plan to move through the major account channel?

4. Is the company prepared to design and make special products or provide special services to meet the needs of these markets?

5. What sales volume is targeted? What percentage is this volume of total company sales? How will these targets be reached?

A Sample List of Major Account Objectives

The following are the objectives of the major account program established for my company:

- To identify and penetrate GSA and other large potential accounts
- To support the dealer network in identifying and closing multi-unit orders
- To increase revenues and maximize profits for the company and its dealers
- To encourage product endorsement by prestigious users
- To provide financial support for dealers through direct billing on large purchases
- To provide information on competitive products to the company's dealers
- To assist dealers in the preparation of bid requests from major accounts, schools, municipalities, and state governments
- To develop standard policies that will eliminate common problems encountered by dealers attempting to sell to major accounts

THE NATIONAL MAJOR ACCOUNT MANAGER'S SECOND STEP

Goals and objectives are nothing more than mountains in the distance. How are these mountains reached? The best way is by mapping a trail. Some call this mapping step developing a plan on how to achieve stated objectives. This is when the head scratching starts. How to get from the lush meadow to the lofty mountaintop? One method is by self-directed questions. The best questions are those that make the NMAM squirm. The following are some of the questions the national major account manager must ask of himself—and answer:

1. How will bids be solicited?
2. Who will be responsible for preparing bid responses?
3. Who will call on the Fortune 1000 prospects in major cities across the country?
4. How will these kind of accounts be serviced on a national basis?
5. If the company is successful in getting products on GSA schedules, how will the thousands of federal government offices across the country be solicited, sold, and serviced?
6. If dealers and distributors are used to service government agency sales, how will they be compensated for sales and service work?

Are you squirming when you look at the above list?

THE NATIONAL MAJOR ACCOUNT MANAGER'S THIRD STEP

What happens after objectives are set and the plan has been developed? Most national major account sales managers reach the conclusion that *they need direct help to get the job done.* Even if the program is limited solely to handling competitive bids, one person cannot do justice to the sheer volume of federal, state, county, and city government agencies and educational institutions which put out bid requests. There must be people strategically located across the country to help out. What is needed in most cases is the establishment of a national major account marketing team, people on the company payroll whose job it is to ferret out all those bid requests and respond to them. Deciding how the major account team will be set up and hiring the right people is what the national major account manager does now.

The Strategic Placement of Major Account Personnel

It isn't necessary to place a major account representative in every company branch or district office throughout the country. Few outfits can afford this drain on the payroll. Many companies will place their major account people at regional offices. This means four or five major account managers in total. Obviously, these aren't enough bodies to discover all the bid opportunities out there, nor can they be expected to thoroughly cover the Fortune 1000. It's up to the regional MAM to maximize his or her efforts by working with and through the personnel in the company's normal selling channels.

Major Account Field Manager's Profile

What's the best type of person to fill those newly opened major account slots? The major account field manager's profile isn't too different from that of the national major account manager with the exceptions that personnel management and strategic planning skills are not needed. In fact, many major account managers don't want and won't accept people responsibility. Why should they? Many earn as much or more than field sales managers and they do it without the headaches of personnel management. When seeking to recruit a MAM, look for a person who:

- Has experience in selling to commercial major accounts or government agencies, or both.
- Works well without direct supervision. (Remember, the major account manager is likely to be placed at a regional office while reporting to the national MAM located in the home office.)
- Is not easily discouraged by long selling cycles.
- Relates and communicates well with the company salespeople working through normal distribution channels. (The best MAMs manage to persuade the territory salespeople and even field sales managers to do a certain amount of bird-dogging for them.)
- Is not easily intimidated by authority figures or red tape. (This character trait can be a mixed blessing. You want the MAM to be comfortable and not easily intimidated when standing before the prospect's executive decision makers and government high level bureaucrats. Those who possess this ability are usually unawed before his or her own company's senior managers.)

Where to Find Major Account Managers

More than any other area of selling, the major account program requires the seasoned sales pro. The stakes are too big, the potential contracts out there too juicy, and the battleground too filled with minefields to make major accounts a training ground for the apprentice. That's why many companies who believe in promoting from within for other sales positions will go outside when recruiting a major account manager. The best sources are:

1. From the competition. Stealing a good person from a competitor can be expensive, but it adds immediate qualified experience to your company's sales effort while taking away an asset from the outfit who has been your biggest headache.

2. From a related industry. It's easier to teach new products and applications than it is major account selling. Someone who understands major accounts and competitive bidding but is new to your industry should not be dismissed as a candidate.

3. From within your company's regular sales team. No, this isn't contradictory. If all MAMs must be experienced, they would necessarily pop out of their attaché cases full grown. While experience is preferred, keep an eye on the territory salesperson within the company who seems to possess a talent and an inclination for major account sales. These will be the boys and girls who always seem to be working on the big deals, making calls on the government agencies, bird-dogging potential major accounts, and so forth. They may deserve a chance in major accounts, particularly in a situation where there is some training and supervision.

MAJOR ACCOUNT COMPENSATION

Most major account salespeople compensation plans are heavy on salary and light on commissions. There are good reasons for setting up the compensation plan this way.

1. The selling cycles for major accounts are long. Many competitive bid situations only come up once a year and major commercial companies ponder forever before changing suppliers. That means it's sometimes a long time between drinks for a major account rep. A good salary helps the major account rep to develop the patience and determination needed to stay with these prospects.

2. When a bid is won or a large commercial contract is signed it often means heavy, heavy order volume. A compensation plan that is heavily weighted on the commission side means that one successful deal could put a major account salesperson on easy street.

3. Most bid situations won't allow a commission schedule with much fat in it. Low commissions that allow lean bid prices are almost a prerequisite to successful bidding.

4. Most good major account salespeople expect a hefty base salary. You won't be able to attract quality people without it.

Just how much will you have to pay to get a good, experienced major account salesperson? Sorry, the kind of person who knows the ropes won't come cheap. Figure a compensation package totaling a minimum of $50,000, most of that in salary. Plus the MAM will demand a commission and bonus schedule that will offer a legitimate shot at $60,000 to $100,000, depending on the industry and circumstances. Other perks depend on the industry; company cars are common.

MAJOR ACCOUNT REPORTING STRUCTURE

If you enjoy betting on sure things, you can safely wager that many companies experience friction between their salespeople in the normal selling channel and major account sales reps. To the sales representatives slogging it out in the territory's trenches, the major account person is a lucky stiff, working a few hours a day on blue-bird deals and not subject to the monthly pressure to achieve quota. To the local district or regional sales manager, the MAM is a prima donna who is bringing in big numbers one month and zilch the next. Some field managers feel that major account reps create personnel problems among members of the sales force. In some cases both the field rep and the field sales manager feel resentment and perhaps a touch of envy.

The very *worst* reporting structure is one in which the MAM reports to a field sales manager. Some reporting structures are set up this way because the region or district receives sales credit for every order brought in by the MAM. The field sales manager can also offer the closest point of supervision. However, if the regional manager is without experience or understanding in how major account sales work, this manager will demand from the MAM a predictable level of performance each and every month. This demand is understandable, but predictability just isn't possible in bid situations where contracts are won or lost by pennies. There will be squabbles, discipline problems, and a breakdown in the local major account program. The regional or local MAM's *must* report to the *national* major account manager if long term objectives are to be met.

Major Account Organization Chart

Exhibit 15 shows a simple major account reporting chart that works. Note that the federal major account specialist is placed off to the side. That's because a good federal contract can impact all regions, and all regions should share in the contract to the extent that goods and services sold to federal agencies under that contract are shipped or serviced into their areas.

HOW TO ASSIGN MAJOR ACCOUNT SALES CREDIT

One of the thorniest problems in major account selling is assigning commission and sales credit for major account contracts. Some companies take the easy way out and just give the credit and commission to the major account manager who brought home the bacon. The territory rep is excluded on the grounds that he or she did nothing to sell the account. This is a simple solution, but companies that use this approach inevitably encounter morale problems. Excluding major account business from territory and regional sales figures is the quickest way to build up resentment and friction between the company's territory salespeople, their managers, and the major account team. For starters, these contracts often carry big numbers, and that attracts the attention and envy of field sales personnel. For another, any exclusions from the territory because of major account designation detracts from that territory's potential. If the territory salespeople can't participate in the program, they will go to great lengths to "hide" potential major accounts *and their managers will help them.* The company has set up a situation in which the salesperson who helps a MAM sign up a local customer is really acting against his or her own best interests.

EXHIBIT 15

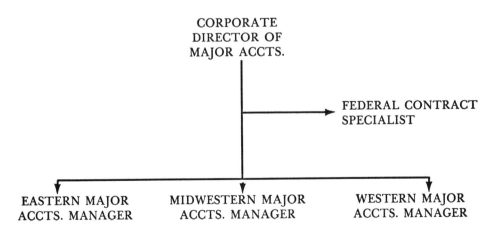

CORPORATE
DIRECTOR OF
MAJOR ACCTS.

FEDERAL CONTRACT
SPECIALIST

EASTERN MAJOR
ACCTS. MANAGER

MIDWESTERN MAJOR
ACCTS. MANAGER

WESTERN MAJOR
ACCTS. MANAGER

The fairest system considers all major account prospects within an area as part of the total sales potential for that territory. Any sales made by the MAM in that territory are credited, not only to the MAM, but also to the local sales rep and to the region covered by the rep's direct superior. Everyone shares. This system of joint credit insures that the MAM will receive full cooperation when working on a bid or a major commercial customer. Leads are quickly forwarded to the MAM. The field sales manager is helpful, even solicitous. The local rep is usually eager to do fetch-and-carry work with the prospect when the MAM is not available. The result is that the company acquires more major accounts and the field sales force is cheering on the major account effort.

How to Handle Split Commissions on Major Account Sales

In many instances a major account signs a contract in one region and the goods are delivered in another. Some companies assign all commission and sales credit to the person who got the order. We have a tendency to reward the person who got the signature on the dotted line. Unfortunately, most products require some kind of after-sale service. Major customers themselves *always* require after-sales service. The salespeople in the region where the goods are shipped are reluctant to offer this service because they don't receive any reward for it. This lack of attention and follow-up will eventually result in losing the major account. If your outfit won't give a major customer attention, someone else will. One of the reasons that major corporations sometimes only want to deal with other major corporations is that they feel big outfits know how to give customer service and support.

The compensation plan that gives all the commission credit to the person who wrote the order won't work in the major account arena. A plan must be drawn that provides compensation for those who will be involved in servicing the account. This means giving both commission and sales credit to both areas on orders that are signed in one place and the goods shipped to another. What kind of commission split? Here's how many companies work:

Commission where product is sold: 40 percent
Commission where product is delivered: 60 percent

Why not a fifty-fifty split? Because the after-sale work such as installation, instruction, and warranty often requires more effort than obtaining the original order. Besides, the person who made the original sale will receive 40 percent of the commission on shipments made all over the country. The salesperson on the receiving end will get 60 percent credit only on products shipped into the local territory.

This commission schedule will work on *exclusive* state contracts as well. In a large state all service for most products cannot be handled outside of the state capital. It is *not* a good idea on contracts that are only hunting licenses (those contracts in which a state or other government agency negotiates price, but allows the local buying entity a choice between two or more vendors). In this situation the local sales person must perform both the selling and the after-sale service.

Working on Small Profit Margins

Commissions should be split with the territory salespeople no matter how small the profit margin is on a particular contract. If the profit is so small it can't be seen without an electron microscope, then make the commission percentage microscopic, *but split it.*

Establishing Sales Credit on Major Account Sales

Who gets the credit toward quota on major account sales? Sometimes a competitive bid contract or a major commercial customer produces big sales numbers, so the question is important. If you want to avoid quarrels, backbiting, and back-room schemes, the answer is that the major account manager, the sales rep in the territory where the major account sales was made, and the field sales manager all should receive *full* credit toward their respective quotas. Quota credit often means more to a sales rep than the commission. Giving it in full to everyone on the scene doesn't cost the company anything, except perhaps in calculating bonuses, but it makes everyone feel that the company recognizes their contribution in landing the big deal.

A PLAN FOR THE GEOMETRIC EXPANSION OF MAJOR ACCOUNT COVERAGE: SHARE THE GLORY

In setting up the structure of a major account selling team, the suggestion was made to start by placing one major account salesperson in every regional office and perhaps another in Washington, D.C. to cover the federal government bureaucracy, with all reporting to the national major account sales manager in the home office. The heavy salaries commanded by good major account salespeople often deter a company from trying for more intensive coverage. Most companies will divide the country into four or five regions. With one major account rep handling an average of ten states, how can that person possibly keep abreast of all the bid opportunities in state governments, county governments, municipalities, university systems, colleges, and school districts within the territory? That answer is simple. The job cannot be handled by one person, even with the assistance of bid-alerts, the advisory systems that provide their subscribers with news of pending bids.

The smart-working major account manager expands his or her own efforts by setting up a team of "bird-dogs" whose job it is to sniff out bid opportunities. Who qualifies as a bird-dog? They are the salespeople, sales managers, dealers, distributors, and others in the company's normal selling channels.

Usually, there's no direct reporting responsibility between the major account team and the company's other salespeople, so how is this cooperation obtained? The MAM can try flattery, pleas of friendship, even outright begging, but the territory salesperson can tell the major account rep to go scratch. What will prompt others in the organization to oblige the major account salesperson when he or she asks that a special effort be made on behalf of the program?

What motivates every bird-dog to splash through that muddy water to retrieve a fallen duck and carry it uneaten back to the hunter? The answer is that the animal later gets a taste of the meat. That's why this chapter has emphasized commission splits and double sales credit on major account orders. The salesperson who received a bit extra in his commission check because of a large bid the company won in his territory will want to find other deals just like it. The regional manager who looks like a managerial wizard because of an exclusive state contract that runs an entire year develops an appetite for bid contracts that won't be satisfied with one deal. This manager will insist that the field salespeople cooperate with the major account salesperson. The independent dealer whose business has tripled because of one order from a Fortune 1000 company will be easier to convince a second time that it sometimes pays to sacrifice margins to increase volume.

As long as everyone shares in the glory and cash, the major account salesperson can make others in the company's sales structure allies, fellow conspirators in the intrigue-filled bidding game. The smart company sets up the compensation program in a way that allows the major account rep to get this kind of assistance.

SERVICING THE MAJOR ACCOUNT SALES NETWORK

As noted in previous chapters, the competitive bid market is a deadline business. If the company's bid isn't in the hopper within the proper time period, the bid is not considered. Very often, the details of an attractive bid opportunity aren't known until the last moment. There isn't much time for bid preparation.

Competitive bids also demand a great many last minute decisions. How much is the company willing to trim its profit margins to get a contract? Is it possible to get cost relief from a supplier on a critical part? Can the company afford to commit to a price for a full year on a contract that requires that kind of price guarantee? What is the competition likely to do in a specific situation? Are there any "kickers" in the specifications that are likely to increase the cost of doing business? Who will handle the service, and what will it cost?

The deadline nature of competitive bids coupled with the need to find answers to questions that change with almost every new bid opportunity means that the company that is serious about the bid marketplace will set up a very good two-way communication link between field major account personnel and the home office. The following ideas on a basic communication link will help support the major account effort.

A Five-Point Program Toward Establishing a Good Major Account Communication Link

1. The national major account manager must be "on call" just about twenty-four hours of every day. The field managers should have the national manager's home phone number and vice-versa.

2. Field major account salespeople should call their offices or answering services at least twice a day.

3. The specifications on each new competitive bid opportunity should be copied *completely,* with one copy forwarded to the home office. When the field person and the national major account manager are discussing that bid, each has a copy.

4. Fax machines are easy to operate and an inexpensive way to reliably transfer information from one part of the country to another. (Ain't technology grand?) Put fax machines in the home and branch offices. Make sure one is near the national major account manager. (Don't send information on bid prices via fax machines unless there is some level of control on the receiving end.) If the company doesn't maintain branch offices, consider placing a fax machine in the field person's home.

5. Let the field person prepare (on the basis of prices, terms, and delivery schedules you supply) and hand deliver as many bid responses as possible. Hand delivery is much surer than the U.S. Postal Service, United Parcel, Red Label, or Federal Express.

CHAPTER SUMMARY

It's a mistake to try to reach the competitive bid and major account markets through a sales force that is not experienced in these areas.

The first step in setting up a national major account marketing effort is hiring a person to head up the program.

The first task of the national major account manager is to develop the goals and objectives of the program.

The most popular major account organization plan for mid-size, and even large, companies is to place one major account field person in each region.

Major account field salespeople should not report to field sales managers in the company's normal selling channels.

Sales and commission credit on major accounts should go to the territory rep and the field sales manager in the area where the sale was made.

The field major account rep can get "help" on needed coverage if sales and commission credit are shared with the regular sales team.

13

MAJOR ACCOUNT HOT BUTTONS

What causes a Fortune 1000 company to select one supplier over another? What causes this same Fortune 1000 company to change a supplier they have used for years? In other words, what prompts the buying decisions at major corporations? The answers to these questions are important. They help guide the company on the threshold of entering the major account arena in developing a successful marketing strategy.

HOW MAJOR CORPORATIONS MAKE BUYING DECISIONS

The first step in understanding how major corporations make buying decisions is to take a close look at the decision makers. In small organizations senior level executives make most of the decisions, including what products to buy and what vendors to buy them from. This isn't true in major corporations—there are just too many decisions to make. In most large corporations the people at the top are strategists. Those directly below them are tacticians who try to make the strategies work. Only when the middle, or third-level, of management is reached are the day-to-day buying decisions made on the countless products used by major corporations. Senior executive committees from Ford and U.S. Steel may negotiate the price and terms for the sheet metal Ford will be putting into their cars next year, and when American Airlines and McDonnell Douglas are discussing the purchase of a jet fleet you can bet the negotiating teams are from the executive suite. But the decisions on most products and services are made by the *product's actual users* with a big assist from the corporation's purchasing department.

Who are these middle managers? For the most part, they fall into two categories:

- The younger managers, ambitious, energetic, and on the way up, with the bright sparkle of a career, still in front of them.
- The older managers who have been slotted. They are cemented in organizational place and they know it. Dreams of glory dashed, their primary goal is to sweat out retirement.

These two corporate middle management types have little in common except when faced with buying decisions. Then they react the same way, basing most decisions on two primary criteria. They are:

- To purchase a product that will do the required job at a price and terms that will provide the best value for the corporation.
- To make a buying decision that won't come back to bite them.

For many managers, the second priority takes precedence over the first.

There are good reasons for the managers to be conservative. The buying decision that trims a few pennies from the cost of a product or cuts delivery time by a few weeks, or even provides a better overall value won't necessarily result in advancement for the manager who made it. The manager who selects a vendor who delivers a poor quality product or messes up delivery can find an unclimbable stone wall set down in the center of his or her career path. Does that tend to make corporate decision makers cautious about choosing suppliers? You bet it does.

FIVE VENDOR CONSIDERATIONS IMPORTANT TO MAJOR ACCOUNT DECISION MAKERS

The need for caution makes the middle manager react predictably when selecting product vendors. The following are some of the points they usually consider:

1. Precedence. The old familiar tune plays well and long at Fortune 1000 companies. If the supplier has been used before without disastrous result, there's little risk to the decision maker in choosing that supplier again. That's why the well-known supplier with a track record can get away with charging high prices or supplying mediocre service and still retain the major account. It isn't that the account doesn't realize there are outfits out there offering better prices or promising superior service. They are aware of these things, but they don't want to risk trying someone new. *The current vendor is a devil they know.*

2. Industry name recognition. The managers from major corporations like to do business with those companies who enjoy solid reputations within their industry. It's a matter of prestige, like driving a BMW or Mercedes, for managers to brag that their companies do business with the best. If the vendor's reputation is good enough, price becomes a secondary consideration. Companies new to the major account marketplace often develop a false sense of security when they learn about an incumbent's price schedules for a major account. The pretender to the business knows there won't be any trouble beating the competitor's prices and perhaps the product offered is superior. The new kid on the block soon learns that price, or even quality, isn't the issue.

3. The vendor has many customers in the same industry. Quick! Follow that sheep! This "follow the guy in front of you" syndrome is based on the rationale that if everyone else in the industry is using a particular vendor, that vendor must be doing a good job. Actually, when the vendor possesses a terrific industry customer list it helps take the onus from the decision maker if things go wrong. He or she is not the only fool in town.

4. Financial stability. A strong balance sheet always helps when soliciting business from major corporations. The corporate buyer wants to be sure the vendor will be around to finish the job, complete the contract, and be there for the fix-it conference when things go wrong. The small company with a shaky Dun & Bradstreet rating has a difficult time instilling confidence in the decision maker.

5. A national presence. Many corporate giants will award small contracts to local companies in the area. It's their way of being good neighbors. The big orders, the ones where product is shipped to the major account's facilities all over the country, the ones with lots of zeros in them, are awarded to companies who can supply on-site service and product training to the customer's scattered facilities.

What's the corporate manager really looking for with these five considerations? It is this: Corporate middle managers want to be comfortable with their buying decisions. They don't want to toss and turn at night because they chose to do business with your company. They don't want worms in the program, ghosts in the machine. If there is any one thing you choose to take away from this chapter it is this:

Find a way to make the corporate decision maker comfortable when buying from your company. Don't make your customers insomniacs. You'll get all the business you can handle.

DEVELOPING A MAJOR ACCOUNT POLICY

How does a vendor out to acquire major accounts develop this comfort index for corporate decision makers? Here's a short list of six steps:

1. The first and most vital step is taken by formulating a major account policy. The policy is written and formalized in a major account policy statement. This policy statement is published and offered to anyone who will read it. The statement demonstrates both to the customer and internally to your company that this is a serious effort to pursue major account business. The cynic might suggest that the policy statement is merely a laundry list of the special concessions you're prepared to make to a major account in return for its business.

2. Develop a special, uniform pricing structure. Good prices are important to Fortune 1000 companies. Rock-bottom prices are not. They often create concern, because major accounts expect service with the product and they expect to pay for it. The Fortune 1000 customer does not normally wish to negotiate a contract that is a losing proposition for the vendor. However, they do expect price concessions based on the quantities they purchase.

3. Demonstrate a national service capability. If you want to do business with a Fortune 1000 company on a national basis, you must be prepared to take care of problems wherever they arise. "Depot" service is not popular with major accounts, though I must admit this attitude is changing slightly as the throwaway mentality begins to prevail.

4. Guarantee parts availability. The Fortune 1000 customer wants to be sure there are parts stored in a warehouse somewhere that can repair the product three and four years down the line when things begin to wear out. One thing that helps prove parts availability is to put your company's products on GSA schedules. The federal government requires that parts for products they purchase be available for seven years.

5. Provide record keeping. Many major accounts expect their vendors to do the record keeping and perform other clerical services related to their business dealing for them. This service could include keeping track of product inventory levels, reordering schedules, and sales made to other corporate locations.

6. Provide a single source of contact (the major account manager responsible for that customer). Fortune 1000 decision makers want an ombudsman within your company who will address complaints, expedite orders, advocate the customer's point of view, and provide an early warning system for potential problems. They want to know that there's a honcho inside your company ready to go to bat for them when necessary.

These six points should all be incorporated into the policy statement. Here's a sample major account policy statement. (Actually it's my company's major account policy statement. See page 186.)

This major account policy statement is part of the presentation used by the major account managers in my company when they solicit business from large companies. That doesn't mean the same statement would work in your industry or is feasible for your company. Different industries require different assurances. The policy statement you write will have to be tailored to address your prospects' discomfort zone. It should be designed to make the managers comfortable.

The policy statement is only the beginning of the major account campaign, and a bare beginning at that. It is a tool in the major account manager's sales kit. Tools don't do much good unless they are used by craftsmen. Policy statements by themselves don't make prospects buy. I never met a major account prospect who was so moved after reading our company's policy statement that he reached for his pen, waited for his emotion to subside, and then signed up.

How to Write Your Company's Major Account Policy Statement

When working on the specifics that should be included in your company's major account policy statement, ask this question: What do the prospects in the industries you've targeted fear most? What are

A SAMPLE MAJOR ACCOUNT POLICY STATEMENT

We guarantee the following to our major account customers:

1. *Prompt deliveries:* Major accounts receive preferred delivery on back-ordered or scarce items.

2. *Most current factory production deliveries:* Major accounts receive the more recently manufactured, factory-fresh machines.

3. *Deliveries by qualified installers:* All installations will be performed by selected personnel qualified to instruct operators.

4. *Service by company-trained technicians:* Required service on any company product will be handled by company-trained technicians.

5. *Price protection:* The company guarantees that the price offered the major account is the lowest price offered for the quantity ordered. Should the company establish a lower price, all product shipped to the major account within the last thirty days will be re-billed at this lower price.

6. *Service and availability on parts:* The company will maintain an adequate parts inventory for all products purchased by the major account.

7. *Single-source contact:* Should any questions or problems arise, the company will maintain a single-source contact, available in person or through an "800" number, who will be responsible for the resolutions of those problems.

8. *Customer record keeping:* The company will furnish upon request, a complete purchase unit of every unit delivered.

their worst nightmares regarding vendor relationships? List all the things you can think of that worry middle managers in the industries you target and address each one of these concerns in the policy statement. Of course much more must be done than just writing assurances on a piece of paper. Systems and procedures must be set in place to make sure these guarantees are met.

THE SECRET VIRTUE NEEDED TO SUCCEED WITH MAJOR ACCOUNTS

You've developed an intelligent major account policy statement that addresses every middle manager's concerns. Your attaché case has a secret compartment with very jazzy major account price schedules. The degree of service you promise is so intensely personal that you've willed your body to be cremated after you die and the ashes sprinkled on the prospect's driveway so his car won't skid in icy weather. Sorry, it's not enough. The orders won't come rolling in. *Don't expect to knock over a number of major account customers with fancy footwork and razzle dazzle.* If it were this easy, good major account salespeople wouldn't command the salaries they do.

The subject of major account call strategy is covered in another chapter, but one point made elsewhere must be made again here. You'll need to possess, or acquire, the virtue of patience to succeed with major accounts. You must make call after call on the major account prospect, slowly wear down the fear of the unknown that changing vendors means. Remember, the middle manager decision maker doesn't like change unless it's absolutely necessary. From the manager's point of view more bad than good things can happen as a result of change. The successful major account salesperson is patient, persistent, develops a relationship, demonstrates industry expertise, is helpful, is honest to the point of candor, and waits for the big chance. Management must be patient too. Don't jeopardize a newly started major account program by expecting results too quickly.

Patience and persistence will eventually pay off. The chance can come when the prospect needs something new that current vendors haven't been supplying. Maybe it's a special part required in small quantity. Perhaps the prospect wants a short-term delivery schedule that the incumbent supplier can't meet. These are opportunities for your company to strut its stuff. Move on them with a first or trial order. Keep the customer informed every step of the way. Always do what you have promised to do. Deliver on time. One warning: The first orders processed by your company for a major account are critical. Of course you're anxious to get the ball rolling with a big customer, but don't be too eager to accept an order if you're not certain that promises can be kept. It's better to pass on an emergency requirement than to miss a delivery promise or ship merchandise that isn't right.

FIVE SIGNS THAT INDICATE A COMPETITIVE SUPPLIER MAY BE IN TROUBLE WITH A MAJOR ACCOUNT CUSTOMER

We all want the major account business that is now enjoyed by our competitors. Sometimes the only way to get it is when the incumbent does something wrong. One of the advantages of patiently making call after call on major accounts even though no business has resulted, is that these calls give you the opportunity to learn when an incumbent supplier is in trouble. Here are some of the signs that indicate the competitive supplier is standing on shaky ground.

1. The major account is surprised by something the supplier does. Major accounts don't like surprises. Once a supplier has established a good reputation for service and quality, the major account customer is remarkably tolerant of small delays in shipping schedules, price increases, and so forth. What they don't like is a shipment that is four weeks late without advance warning. They don't like unannounced changes in specifications or materials, orders that are billed at increased prices without prior notice, or a newspaper article noting that the vendor has just signed the major account's biggest competitor. If the major account prospect you've been patiently nurturing bitterly complains that his current supplier has delivered a surprise, listen carefully. You may be on the threshold of an opportunity.

2. Absence. It's crazy, but some vendors take their major account customers for granted. They take their orders over the phone, send them new pricing data by mail, and generally devote time to obtaining new customers instead of treasuring the customers they have. All customers want their business to be appreciated. The major account wants the degree of attention and hand-holding that the volume of business his company is buying deserves. If you're at the prospect's office often enough and the incumbent is off gathering daisies in distant fields, your roles will eventually reverse.

3. An unwillingness to make things right. One of the most frequent, and most avoidable, causes of major accounts switching vendors is a squabble about a product or a performed service. Perhaps the major account feels a certain shipment is not up to standard while the supplier *knows* the products in that shipment met all quality specifications. The customer wants to return what it calls junk and the vendor claims that return would be a violation of contract. These squabbles can escalate, egos get involved, the letter of the contract is invoked by both sides, righteous indignation flares like sunspots, until long-term relationships come to an inglorious end. Be on the lookout for developing squabbles when making calls on major account prospects. Guess whose side you should take?

4. Uneven dealing. If a major account learns that another company is getting the benefit of better pricing terms for similar products and quantities or favored delivery and payment treatment, look out. Sometimes major account salespeople have an opportunity of creating a problem for a current supplier by bringing in *public information,* such as a newspaper or magazine article, about that supplier's business dealings. But never pass out confidential information that has somehow come into your possession. First, you are not James Bond or Mata Hari, in the secret information business. Second, the material may not be accurate. You may find yourself on the receiving end of a slander suit. This isn't a concern with information that has been made public. If something untrue or slanderous has appeared in *Time* or the *Wall Street Journal* the onus is on the publication.

5. Changes. The supplier changes something: Perhaps it's the specifications on the product the major account buys. Maybe the production is moved to a new plant. Perhaps it's the discount schedule. Maybe the incumbent supplier assigns a new person to the account. No matter what it is, the person making the decision is being moved, unwillingly to unfamiliar ground. That creates apprehension in the manager's mind and apprehension translates to opportunity for you.

Any of these situations gives the major account salesperson who has been making the calls consistently an opportunity to take over from an incumbent supplier. The trick is to recognize these events as they are occurring so you are ready to take advantage of them. You should also recognize these situations as possible danger areas once you acquire the account. Don't let the same thing happen to you.

CHAPTER SUMMARY

Middle managers make most of the product and vendor decisions at major corporations.

The most important concern of middle managers when choosing an equipment or service vendor is not to make a mistake.

For major account middle managers, their primary hot button is that they want to feel comfortable about their buying decisions.

One of the ways for these decision makers to feel comfortable is to do what has been done before. That's why it is difficult to get them to change.

The first step in establishing a major account marketing plan is by writing a major account policy statement.

The policy statement attempts to address all the decision maker's concerns in doing business with a new supplier.

The major account wants guarantees on fair prices, national service, spare parts availability, record keeping, and lots of personal hand-holding.

Many major accounts are lost because the supplier took the business for granted.

One of the surest ways to lose a major account is to offer another customer a better deal on the same product with similar quantities.

The most important virtue when calling on major accounts is patience. Trust must be established before any business is written.

Take advantage of a small order opportunity to build credibility and demonstrate your firm's capability. Turn down an order when you have concerns about your company's ability to perform to the customer's requirement. Wait for some other opportunity that better suits your company.

There are certain signs that indicate when an incumbent supplier may be in trouble. Learning to read these signs gives you a better opportunity to step into the breach.

Once a major account is acquired, learn to read the danger signs that indicate trouble may be ahead.

14

THE NITTY-GRITTY OF COMPETITIVE BIDDING AND MAJOR ACCOUNT SELLING

WHY GOVERNMENT RED TAPE IS A LEGITIMATE CONCERN

One of the reasons that many companies don't vigorously pursue business with government agencies, either federal, state, or local, is that they are apprehensive about the amount of paperwork and red tape involved. Some of this concern about bureaucratic snarls is well founded. All government agencies must follow strict rules and regulations. They find satisfaction and joy in rigid procedures. For many bureaucrats, the carbon interleaved triplicate form is an art statement. Some find it difficult to understand why their vendors don't feel the same sense of romance when they confront a regulation. True, the government is an excellent credit risk because the bills always get paid. The catch is that the bill must be presented properly. A tiny mistake, such as a misplaced comma, can take forever to get corrected. An order that isn't properly documented, an invoice that is incomplete or a missing number or, saints preserve us, a transposed number on a requisition, can mean

191

backtracking, rechecking, verifying, sending a duplicate or triplicate set of invoices, and incredibly long delays before the company gets paid.

DOCUMENTATION: THE KEY TO GETTING PAID ON GOVERNMENT ORDERS

It's important when doing business with government agencies to set up a procedure that will provide the kind of documentation needed to produce an invoice the government agency will pay without question. That means getting the order off to the right start, and the right start means documenting everything from the very beginning. The following simple procedure outlines a right start that will ensure that any government agency will promptly pay for the products they purchase.

An Eleven-Step Fail-Safe Government Order Processing System

1. Never accept a verbal purchase order from a government employee. If the agency is in a big hurry for the product, it can move quickly to cut you a purchase order. With today's facsimile machines, a copy of the typed order can be in your office in five minutes. Never make shipments on verbal orders that your government contact tells you "are sure to be approved."

2. Don't allow your regional, district, or branch offices to process government orders. Send them to a central location and have them checked and processed by an order administrator who is familiar with government procedures and requirements. Despite the extra time it takes to send the orders to a central location, this procedure should speed things up rather than slow them down. The experienced administrator can process the government orders faster. A central invoicing center will also ensure that the bills are sent out correctly prepared.

3. The order administrator should check all incoming orders to make sure that they are made out properly, all requisition numbers are included, the pricing is correct per the terms of any contracts that may be in force, the billing and shipping points are noted, and so forth. This editing and checking procedure weeds out incorrect orders before they get into the system.

4. The order administrator should note how the order is addressed. If your company sells through dealers or agents, but bills government accounts directly, the order may come to your company

"Care Of" the dealer who obtained it. The problem is that the "Care Of" address is what is recorded on the government agency computer file. The agency may send the payment check to the dealer rather than to your company no matter what instructions are on the invoice regarding payment. At the very least there will be a delay in the funds reaching your company.

5. The administrator should establish an order log to control each incoming government order. The log should maintain a sequential numbering system, the date the order was placed, the government agency, the product ordered, the price, the requisition number on the order, the contract number, if applicable, and the expected shipping date. This log can be used as a referral when checking on the status of the order.

6. The administrator should complete the order entering miscellaneous information pertinent to the company such as department number, salesperson's number, commission splits, and terms.

7. An order acknowledgment should be sent to the salesperson or dealer who obtained the sale. This acknowledgment provides a final check that the order was entered correctly.

8. When the order is prepared for shipment a shipping control number should be assigned.

9. Once the shipping control number has been created, the order should be immediately shipped. Attached to the order should be the following:

- A packing slip
- A proof of delivery form coded with the order log sequential number pertinent to that order
- A return envelope stamped with the department so the proof of delivery can be recorded upon return

10. After the shipment has been made, the shipping control will be held in a separate file pending the return of the proof of delivery. When this is received, a completion entry is made.

11. The invoice to the government agency can now be cut and mailed according to the instructions on the government purchase order.

Setting up this kind of system will ensure that orders are entered correctly. You will know the status of orders in the system, you know that all orders are shipped with proper documentation, and you can be confident that the invoice will get paid promptly. This system provides audit trails that can be accessed to determine what and when things happened with all government orders. The audit trail becomes a way to track things down when there is a question on an order. It also enables the company to send duplicate copies when the government agency "loses" your invoice. (Yes, this happens frequently. Sometimes the second set of documents must be followed by a third).

The proof of delivery forms and invoice copies can also be used to calculate commission schedules for salespeople, dealers, and others who may have contributed to the sale.

The following are copies of a sample order acknowledgment, a proof of delivery, and a commission calculation sheet.

TEN THINGS TO INCLUDE WHEN PRINTING A GSA CATALOG

Once your company's product is on GSA schedule, it's very important to your sales effort to print up and distribute a GSA catalog. How are federal government agencies out in the hinterlands going to know what you have to sell unless you tell them? The catalog should include the following information:

- The company's GSA account number and the term of the contract.
- A list of the products, preferably with pictures, on GSA schedule. Include product description and lists of features.
- The GSA pricing on the products under contract, including pricing on supplies.
- A listing of the payment terms and the warranty period.
- Instructions on how to order and where to send that order.
- A list of company offices, including addresses and phone numbers.
- A contact or contacts within your company who are familiar with the terms of the contract and the products listed. A toll-free "800" number is also a good idea if your company can afford it. Fax numbers are also becoming popular.
- If your company uses dealers, distributors, or manufacturer's reps to market, the catalog should include the names, phone numbers and addresses, and other pertinent data regarding these agencies.
- Provide the details of your company's policy regarding trade-ins, demonstrations, and trials.

If possible, have the catalog prepared by professionals and present the products attractively. Often, this catalog will be your only selling

EXHIBIT 16

ORDER ACKNOWLEDGMENT

CUSTOMER #_____   SALESPERSON'S #_____   ACKNOWLEDGMENT #_____

DATE_____   DATE RECEIVED _____   CUSTOMER P.O.#_____
                                              REQUISITION #_____
                                              CONTRACT #_____

BILL TO_____   SHIP TO _____

STREET_____   _____

CITY_____   _____

STATE & ZIP CODE_____   _____

PRODUCT #	DESCRIPTION	QUANTITY	PRICE	EXTENSION

SHIPPING DATE_____   VIA _____   AMOUNT DUE _____
TERMS_____

PLEASE CONTACT US IMMEDIATELY ABOUT ANY DISCREPANCIES BETWEEN YOUR
PURCHASE ORDER AND THIS ACKNOWLEDGMENT.

tool in thousands of government offices. Print as many copies of this
catalog as you can afford to send to federal government offices all over
the country. As mentioned previously, don't forget to send copies of
the catalog to state and municipal agencies and educational institutions.
It's a good way to cash in on your federal government contract because
many local government agencies will often choose to buy at GSA price
schedules rather than send out requests for competitive bids.

EXHIBIT 17

BROTHER INTERNATIONAL CORP.

PROOF OF DELIVERY

O/C#

| DEALER NAME & ADDRESS | PURCHASE ORDER NO. |

| DELIVERED TO | BROTHER USE ONLY |

PLEASE HAVE THE ATTACHED PROOF OF
DELIVERY SIGNED UPON DELIVERY OF
MERCHANDISE. RETURN TO
BROTHER INTERNATIONAL CORP
20 GOODYEAR
IRVINE. CA 92718
ATTN. GSA BILLING
UPON OUR RECEIPT WE WILL BE ABLE TO DO
BILLING AND COMMISSIONS

MODEL	SERIAL NUMBER	MODEL	SERIAL NUMBER

HAVE RECEIVED SATISFACTORY INSTRUCTION ON THE OPERATION OF THE MACHINES DELIVERED.

SIGNATURE _____

RECEIVED BY		DATE	DELIVERED BY
SIGNATURE	PRINT NAME	/ /	PRINT

BEST PRINTING INC • (714) 951 4636

Mail completed form to Brother International Corporation, 20 Goodyear, Irvine, CA 92718, Att.: GSA

SELLING FOR LESS THAN GSA CONTRACT TERMS

GSA negotiators insist that the federal government be quoted the very lowest pricing the company can offer. The prices offered on GSA contract should be your company's best prices, based on similar terms and conditions. If your company is found selling a product on GSA contract to others, such as a state government agency, for less than the federal government negotiated price, the GSA can demand that your company do the following:

EXHIBIT 18

COMMISSION CALCULATION SHEET

MONTH _____   YEAR _____   SALESPERSON _____   SALES NO. _____

INVOICE #	DATE SHIPPED	CUSTOMER #	$ AMOUNT	COMMISSION %	COMMISSION $

TOTAL $ INVOICED _____   TOTAL COMMISSION DUE _____

- Roll back your prices and refund the federal government the difference on all products purchased during the contract.
- Deliver all future orders for that product based on the lower price.

It's important to remember these restrictions when bidding state and local contracts. A state bid request often carries the same terms and conditions as the federal contract. Don't be so anxious to win a state plum that you bid lower in this circumstance. You could jeopardize the federal award or subject your company to penalities. If a bid to a state or local government agency is lower, unless you can prove differences in the terms and conditions, the GSA may demand a price rollback and a rebate. Don't think you can do it on the sly. If you offer lower terms elsewhere, you can bet your competitors will be sure the information gets into the right hands in Washington.

When the company has a GSA contract, be sure that every order under that contract is billed at the negotiated price. *Never* bill a federal government agency a lower price because your company is overstocked or some other business conditions have changed. The GSA may assume that one lower invoice is a new offer and demand that all future products be delivered under this pricing schedule. They may even demand a rebate on past products shipped.

Of course it is perfectly acceptable to lower prices to the government on products covered by a GSA schedule. The way to this is via written notification to GSA personnel in Washington. Don't begin by lowering the product price on an order sent in by some army base in the hinterlands. Warning: Lowering prices on products under GSA schedule seldom results in increased volume of government orders. So why do it?

HOW TO PREPARE A BID REFERENCE BOOK: NINETEEN THINGS TO INCLUDE

If your company is large enough to have major account representatives placed in regions all over the country, they're probably working on bid requests all the time. Many of these bid requests require information about the company submitting the bid. They want to know if the company making the proposal is a reliable supplier.

The director of major accounts in the home office will be continually bombarded with questions from the field related to bid preparation. These questions require detailed knowledge of the company, its history, and how it operates. As previously stated, it's important to fill out each little box in a bid request, or the bid may be rejected. The field major account manager may not possess some of the detailed information required on some bids.

If the director of major accounts doesn't want to spend all of his or her time on the phone feeding this data to anxious major account people working on a deadline to get a bid in, the answer may be a bid reference book. This reference book should contain all the data usually needed on bid requests. Put it in the hands of all personnel authorized to submit bids on behalf of the company. Here's a list of the kind of information government agencies ask for on their bid requests:

• The address and phone number of the company's home office

- The kind of company (corporation, partnership, minority owned, small business, manufacturer, dealer, distributor, etc.)
- If a corporation, where incorporated and in what year
- How long the company has been in business
- The company's federal and local tax identification numbers
- The company's Dun & Bradstreet number
- The square footage of the plant, the warehouse, and the office
- The total number of company employees
- The details of the company's affirmative action plan (Some bid requests will ask that the bidder fill out survey forms with details on the ethnic mix of employees, number of women and minorities in supervisory position, and so forth)
- The value of the company's inventory
- The company's gross sales for each of the past several years
- The names of the company's insurance carriers and the type of insurance carried
- The company's bank references
- Representative customer lists
- Representative vendor lists
- The names of corporate officers
- A current financial report
- The company's interest or plants or dealings in South Africa, if any (many local government agencies and particularly our universities won't do business with companies that have substantial business interests in South Africa).
- If a foreign owned company, the country and city of origin

No single bid request is likely to ask for all the information that is listed here. However, many government agencies will request at least part of this data enough times so that it becomes prudent to keep it readily available. If you do much competitive bidding, you'll find preparing a reference book of this kind made up for your company will be invaluable. Give it to those with the authority to submit bids. They will save time digging out all this data and avoid last minute emergencies, and possibly lost opportunities, while vital bits of information are researched.

THE ADVANTAGES AND DISADVANTAGES OF USING AN INDEPENDENT FEDERAL MARKETING GROUP

The Advantages:

For many companies, the federal government marketplace with its bewildering maze of rules, regulations, barriers, offices, and bureaucrats seems too confusing and intimidating to approach. Yes, these companies recognize that the federal government is a big "consumer" of all kinds of products. However, the time, attention and expense required to squeeze even a small volume of orders from this impenetrable jungle seems to be prohibitive. How can the small company with limited resources even hope to achieve any success here? Most don't even know where to begin and few have the staying power it takes to get results.

The small companies who want a piece of the government pie can turn to marketers, specialized manufacturer's reps with experience and expertise in calling on the federal government marketplace. These marketers can provide a variety of functions, from helping a company to get its products on GSA schedules, to selling directly to government agencies in Washington, to creating a demand for products by increasing their visibility to potential end users. Charges for their services may include up-front fees (a company that will assist your company in getting its product on GSA schedule will certainly charge your company a hefty fee for its efforts), retainers, or commissions on sales, or all of these. The advantages of using these so-called experts are as follows:

1. The good ones understand the federal bureaucracy and the red tape that is a foot deep in the nation's capital. They know their way around Washington and they know many important decision makers.

2. These insiders can reduce the time it takes to get a product on GSA schedule simply because they know how to go about it.

3. These consultants know how the negotiating game works with GSA employees. Sometimes their negotiating skills help your company get a better price for its product. This skill alone can more than pay for their consulting fees.

4. A skillful marketing group can offer objective advice on needed product changes or revised price schedules that might make your product more attractive to government agencies.

In short, they are trail guides that know all the shortcuts from point *A,* (waiting for a limo at Dulles airport and wondering where to go first) to point *B*, (a successful GSA or competitive bid contract that will mean many dollars in additional revenue for your company).

The Disadvantages

The advantages listed above don't mean that you should rush out and hire a group of Washington-based hotshots to move product for your company in that reclaimed swamp also known as "Foggy Bottom." There is a downside to this tactic, and it is a long step down. Here are a few of the negative aspects of using independent consultants that should concern you:

1. One definition of an "expert" is anyone who is more than fifty miles away from home. Many of the so-called Washington consultants couldn't sell snow shovels in Fairbanks, Alaska. These "experts" take your money, make you promises, but your product never gets on GSA schedule.

2. You may think you've negotiated a deal on a set fee basis. You pay a certain amount up front and the job gets done. That's the contract. Read the fine print that's only exposed when you rub lemon juice on the back of the page. On many of these deals the meter runs on and on, and the consultant claims that you're always a few short weeks away from success. The unforeseen delays add charges that keep piling up and up. In this matter, the consultants sometimes can't be blamed. It's very difficult to determine the exact time and effort needed to negotiate a GSA contract with Uncle Sam.

3. The team of experts may know Washington and the bars where the driest martinis are served, but they don't know your company's product. Someone may be needed to provide the necessary expertise. The consultants need someone close at hand to consult with them on product. If you must keep someone in Washington for this purpose, where is the savings in man-hours?

4. The specialists may represent many different manufacturers and many different products. How much time, devotion and dedication will be given to your project? That's anybody's guess. Of course the consultants will tell you they're tending to your company's affairs. Like lawyers, they'll give you an invoice detailing "billable hours." How do you go about verifying those hours from hundreds or thousands of miles away?

Do the advantages outweigh the disadvantages? It's a difficult call. Hiring a manufacturer's rep who is paid on straight commission to represent your company in Washington obviously isn't going to cost you anything, except perhaps missed opportunities. Hiring a consultant for a fee to get a product on GSA schedule will be more expensive and a bit more hazardous. You may spend a lot of money and still leave the capitol empty-handed. Remember, only a third of all companies who try to get on GSA schedule succeed. Those who make it are faced with high administrative costs, tight requirements, and price ceilings. Being on schedule doesn't automatically guarantee sales. Unless you have a plan to exploit a GSA contract award, it often doesn't pay to make the effort.

SELLING CLOSE-OUTS AND DISTRESS MERCHANDISE THROUGH COMPETITIVE BIDDING

If competitive bids require such a sharp pencil, isn't this marketplace a terrific place to get rid of obsolete merchandise? Many people get the brainstorm that moving old-model equipment, the stuff that's gathering dust in a far corner of the warehouse, is a wonderful idea. After all, selling the product to schools and government agencies won't clog the commercial marketplace for the new stuff that's coming along. The old product meets specs, mind, and it's all good stuff. Let's clean out the warehouse. So what if the product is a little bit dated? Those yokels who never faced a payroll or a deadline will never know the difference.

Unfortunately, the "yokels" do know the difference. Most competitive bids call for products that are in "current production." Discontinued items don't qualify. If you bid such an item, your competitors are sure to protest when you're the low bidder. The federal government requires seven-year parts availability for items on GSA schedule. Sorry, but you'll have to find another market for those obsolete products somewhere else.

LIFE CYCLE COSTING: HOW TO WIN BIDS EVEN THOUGH YOUR PRODUCT CARRIES A HIGH PRICE TAG

Does your product carry a high price tag that makes it unattractive in bid situations? Maybe it offers excellent quality, perhaps the best on the market, but the competitors are able to deliver products with similar features for less money. Don't give up and leave the field to others. The government marketplace isn't closed to you if you can demonstrate *life cycle efficiency*.

Government procurement officers are beginning to realize that there is a razor blade factor in most products. It isn't the initial cost of the razor that matters, it's what you pay for the blades. In the past, some vendors anxious to acquire big-volume orders have bid products near cost, or even below cost, because they hoped to make a profit from the follow-up supply and service requirement. For many products the cost of supplies or service over the product's lifetime can vastly exceed the initial purchase price.

Has the government agency made a good deal by accepting a lowball bid on an item and then ever after paying exorbitant prices for needed supplies? Many government procurement officers think not. They are now framing bid proposals that take into account all the factors related not only to the initial price of the product, but the cost to operate it over its anticipated lifetime. (The lifetime of a product is usually considered to be five to seven years). These factors added together are called life cycle costs.

Here are some of the factors usually included in life cycle cost calculations:

- The bid or original price of the product
- The cost, per year, for the supplies (The bidders may be required to guarantee supply costs over a period of time or to include a certain quantity of supplies with each product delivered.)
- The estimated cost for maintenance per year (based on historical records)
- The energy costs per year
- The residual value after five or seven years (subtracted from the costs), obtained by industry polls.

The actual formulas used are a bit more complicated than the simple list presented here because they calculate supply costs based on price *divided* by yield. If two cans of shave cream are the same price, but one contains twice as many ounces, obviously it is the one that is less expensive. Most life cycle formulas divide yield by price to arrive at true cost.

Supplies, over the lifetime of the product, represent the biggest percentage cost factor for most products. That's why the life cycle formulas used by government agencies attach more weight to them.

It seems like a paradox, but life cycle costing is an opportunity to sell high priced products to government agencies, particularly via bid requests. All that's needed to sell items at higher prices than your competitors charge is to reduce the cost of product supplies below those of your competitors or increase the yield on supplies without increasing the cost. Because supply costs carry a heavier weight than original equipment costs, you'll win many bids at excellent profit margins.

Many federal government agencies use life cycle cost figures to award bid contracts, and state agencies are beginning to use it as well. When bidding a life cycle contract remember this simple strategy:

1. Bid the product high.
2. Bid the supplies low.
3. As an alternative, increase the yield on the supplies.

GOVERNMENT BANDING

Sometimes the federal government bids sole-source contracts, awarding all product used in a category to a single vendor, and sometimes it will contract with many different vendors in a product category, negotiating price with the vendors via GSA contract and allowing the end users to choose the models they prefer. Two manufacturers can thus have products with similar specifications on contract, but with vastly different prices. How do the administrators "tilt" the prospective buyers to the product carrying the lower price tag? They do it through a process they call "banding."

On multiple award categories, GSA administrators decide which products on contract offer the best value based on life cycle cost studies previously described. These products are given a "green banding" label. Green banding simply means that any government agency with available funds in its particular budget can buy that product through the normal requisition procedure. Purchasing a green-banded product is simple, without red tape (by government standards), and the decision is rarely questioned.

Products on contract with slightly higher price tags, or that have higher life cycle costs are given "yellow banding" tags. An agency with available funds can still purchase this product, but a justification must be written as to why a green-banded product wouldn't do. This justification could be the required use of a special feature on a certain machine. It is rarely questioned, but still time must be taken to give an explanation. That alone is a discouragement.

Products on contract bearing the highest price tags or worst life cycle costs are given "red banding" labels. The justification requirements for the agency that wants to buy a red-banded product are stiffer. The reasons for not buying a green- or yellow-banded product must go through scrutiny. Approval for purchase must be signed off by managers two levels higher. Some requests for red-banded products will get turned down.

Banding is thus a bureaucratic solution to the free choice that multiple-award contracts apparently allow. The color bands "steer" the using agencies to the products GSA administrators want them to buy. The steering mechanism is a bureaucratic snarl. Buy the green-banded stuff and avoid any problems. Be stubborn, the GSA suggests, buy the red banded-stuff and learn just how bureaucratic we can become.

KEEPING THE RIGHT PERSPECTIVE ABOUT BID BUSINESS

Competitive bidding is a quick way for a small or medium-size company to build sales volume. However, for some companies that enjoy success with this market strategy, bidding can become a narcotic. It's possible to have too much of a good thing. Winning a large bid seems like such an easy solution to sales volume problems, that some companies spend more and more time on this activity. The company's regular business suffers, as those in charge run after rainbows, chase down bluebirds. For some companies, successful bids become plugged into next year's sales projections and budgets, so repeating as the contract winner next year becomes mandatory to achieving objectives. When business drops in other areas, the solution is to replace the loss with still more bid business.

The problem with this approach is that competitive bid business often requires the company to deliver goods at slimmer margins. Winning a few bids to hike sales volume while mixing with more profitable commercial business is fine. But a small or medium-size company should set limits on the percentage of competitive bid sales contracts it processes. There is danger when the percentage of bid business becomes too high. Not only do margins drop, but annual sales become less predictable. Several bids lost by a few pennies each could dramatically affect the company's sales projection.

The reason competitive bidding is such an easy way to build volume is there is absolutely no customer loyalty to reckon with. By government regulation, the contract must be given to the lowest qualified bidder meeting all the specifications. The fact that your company wins a contract one year is no guarantee it can keep it next year. The same regulations that help you gain that contract make it fair game for every competitor who wants to have a stab at it. If competitive bidding is an easy market for your company, it is also an easy market for others like yours.

That's why the percentage of sales volume competitive bid business contributes to your company should be limited. For the small or middle-size nondefense company, 25 percent of product sold through the competitive bid process is a good upper limit. If your company exceeds that figure one year through astute bidding, or blind luck, an effort should be made to increase business to the commercial marketplace.

There's another reason to limit the amount of business your company does through competitive bidding. Government agencies occasionally go through administrative crises. They don't pay their bills on time because of administrative snafus. The Defense Contract Administrative Service in Los Angeles, a Department of Defense agency that is responsible for paying contractors in nine western states, is notorious for slow and late payment. The delays are so serious that some small companies lacking the financial resources to weather the storm have been forced to close their doors. The Defense Department is creating a new national payment center in Columbus, Ohio, but some feel that will only complicate problems until the center goes through a shakedown phase.

Slow payment on a limited number of invoices is expensive but bearable because the government always pays legitimate bills eventually. However, the company that relies too heavily on bid contracts can be thrown into bankruptcy when revenue is late in arriving. That's as good a reason as any to limit the amount of business your company does through the competitive bid process.

CHAPTER SUMMARY

For the company wishing to enter the competitive bid marketplace, government red tape is a legitimate concern.

All government purchase orders should be fully documented.

The system set up to process government orders should contain built-in audit trails.

When printing a GSA catalog, include as much information about the product as possible. In many cases the catalog is your company's primary selling tool.

GSA negotiators demand that the federal government be offered the company's best price. Never bid a product on GSA contract to a local agency at a lower price.

A bid reference book can save your company countless hours in bid preparation.

A quick way to get started in federal government marketing is to use an independent marketing group that understands the nation's capital.

Don't try to sell close-outs or distress merchandise through the competitive bid process.

Life cycle costing is one way to sell high-priced products to government agencies.

The GSA administration uses color band coding to steer government agencies towards products it considers best buys.

The small or medium-size nondefense company should try to set percentage limits on the amount of competitive bid business it goes after.

15

YOUR DATABASE TO BID CONTRACT OPPORTUNITIES

MILITARY BASES

One of the most important sources for federal government business are on nation's military bases. They are small cities, in some cases dwarfing the size of surrounding communities. Military bases need everything a civilian community needs and much more. Most have a policy of doing as much business with local merchants as possible. The commanders of these bases realize the public relations value of being good neighbors. Some commanders even sponsor business shows where local merchants can show their products to base personnel.

It's easier to sell to a military base if your company's products are on GSA schedule. However, the military market should not be neglected by a local company just because the products or services it offers have not been placed on federal government buying schedules. The procurement officers for military bases have the authority to purchase many items off contract. The following is a list of the country's bases. At least one may be within geographical reach of your company. They all represent excellent opportunities to increase sales volume.

Major Military Installations

ALABAMA

Anniston Army Depot	Anniston
Ft. McClellan	Anniston
Ft. Rucker	Ozark
Gunter A.F.S.	Montgomery
Marshall Space Flight Center	Huntsville
Maxwell A.F.B.	Montgomery
Mobile C.G.B.	Mobile
Redstone Arsenal	Huntsville

ALASKA

Adak N.S.	Adak
Eilson A.F.B.	Fairbanks
Elmendorf A.F.B.	Anchorage
Ft. Greely	Big Delta
Ft. Jonathan Wainwright	Fairbanks
Ft. Richardson	Anchorage
Ketchikan C.G.B.	Ketchikan
Kodiak C.G.A.S.	Kodiak
Shemya A.F.B.	Anchorage
Sitka C.G.A.S.	Sitka

ARIZONA

Davis-Monthan A.F.B.	Tucson
Ft. Huachuca	Douglas
Luke A.F.B.	Glendale
Williams A.F.B.	Chandler
Yuma M.C.A.S.	Yuma
Yuma Proving Ground	Yuma

ARKANSAS

Ft. Chaffee	Fort Smith
Blytheville A.F.B.	Blytheville
Little Rock A.F.B.	Jacksonville
Pine Bluff Arsenal	Pine Bluff

CALIFORNIA

Alameda N.A.S.	Alameda
Beale A.F.B.	Marysville
Camp Pendleton M.C.B.	Oceanside
Castle A.F.B.	Merced
China Lake Naval Weapons Center	Ridgecrest
Concord Naval Weapons Station	Concord
Coronado Naval Amphibious Base	Coronado
Dryden Flight Research Center	Edwards
Edwards A.F.B.	Edwards
El Toro M.C.A.S.	Santa Ana
Ft. Hunter Liggett	Jolon
Ft. Ord	Monterey
George A.F.B.	Victorville
Humboldt Bay C.G.A.S.	McKinleyville
Lemoore N.A.S.	Lemoore
Long Beach Naval Shipyard	Long Beach
Los Angeles A.F.S.	El Segundo
McClellan A.F.B.	Sacramento
March A.F.B.	Riverside
Mare Island Naval Shipyard	Vallejo
Mather A.F.B.	Sacramento
Miramar N.A.S.	San Diego
Moffett Field N.A.S.	Mountain View
Naval Construction Battalion Center	Port Hueneme

North Island N.A.S.	San Diego
Norton A.F.B.	San Bernardino
Oakland Army Base	Oakland
Pacific Missile Test Center–Point Magu	Oxnard
Presidio of Monterey	Monterey
Presidio of San Francisco	San Francisco
Sacramento Army Depot	Sacramento
San Diego N.S.	San Diego
San Francisco C.G.A.S.	San Francisco
Seal Beach Naval Weapons Station	Seal Beach
Sharpe Army Depot	Stockton
Stockton Naval Comm. Station	Stockton
Terminal Island C.G.B.	San Pedro
Travis A.F.B.	Fairfield
Twentynine Palms M.C.B.	Twentynine Palms
Vandenberg A.F.B.	Lompoc

COLORADO

Fitzsimmons Army Medical	Aurora
Ft. Carson	Colorado Springs
Lowry A.F.B.	Denver
Peterson A.F.B.	Colorado Springs
Rocky Mountain Arsenal	Denver
U.S. Air Force Academy	Colorado Springs

CONNECTICUT

New London Submarine Base	Groton
U.S. Coast Guard Academy	New London

DELAWARE

Dover A.F.B.	Dover

DISTRICT OF COLUMBIA

Bolling A.F.B.	Washington, D.C.
Ft. McNair	Washington, D.C.
Washington Navy Yard	Washington, D.C.

FLORIDA

Cecil Field N.A.S.	Jacksonville
Clearwater C.G.A.S.	Clearwater
Coastal Systems Laboratory	Panama City
Corry Station N.T.C.	Pensacola
Eglin A.F.B.	Valparaiso
Homestead A.F.B.	Homestead
Jacksonville N.A.S.	Orange Park
J.F. Kennedy Space Center	Cape Canaveral
Key West N.A.S.	Key West
Macdill A.F.B.	Tampa
Mayport N.S.	Mayport
Miami C.G.A.S.	Opa Locka
Miami Beach C.G.B.	Miami Beach
Orlando N.T.C.	Orlando
Patrick A.F.B.	Cocoa
Pensacola N.A.S.	Pensacola
Tyndall A.F.B.	Springfield
Whiting Field N.A.S.	Milton

GEORGIA

Atlanta N.A.S.	Marietta
Dobbins A.F.B.	Marietta
Ft. Benning	Columbus
Ft. Gordon	Augusta
Ft. McPherson	Atlanta

Ft. Stewart	Hinesville
Hunter Army Airfield	Savannah
Marine Corps Supply Center	Albany
Moody A.F.B.	Valdosta
Robins A.F.B.	Warner Robins

HAWAII

Barbers Point N.A.S.	Ewa Beach
Camp H.M. Smith M.C.B.	Hawawa Heights
Ft. Shafter	Honolulu
Hickam	Honolulu
Kaneohe Bay M.C.A.S.	Kallua
Pearl Harbor Nav. Res.	Honolulu
Schofield Barracks	Wahiawa
Wheeler A.F.B.	Wahiawa

IDAHO

Mountain Home A.F.B.	Mountain Home

ILLINOIS

Chanute A.F.B.	Rantoul
Ft. Sheridan	Highwood
Glenview N.A.S.	Glenview
Great Lakes Naval Training Center	North Chicago
Joliet Army Ammunition Plant	Joliet
Rock Island Arsenal	Rock Island
Scott A.F.B.	Belleville

INDIANA

Crane Naval Weapons Support Center	Crane
Ft. Benjamin Harrison	Indianapolis
Grisson A.F.B.	Peru

Jefferson Proving Ground	Madison
Naval Avionics Center	Indianapolis

KANSAS

Ft. Leavenworth	Leavenworth
Ft. Riley	Junction City
McConnell A.F.B.	Wichita

KENTUCKY

Ft. Knox	Louisville
Lexington Bluegrass Army Depot	Lexington
Navy Ordinance Station	Louisville

LOUISIANA

Barksdale A.F.B.	Shreveport
England A.F.B.	Alexandria
Ft. Polk	Leesville
New Orleans C.G.B.	New Orleans
New Orleans N.A.S.	New Orleans
New Orleans Naval Support Activity	New Orleans

MAINE

Brunswick N.A.S.	Brunswick
Loring A.F.B.	Limestone
South Portland C.G.B.	Portland
Southwest Harbor C.G.B.	Southwest Harbor

MARYLAND

Aberdeen Proving Ground	Aberdeen
Andrews A.F.B.	Camp Springs
Ft. Detrick	Frederick

Ft. Meade	Odenton
Ft. Ritchie	Cascade
Indian Head Naval Ordinance Station	Indian Head
N.A.T.C. Patuxent River	Patuxent River
U.S. Naval Academy	Annapolis

MASSACHUSETTS

Ft. Devins	Ayer
Hanscom A.F.B.	Bedford
Natick Laboratories	Natick
Otis A.F.B.	Falmouth
South Weymouth N.A.S.	South Weymouth
Westover A.F.B.	Chicopee
Woods Hole C.G.B.	Woods Hole

MICHIGAN

Detroit Arsenal	Warren
Detroit C.G.B.	Detroit
K.I. Sawyer A.F.B.	Gwynn
Michigan Army Missile Plant	Detroit
Sault Ste. Marie C.G.B.	Sault Ste. Marie
Traverse City C.G.A.S.	Traverse City
Wurtsmith A.F.B.	Oscoda

MISSISSIPPI

Columbus A.F.B.	Columbus
Keesler A.F.B.	Biloxi
Meridian N.A.S.	Meridian
Naval Construction Battalion Center	Gulfport

MISSOURI

Ft. Leonard Wood	Waynesville
Richards-Gebaur A.F.B.	Grandview
St. Louis C.G.B.	St. Louis
Whiteman A.F.B.	Knobnoster

MONTANA

Malmstrom A.F.B.	Great Falls

NEBRASKA

Offutt A.F.B.	Omaha

NEVADA

Nellis A.F.B.	Las Vegas
Fallon N.A.S.	Reno
Sierra Army Depot	Reno

NEW HAMPSHIRE

Pease A.F.B.	Portsmouth
Portsmouth Naval Shipyard	Portsmouth

NEW JERSEY

Bayonne Military Ocean Terminal	Bayonne
Cape May C.G.A.S.	Cape May
Ft. Dix	Wrightstown
Ft. Monmouth	Oceanport
McGuire A.F.B.	Wrightstown
Picatinny Arsenal	Dover

NEW MEXICO

Cannon A.F.B.	Clovis
Holloman A.F.B.	Alamongordo
Kirtland A.F.B.	Albuquerque
Sandia Base	Albuquerque
White Sands Missile Range	Las Cruces

NEW YORK

Buffalo C.G.B.	Buffalo
Ft. Drum	Watertown
Ft. Hamilton	New York
Griffiss A.F.B.	Rome
Plattsburgh A.F.B.	Plattsburgh
Seneca Army Depot	Romulus
U.S. Military Academy	West Point
Watervliet Arsenal	Watervliet

NORTH CAROLINA

Camp Lejeune M.C.B.	Jacksonville
Cherry Point M.C.A.S.	Havelock
Elizabeth City C.G.A.S.	Elizabeth City
Ft. Bragg	Fayetteville
Ft. Macon C.G.B.	Atlantic Beach
New River M.C.A.S.	Jacksonville
Pope A.F.B.	Springlake
Seymour Johnson A.F.B.	Goldsboro

NORTH DAKOTA

Grand Forks A.F.B.	Grand Forks
Minot A.F.B.	Minot

OHIO

Newark A.F.S.	Heath
Rickenbacker A.F.B.	Columbus
Wright-Patterson A.F.B.	Dayton

OKLAHOMA

Altus A.F.B.	Altus
Ft. Sill	Lawton
McAlester Army Ammunition Plant	McAlester
Tinker A.F.B.	Oklahoma City
Vance A.F.B.	Enid

OREGON

Astoria C.G.B.	Astoria
North Bend C.G.A.S.	North Bend

PENNSYLVANIA

Carlisle Barracks	Carlisle
Frankford Arsenal	Philadelphia
Ft. Indiantown Gap	Annville
Letterkenny Army Depot	Chambersburg
New Cumberland Army Depot	New Cumberland
Philadelphia Naval Shipyard	Philadelphia
Tobyhanna Army Depot	Scranton
Warminister Naval Air Development Center	Warminister
Willow Grove N.A.S.	Willow Grove

SOUTH CAROLINA

Beaufort M.C.A.S.	Beaufort
Charleston A.F.B.	Charleston
Charleston C.G.B.	Charleston

Charleston Naval Shipyard	Charleston
Charleston N.S.	Charleston
Charleston Naval Weapons Station	Charleston
Ft. Jackson	Columbia
Myrtle Beach A.F.B.	Myrtle Beach
Parris Island Marine Corps Recruit Depot	Beaufort
Shaw A.F.B.	Sumter

SOUTH DAKOTA

Ellsworth A.F.B.	Box Elders

TENNESSEE

Ft. Campbell	Clarksville
Memphis N.A.S.	Millington

TEXAS

Bergstrom A.F.B.	Austin
Brooks A.F.B.	San Antonio
Carswell A.F.B.	Fort Worth
Chase Field N.A.S.	Beeville
Corpus Christi C.G.A.S.	Corpus Christi
Corpus Christi N.A.S.	Corpus Christi
Dallas N.A.S.	Dallas
Dyess A.F.B.	Abilene
Ft. Bliss	El Paso
Ft. Hood	Killeen
Ft. Sam Houston	San Antonio
Galveston C.G.B.	Galveston
Goodfellow A.F.B.	San Angelo
Houston C.G.A.S.	Houston
Kelly A.F.B.	San Antonio

Kingsville N.A.S.	Kingsville
Lackland A.F.B.	San Antonio
Laughlin A.F.B.	Del Rio
Lyndon B. Johnson Space Center	Houston
Randolph A.F.B.	Universal City
Red River Army Depot	Texarkana
Reese A.F.B.	Lubbock
San Antonio A.F.S.	San Antonio
Sheppard A.F.B.	Wichita Falls

UTAH

Dugway Proving Ground	Dugway
Hill A.F.B.	Ogden
Tooele Army Depot	Tooele

VIRGINIA

Ft. Belvoir	Alexandria
Ft. Eustis	Newport News
Ft. Lee	Petersburg
Ft. Monroe	Hampton
Ft. Myer	Arlington
Langley A.F.B.	Hampton
Little Creek Naval Amphibious Base	Norfolk
Norfolk N.A.S.	Norfolk
Norfolk N.S.	Norfolk
Norfolk Naval Shipyard	Portsmouth
Oceana N.A.S.	Virginia Beach
Quantico M.C.A.S.	Quantico
Yorktown Naval Weapons Station	Yorktown

WASHINGTON

Bangor Naval Submarine Base	Bremerton
Fairchild A.F.B.	Spokane
Ft. Lewis	Tacoma
McCord A.F.B.	Tacoma
Port Angeles C.G.A.S.	Port Angeles
Puget Sound Naval Shipyard	Bremerton
Seattle Naval Support Activity	Seattle
Whidbey Island N.A.S.	Oak Harbor

WISCONSIN

Ft. McCoy	Sparta
Milwaukee C.G.B.	Milwaukee

WYOMING

Francis E. Warren A.F.B.	Cheyenne

THE NATION'S LARGEST MILITARY CONTRACTORS

The following is a list of the United States' top twenty-two defense contractors. Each of these companies has sold more than one billion dollars in products and services *annually* to the military in past years. Their contracts with the government requires them to subcontract a percentage of their work to small business and minority-owned firms. They are wonderful prospects for the small business that can deliver reliable products on time.

Addresses and phone numbers are not included because these companies maintain plants, divisions, and offices in many locations across the country. These facilities try to procure products locally whenever they can. If one of these companies maintains a facility in your area, contact their procurement office. Ask for the purchasing agent in charge of small business or minority set-asides. Very likely you'll be mailed a form to fill out with questions about your company's size, number of employees, product line, delivery capabilities, etc. If your company qualifies as a small business with a product or service they need to fulfill a contract, they'll be *anxious* to establish a business relationship with you. This business could be on the basis of a competitive bid or a direct award.

The following list is in rough order of the value of each company's contract awards in 1988. There's some jockeying for position from one year to the next, but the players stay remarkably the same.

McDonnell Douglas Corporation
General Dynamics Corporation
General Electric Company
Tenneco Incorporated
Raytheon Company
Martin Marietta Corporation
General Motors Corporation
Lockheed Corporation
United Technologies Corporation
The Boeing Company
Grumman Corporation
Litton Industries, Incorporated
Westinghouse Electrical Corporation
Rockwell, International Corporation
Unisys Corporation
Honeywell Bull Incorporated
Textron Incorporated
TRW Incorporated
Texas Instruments Incorporated
International Business Machines
General Telephone and Electric
LTV, Inc.

The following lists include all State central purchasing offices, the one hundred largest county and local government purchasing offices and the one hundred largest school districts. Outside the Federal government, these agencies represent the biggest and best bidding opportunities. Use the methods suggested in this book to get on the bid lists of those agencies your company can service. This is the first step in taking a seat at the high stakes bidding game. Good luck!

STATE PURCHASING OFFICES

ALABAMA

Howard L. White, Jr.
Director of Purchasing & Stores
Dept. of Finance
Rm. 204, State Capitol
Montgomery, AL 36130
(205) 261-3128

ALASKA
Bob Link
Director
General Services & Supply Div.
Dept. of Administration
P.O. Box C-0210
Juneau, AK 99811
(907) 465-2250

ARIZONA

Wayne A. Casper
State Purchasing Director
Purchasing Office
Dept. of Administration
1688 W. Adams St.
Rm. 220
Phoenix, AZ 85007
(602) 255-5511

ARKANSAS

Edward Erxleben
Administrator
Office of State Purchasing
Finance & Administration Dept.
P.O. Box 3278
Little Rock, AR 72201
(501) 371-2336

CALIFORNIA

John S. Babich
Deputy Director
Office of Procurement
Dept. of General Services
1823 14th St., Box 1612
Sacramento, CA 95807
(916) 445-6942

COLORADO

E.R. Roon
Director
Div. of Purchasing
Dept. of Administration
1525 Sherman St., 7th Fl.
Denver, CO 80203
(303) 866-3261

CONNECTICUT

John W. Otterbein
Deputy Commissioner
Bureau of Services
Administrative Services Dept.
460 Silver St.
Middletown, CT 06457
(203) 344-2067

DELAWARE

Richard Cathcart
Director
Div. of Purchasing
Dept. of Administrative Services
P.O. Box 299
Delaware City, DE 19706
(302) 571-3070

FLORIDA

William Monroe
Director
Div. of Purchasing
Dept. of General Services
613 Larson Bldg.
Tallahassee, FL 32301
(904) 488-1194

HAWAII

Earl B. Dedell
Chief
Purchasing & Supply Div.
Accounting & General Services Dept.
1151 Punchbowl St.
Honolulu, HI 96813
(808) 548-4057

ILLINOIS

Michael Tristano
Director
Dept. of Central Management Services
715 Stratton Bldg.
Springfield, IL 62706
(217) 782-2141

IOWA

Bob Soldat
Administrator
Div. of Purchasing
Dept. of General Services
Hoover State Office Bldg.
Des Moines, IA 50319
(515) 281-6285

KENTUCKY

Mike Diehl
Director
Div. of Purchases
Finance & Administration
Cabinet
Capitol Annex
Frankfort, KY 40601
(502) 564-4510

GEORGIA

Thomas M. Bostick
Director
Purchasing & Surplus
Property Div.
200 Piedmont Ave.
#1302 W.
Atlanta, GA 30334
(404) 656-3240

IDAHO

Coleen Grant
Administrator
Div. of Purchasing
Dept. of Administration
801 Reserve St.
Boise, ID 83720
(208) 334-2465

INDIANA

Orval Lundy
Commissioner
Dept. of Administration
507 State Office Bldg.
160 N. Senate Ave.
Indianapolis, IN 46204
(317) 232-3114

KANSAS

Nicholas B. Roach
Director
Div. of Purchases
Dept. of Administration
1st Fl., State Off. Bldg.
Topeka, KS 66614
(913) 296-2376

LOUISIANA

Stephanie L. Alexander
Commissioner
Div. of Administration
P.O. Box 94095
Baton Rouge, LA 70804
(504) 922-0064

MAINE

Ronald S. Lord
State Purchasing Agent
Bureau of Purchasing
Dept. of Admbinistration
State House Station #9
Augusta, ME 04333
(207) 289-3521

MASSACHUSETTS

Daniel D. Carter
Director of Purchasing
Executive Office of Administration &
Finance
John McCormick Off. Bldg.
One Ashburton Pl., Rm. 1011
Boston, MA 02108
(617) 727-2882

MINNESOTA

John Hagerty
Director
Materials Management Div.
Dept. of Administration
Rm. 112, 50 Sherburne Ave.
St. Paul, MN 55155
(612) 296-1442

MISSOURI

Thomas F. Blaine, Jr.
Director
Div. of Purchasing
Office of Administration
Truman Bldg., Box 809
Jefferson City, MO 65102
(314) 751-3273

NEBRASKA

Barbara A. Lawson
Purchasing, Material Div.
Administrative Serviccs Dept.
P.O. Box 94847
Lincoln, NE 68509
(402) 471-2401

MARYLAND

Paul T. Harris, Sr.
Chief
Purchasing Bureau
Dept. of General Services
301 W. Preston St., Rm. M2
Baltimore, MD 21201
(301) 225-4620

MICHIGAN

Wiliam Warstler
Director
Purchasing Div.
Dept. of Management & Budget
P.O. Box 30026
Lansing, MI 48909
(517) 373-0300

MISSISSIPPI

Oren Segrest
Director
Purchase Bureau
Fiscal Management Board
1504 Sillers Bldg.
Jackson, MS 39202
(601) 359-3402

MONTANA

Mike Muskiewicz
Administrator
Purchasing Div.
Dept. of Administration
Capitol Station
Helena, MT 59620
(406) 444-2575

NEVADA

Terry Sullivan
Director
Purchasing Div.
Dept. of General Services
Capitol Complex
Carson City, NV 89710
(702) 885-4094

NEW HAMPSHIRE

Timothy Gibney
Plant & Property Mgt.
Administrative Services
Dept.
102 State House Annex
Concord, NH 03301
(603) 271-1110

NEW MEXICO

Ronn Jones
Director
Purchasing Div.
Dept. of General Services
1100 St. Francis Dr.
Santa Fe, NM 87501
(505) 827-0472

NORTH CAROLINA

Max Baldwin
Purchasing Officer
Div. of Purchase & Contract
Dept. of Administration
116 W. Jones St.
Raleigh, NC 27611
(919) 733-3581

OHIO

Steven Hunter
State Purchasing Administrator
Div. of Office Services
Administrative Services Dept.
183 E. Mound St.
Columbus, OH 43266
(614) 466-8218

OREGON

Kay Toran
Administrator
Div. of Purchasing
Dept. of General Services
1225 Ferry St., SE
Salem, OR 97310
(503) 378-4643

NEW JERSEY

Giulio Mazzone
Supervisor
Bureau of Purchasing
Dept. of Treasury
135 W. Hanover St.
Trenton, NJ 08625
(609) 292-4751

NEW YORK

John Egan
Commissioner
Office of General Services
Empire State Plaza
Corning Tower Bldg.
Albany, NY 12242
(518) 474-5991

NORTH DAKOTA

Bud Walsh
State Purchasing Agent
Purchasing Div.
Office of Management & Budget
4th Fl., State Capitol
Bismarck, ND 58505
(701) 224-2680

OKLAHOMA

Ray Lazenby
Director
Office of Public Affairs
Central Purchasing Div.
B-4 State Capitol
Oklahoma City, OK 73105
(405) 521-2115

PENNSYLVANIA

James W. Brown
Secretary
Dept. of General Services
515 N. Office Bldg.
Harrisburg, PA 17120
(717) 787-5996

RHODE ISLAND

Dennis M. Lynch
Purchasing Agent
Div. of Purchases
Dept. of Administration
301 Promenade St.
Providence, RI 02908
(401) 277-2321

SOUTH DAKOTA

Mike Melhaff
Director
Purchasing & Printing
Foss Bldg., Rm. 119
Pierre, SD 57501
(605) 773-3405

TEXAS

Lias B. Steen
Executive Director
Purchasing & General Services
Commission
Box 13047
Capitol Station
Austin, TX 78711
(512) 463-3446

VERMONT

Patricia L. Thomas
Commissioner
Dept. of General Services
128 State St.
Montpelier, VT 05602
(802) 828-3331

WASHINGTON

Meredith Jennings
Director
Purchasing Div.
General Administration Dept.
P.O. Box 1529, M/S
TB-01
Auburn, WA 98071
(206) 931-3931

SOUTH CAROLINA

Virgil V. Carlsen
Director of State Procurement
Materials Management
Div. of General Services
800 Dutch Sq., #250
Columbia, SC 29210
(803) 737-8910

TENNESSEE

Alvin Cohen
Div. of Purchasing
Dept. of General Services
C2-211 Central Services Bldg.
Nashville, TN 37219
(615) 741-1035

UTAH

Doug Richins
Director
Div. of Purchasing
Administrative Services Dept.
2112 State Off. Bldg.
Salt Lake City, UT 84114
(801) 533-4620

VIRGINIA

Donald F. Moore
Director
Div. of Purchases & Supply
Dept. of General Services
P.O. Box 1199
Richmond, VA 23209
(804) 786-3846

WEST VIRGINIA

Kathy Klein
Director
Purchasing Div.
Dept. of Finance & Administration
State Capitol Complex
Charleston, WV 25305
(304) 348-2309

WISCONSIN

Larry Eisenberg
Director
Bureau of Procurement
Dept. of Administration
P.O. Box 7867
Madison, WI 53707
(608) 266-0974

WYOMING

Frank Bonds
Administrator
Purchasing & Property Control
Administration & Fiscal Control Dept.
Emerson Bldg.
Cheyenne, WY 82002
(307) 777-7253

DISTRICT OF COLUMBIA

Bruce Marshall
Administrator
Dept. of Administrative Services
Materiel Management Administration
613 G St., NW,
Rm. 1014
Washington, DC 20001
(202) 639-1170

AMERICAN SAMOA

Ben Tau
Director
Office of Material Mgt.
Pago Pago, AS 96799
(684) 639-1170

NORTHERN MARIANA ISLANDS

Antonio I. Taisacan
Acting Chief
Procurement & Supply Div.
Finance & Accounting Dept.
Office of the Governor
Saipan, CM 96950
(670) 322-9441

PUERTO RICO

Blas Contreras
Administrator
General Services Administration
P.O. Box 7428
Santurce, PR 00916
(809) 721-7370

VIRGIN ISLANDS

Delma Hodge
Commissioner
Dept. of Property & Procurement
Subbase Bldg., #1
St. Thomas, VI 00802
(809) 774-0828

THE FIFTY LARGEST CITY PURCHASING AGENCIES

CITY OF NEW YORK

Charlotte Frank
Director of Procurement
1 Center Street
New York, NY 10007
(212) 669-8520

CITY OF CHICAGO

Mary Skipton
Purchasing Dept.
121 N. La Salle, Room 403
Chicago, IL 60602
(312) 744-4900

CITY OF PHILADELPHIA

Joseph Handel
Purchasing Manager
15 & J.F.K. Blvd.
Room 1370, MSB
Philadelphia, PA 19102-1686
(215) 686-4751

CITY OF DALLAS

Joseph Pippin
Purchasing Department
1500 Marilla
Dallas, TX 75209
(214) 670-3329

CITY OF AUSTIN

Fred Wiley
Purchasing Officer
Purchasing Department
P.O. Box 1088
Austin, TX 78767-8845
(512) 499-2000

CITY OF PHOENIX

Bill Bengert
Dir. of Purchasing
Materials Management Dept.
251 W. Washington
Phoenix, AZ 85003
(602) 262-7181

CITY OF LOS ANGELES

A.R. Riolo
Purchasing Department
200 N. Main Street
Room 850, City Hall East
Los Angeles, CA 90012
(213) 485-2121

CITY OF HOUSTON

Phil Lightfoot
Director of Purchasing
901 Bagby
Houston, TX 77001
(713) 247-1000

CITY OF DETROIT

Oreese Collins, Jr.
Purchasing Department
2 Woodward
912 City County Bldg.
Detroit, MI 48226
(313) 224-4600

CITY OF SAN DIEGO

Ralph Shackelford
Purchasing Department
1010 Second Ave.
San Diego, CA 92101
(619) 236-6210

CITY OF LONG BEACH

Harry Lipton
Director of Purchasing
333 W. Ocean
Long Beach, CA 90802
(213) 590-6555

CITY OF SAN ANTONIO

R.G. Tetchman
Purchasing Department
131 W. Nuevo
San Antonio, TX 78204
(512) 299-7260

CITY OF BALTIMORE

Ella Pierce
Bureau of Purchases
111 N. Calvert
Baltimore, MD 21202
(301) 396-5706

CITY OF INDIANAPOLIS

Stephen Millspaugh
Purchasing Department
1522 City–County Bldg.
Indianapolis, IN 46204
(317) 236-4900

CITY OF MEMPHIS

Glen Campbell
Purchasing Department
125 Mid America, Room 374
Memphis, TN 38103
(901) 576-6683

CITY OF TULSA

John Ogren
Director of Purchasing
200 Civic Center
Tulsa, OK 74103
(918) 592-7777

CITY OF DENVER

Leo Pearlman
Purchasing Department
303 W. Colfax
Denver, CO 80204
(303) 575-2382

CITY OF MILWAUKEE

Edward A. Witkowski
Purchasing Department
200 E. Wells St.
Milwaukee, WI 53202
(414) 278-3501

CITY OF SAN FRANCISCO

Marvin Geistlinger
Director of Purchasing
McAllister & Venice
City Hall, Room 270
San Francisco, CA 94102
(415) 554-6743

CITY OF SAN JOSE

Sam Gaetz
Purchasing Department
1608 Las Plumas Ave.
San Jose, CA 95133
(408) 277-4413

CITY OF HONOLULU

Haruo Schigezawa
Purchasing Department
530 S. King, Room 115
Honolulu, HI 96813
(808) 527-5692

CITY OF MIAMI

Ron Williams
Director of Purchasing
1390 NW 20th Street
Miami, FL 33142
(305) 579-6093

CITY OF SEATTLE

Comi Teral
Purchasing Department
400 Yesler Bldg., Rm. 405
Seattle, WA 98104
(206) 684-0444

CITY OF NEW ORLEANS

Deborah Roberts
Director of Purchasing
1300 Perdido
New Orleans, LA 70112
(504) 586-4284

CITY OF JACKSONVILLE

Daniel Haskell
Director of Purchasing
Room 301, City Hall
220 E. Bay Street
Jacksonville, FL 32202
(904) 630-1194

CITY OF BOSTON

Tony Streeter
Director of Purchasing
City Hall Purchasing Dept.
City Hall Plaza, Room 808
Boston, MA 02201
(617) 725-4554

CITY OF CINCINNATI

Ann Degroot
Director of Purchasing
801 Plum
Cincinnati, OH 45202
(513) 352-3000

CITY OF NASHVILLE-DAVIDSON

Everett Madlin
Director of Purchasing
1001 Stahlman Bldg.
Nashville, TN 37201
(615) 259-5000

CITY OF OKLAHOMA CITY

Rana Bohan
Director of Purchasing
201 Channing Square, Room B-14
Oklahoma City, OK 73102
(405) 231-2011

CITY OF ST. LOUIS

Rita M. Kirkland
Director of Purchasing
1200 Market St., Room 324
St. Louis, MO 63103
(314) 622-4000

CITY OF WASHINGTON, D.C.

Mr. J.W. Lanum
Director of Purchasing
613 G St. N.W., Room 1014
Washington, D.C. 20001
(202) 727-0171

CITY OF COLUMBUS

Barbara Johnson
Director of Purchasing
95 West Long Street
Columbus, OH 43215
(614) 222-8315

CITY OF BATON ROUGE

Jimmy Kilshaw
Director of Purchasing
P.O. Box 1471
Baton Rouge, LA 70821
(504) 389-3000

CITY OF EL PASO

Ted Arellano
Director of Purchasing
2 Civic Center Plaza
El Paso, TX 79901-1196
(915) 541-4000

CITY OF KANSAS CITY

Charles Young
Director of Purchasing
414 E. 12th St.
Kansas City, MO 64106
(816) 274-2000

CITY OF ATLANTA

Gary S. Walker
Director of Purchasing
197 Central Ave. SW
Atlanta, GA 30335
(404) 658-6000

CITY OF FT. WORTH

Lynn Spruiell
Director of Purchasing
1000 Throckmorton
Purchasing Department
Ft. Worth, TX 76102
(817) 870-8360

CITY OF PORTLAND

Carlton Chayer
Director of Purchasing
1120 SW 5th, Room 1313
Portland, OR 97204
(503) 796-6855

CITY OF MINNEAPOLIS

Harold Beetsch
Director of Purchasing
A-2203, 300 S. 6th St.
Minneapolis, MN 55487
(612) 348-3000

CITY OF ALBUQUERQUE

Mike Warner
Director of Purchasing
P.O. Box 1293
Albuquerque, NM 87103
(505) 768-2000

CITY OF BUFFALO

Daniel Bohen
Director of Purchasing
1902 City Hall
65 Niagara Square
Buffalo, NY 14202
(716) 851-4200

CITY OF CHARLOTTE

Mr. B.C. Brown
Director of Purchasing
600 E. 4th Street
Charlotte, NC 28202
(704) 336-2040

CITY OF PITTSBURGH

Don Botsford
Director of Purchasing
City-County Building
414 Grant
Pittsburgh, PA 15219
(412) 255-2100

CITY OF TUCSON

David V. Mackey
Director of Purchasing
P.O. Box 27210
Tucson, AZ 85726-7210
(602) 791-4911

CITY OF OAKLAND

James Ashley
Director of Purchasing
7101 Edgewater Dr.
Oakland, CA 94621
(415) 273-3521

CITY OF TOLEDO

John E. Bibish & Kim Bliss
Director of Purchasing
No. 1 Government Center
Jackson & Erie
Toledo, OH 43604
(419) 245-1000

CITY OF OMAHA

Ken Braymen
Director of Purchasing
1819 Farnam St.
Room 1003, Civic Center
Omaha, NE 68183
(402) 444-5400

CITY OF NEWARK

Louis Lucarelli
Director of Purchasing
828 Broad Street
Newark, NJ 07102
(201) 733-3776

CITY OF VIRGINIA BEACH

Judy Robertson
Director of Purchasing
Purchasing Department
Room 320, Municipal Center
Virginia Beach, VA 23456
(804) 427-4438

CITY OF CLEVELAND

William Moon
Director of Purchasing
601 Lakeside
Cleveland, OH 44114
(216) 664-2000

THE FIFTY LARGEST COUNTY PURCHASING AGENCIES

COUNTY OF SACRAMENTO

Andrew T. Reshke
Purchasing Agent
3284 Ramos Circle
Sacramento, CA 95827
(916) 366-2023

COUNTY OF RIVERSIDE

Frank McGraw
Purchasing Department
2980 Washington
Riverside, CA 92504-4698
(714) 787-2898

COUNTY OF LOS ANGELES

Gene Davis
Director of Purchasing
2500 S. Garfield Ave.
Commerce, CA 90040
(213) 720-6804

COUNTY OF VENTURA

Gene Aviles
Director of Purchasing
800 S. Victoria
Ventura, CA 93009
(805) 654-3750

COUNTY OF SAN FRANCISCO

Marvin Geistlinger
Director of Purchasing
McAllister & Venice
City Hall, Room 270
San Francisco, CA 94102
(415) 554-6743

COUNTY OF SAN DIEGO

James Tapp
Director of Purchasing
5555 Overland Ave.
Building 11
San Diego, CA 92123
(619) 694-2940

COUNTY OF SANTA CLARA

Jack Bunsch
Director of Purchasing
Purchasing Department
1553 Berger Dr., Bldg. 1
San Jose, CA 95112
(408) 299-2121

COUNTY OF SAN BERNAR-DINO

John F. Michaelson
Director of Purchasing
Purchasing Department
777 E. Rialto Ave.
San Bernardino, CA 92145
(714) 387-5563

ALAMEDA COUNTY

Gary Holm
Director of Purchasing
General Services
4400 McArthur Blvd.
Oakland, CA 94619
(415) 530-9660

COUNTY OF ORANGE

GSA Purchasing
Chris Barnes
Manager
1300 S. Grand Ave., Bldg. A
Santa Ana, CA 92714
(714) 567-7300

COUNTY OF COOK COUNTY

William Donovan
Purchasing Agent
118 N. Clark St., Room 1018
Cook County, IL 60602
(312) 443-5500

COUNTY OF WESTCHESTER

Charles J. Oleson
Purchasing Agent
Bureau of Purchase & Supplies
Grasslands Reservation
Valhalla, NY 10595
(914) 347-6100

COUNTY OF NASSAU

Philip Munda
Director of Purchasing
1551 Franklin Ave.
Mineola, NY 11501
(516) 535-3131

COUNTY OF SUFFOLK

Chief Purchasing Agent
10 Oval Drive
Hauppauge, NY 11788
(516) 360-4000

CONTRA COSTA COUNTY

Cliff Baumer
Purchasing Department
630 Court Street
P.O. Box 31
Martinez, CA 94553
(415) 646-2174

COUNTY OF SAN MATEO

Carmen Redmond-Brown
Supervisor
General Services
590 Hamilton St.
Redwood City, CA 94063
(415) 363-4323

COUNTY OF DUPAGE

Cliff Williams
Director of Purchasing
421 N. County Farm Road
Wheaton, IL 60187
(312) 682-7000

COUNTY OF NEW YORK CITY

Susan Weisenfeld
Director of Purchasing
1 Center Street
Municipal Bldg., 68th Fl.
New York, NY 10007
(212) 669-8562

COUNTY OF ERIE

Joseph Heleniak
Director of Purchasing
95 Franklin St.
Buffalo, NY 14202
(716) 846-6315

COUNTY OF QUEENS

Marilyn Willoughby
Director of Purchasing
Queens General Hospital Ctr.
Purchasing Department
Goethals Ave. & Parsons Blvd.
Jamaica, NY 11432
(718) 990-2995

COUNTY OF BERGEN

Frank Marinello
Director of Purchasing
21 Main Street
Hackensack, NJ 07601
(201) 646-2000

COUNTY OF DADE

Rick Grimm
Director of Purchasing
111 NW 1st St., 23rd Floor
Miami, FL 33128
(305) 375-5311

COUNTY OF PINELLAS

Steve Carroll
Director of Purchasing
315 Court Street
Clearwater, FL 34616
(813) 462-3000

COUNTY OF HILLSBOROUGH

Ted Grable
Director of Purchasing
P.O. Box 1110
Tampa, FL 33601
(813) 272-5000

COUNTY OF ALLEGHENY

Robert C. Huckenstein
Director of Purchasing
Room 202, Courthouse
Pittsburgh, PA 15219
(412) 355-5199

COUNTY OF OAKLAND

Lloyd Hampton
Director of Purchasing
1200 N. Telegraph
Pontiac, MI 48053
(313) 858-0480

COUNTY OF ESSEX

Burt Martone
Director of Purchasing
Hall of Records, Rm. 405
465 Martin Luther King, Jr. Blvd.
Newark, NJ 07102
(201) 621-4400

COUNTY OF BROWARD

Glen Cummings
Director of Purchasing
115 S. Andrews Ave.
Ft. Lauderdale, FL 33301
(305) 357-7585

COUNTY OF PALM BEACH

John Weyrauch
Director of Purchasing
1280 N. Congress Ave.
W. Palm Beach, FL 33409
(407) 233-1500

COUNTY OF PHILADELPHIA

Marilyn Pearson
Director of Purchasing
Procurement Dept., Rm. 1370
Municipal Services Bldg.
Philadelphia, PA 19102
(215) 686-1776

COUNTY OF WAYNE

Pamela T. Parris
Director of Purchasing
600 Randolph Street
First Floor, Room 146
Detroit, MI 48226
(313) 224-5155

COUNTY OF DALLAS

Director of Purchasing
601 Elm Street
Dallas, TX 75202
(214) 653-7431

COUNTY OF HARRIS

Jack R. McCown
Director of Purchasing
1001 Preston, 6th Floor
Houston, TX 77002
(713) 221-5000

COUNTY OF BEAR

Charles Eads
Director of Purchasing
Bear County Courthouse
San Antonio, TX 78205
(512) 220-2201

COUNTY OF MARICOPA

Joseph Warnas
Director of Purchasing
320 W. Lincoln St.
Phoenix, AZ 85003
(602) 262-3011

COUNTY OF CUYAHOGA

Michael Kochan
Director of Purchasing
Room 100, Annex Bldg.
112 Hamilton Ave.
Cleveland, OH 44114
(216) 443-7000

COUNTY OF HAMILTON

Richard K. Powers
Director of Purchasing
138 E. Court St., Room 607
Cincinnati, OH 45202
(513) 632-8261

COUNTY OF TARRANT

Sharan Gunn
Purchasing Agent
100 E. Weatherford St.
Room 303
Ft. Worth, TX 76196
(817) 334-1195

KING COUNTY PURCHASING AGENCY

David Leach
Director of Purchasing
620 King County Administration Bldg.
500 4th Ave.
Seattle, WA 98104
(206) 344-4100

COUNTY OF HONOLULU

Haruo Shigezawa
Director of Purchasing
Purchasing Division
Dept. of Finance
Honolulu Halle
Honolulu, HI 96813
(808) 523-4616

COUNTY OF FRANKLIN

Bob Baumbartner
Director of Purchasing
410 S. High
Columbus, OH 43215
(614) 462-3322

COUNTY OF MIDDLESEX

Carol Kelley
Director of Purchasing
40 Thorndike St.
East Cambridge, MA 02141
(617) 494-4000

COUNTY OF HENNEPIN

Bill Binger
Director of Purchasing
Hennepin County Purchasing
300 S. 6th Street
Minneapolis, MN 55487-0225
(612) 348-3181

COUNTY OF ST. LOUIS

Rita M. Kirkland
Director of Purchasing
1200 Market St., Room 324
St. Louis, MO 63103
(414) 278-4223

COUNTY OF INDIANAPOLIS-MARION

Stephen Millspaugh
Director of Purchasing
1522 City–County Building
Indianapolis, IN 46204
(317) 236-3200

COUNTY OF FAIRFAX

Larry Wellman
Director of Purchasing
4100 Chain Bridge Road
Fairfax, VA 22030
(703) 246-3201

COUNTY OF CLAYTON

Bruce Kendrick
Director of Purchasing
41 S. Central
Clayton, MO 63105
(314) 889-2000

COUNTY OF MILWAUKEE

Daniel H. Kazmierczak
Purchasing Administrator
9508 Watertown Plank Road
Wauwatosa, WI 53226
(317) 236-3200

COUNTY OF SHELBY

Harold Lawler
Director of Purchasing
160 N. Mid-America Mall
Suite 1109
Memphis, TN 38103
(901) 576-4360

THE HUNDRED LARGEST SCHOOL DISTRICTS

The following is a list of more than 100 of the largest school districts in the United States with names, addresses, phone numbers, and contacts. Each of these school districts has a minimum population of 10,000 students. They are only a small portion of the more than 15,000 school districts in the United States, but because of their size they have enormous buying potential.

CALIFORNIA

Los Angeles Unified School District
1425 S. San Pedro
Los Angeles, CA 90051
Robert Haley, (213) 742-7151

San Francisco Unified School District
1000 Selby Street
San Francisco, CA 94124
John Carriere, (415) 824-5880

San Jose Unified School District
250 Stockton
San Jose, CA 95126
Dick Niblock, (408) 998-6000

San Diego School District
2351 Cardinal Lane
San Diego, CA 92123
Cordilla Mendoza, (619) 234-8701

Sacramento City School
P.O. Box 2271
Sacramento, CA 95810
Betty Willett, (916) 454-8011

Glendale Unified School District
223 North Jackson
Glendale, CA 91206
Benny Lorenz, (818) 241-3111

Garden Grove School District
10331 Stanford Ave.
Garden Grove, CA 92640
Martha Row, (714) 638-6000

Anaheim School District
501 Crescent Way
Anaheim, CA 92801
Fred Dagne, (714) 999-3511

Antelope Valley Union High School District
45024 N. Third Street East
Lancaster, CA 93535
Sharon Orona, (805) 948-7655

Oakland Unified School District
900 High Street
Oakland, CA 94601
Dean Riley, (415) 836-8261

Whittier School District
9407 S. Painter
Whittier, CA 90605
Shirley Murphey, (213) 698-8121

FLORIDA

Pinellas County School Board
P.O. Box 4688
Clearwater, FL 34618
G. Clark, (813) 442-1171

Palm Beach County Schools
1901 NW 16th St.
Belle Glade, FL 33430
M. Little, (305) 996-4900

Lee County School District
2055 Central Ave.
Fort Meyers, FL 33901
Michael Bowen, (813) 334-1102

Dade County South Area
9040 W. 79th St.
Miami, FL 33156
(305) 595-7022

Dade County North Central Area
1080 La Baron Drive
Miami Springs, FL 33166
(305) 885-2543

Broward County School District
P.O. Box 5408
Ft. Lauderdale, FL 33312
Adrian Villares, (305) 765-6000

Dade County School District
1450 NE Second Ave.
Miami, FL 33132
Dr. Richard Hinds, (305) 376-1000

Orange County Public Schools
P.O. Box 271
Orlando, FL 32802
James Calvin, (305) 422-3200

GEORGIA

Atlanta Public Schools
210 Pryor Street
Atlanta, GA 30335
Ms. M. Andrews, (404) 827-8787

Savannah–Chatam County School District
208 Bull Street
Savannah, GA 31401
William Wise, (912) 651-7000

ILLINOIS

Springfield School District 186
1900 W. Monroe St.
Springfield, IL 62704
Dr. James Chenry, (217) 525-3000

Chicago Public Schools
1819 W. Pershing Rd.
Chicago, IL 60609
Martin Lacny, (312) 890-8000

East St. Louis School District 189
1005 State Street
East St. Louis, IL 62201
Donald Allen, (618) 875-8800

Waukegan School District 60
1201 N. Sheridan Rd.
Waukegan, IL 60085
Gerry Yeggy, (312) 336-3100

Township High School District 214
799 W. Kensington Rd.
Mt. Prospect, IL 60056
John Swanson, (312) 259-5300

INDIANA

Indianapolis School District
120 East Walnut Street
Indianapolis, IN 46204
Rodney Black, (317) 266-4411

IOWA

Des Moines Independent School District
1800 Grand Ave.
Des Moines, IA 50307
Arch Rohden, (515) 242-7911

KANSAS

Wichita Unified School District
428 South Broadway
Wichita, KS 67702
Dr. Martin Hartley, (316) 833-2000

Shawnee Mission District 512
7235 Antioch
Shawnee Mission, KS 66204
B. Hodges, (913) 831-1900

KENTUCKY

Jefferson County Schools
P.O. Box 34020
Louisville, KY 40232
George Simpson, (502) 456-3357

LOUISIANA

Orleans Parish School District
4100 Touro St.
New Orleans, LA 70122
Fred Palumbo, (504) 286-2700

Calcasieu Parish School District
P.O. Box 800
Lake Charles, LA 70602
Wayne Richard, (318) 433-6321

East Baton Rouge Parish District
P.O. Box 2950
Baton Rouge, LA 70821
Ms. Lillian Harrison, (504) 922-5400

MARYLAND

Washington County School District
P.O. Box 730
Hagerstown, MD 21740
Charles Plummer, (301) 791-4000

Baltimore County School District
6901 N. Charles Street
Randall Town, MD 21204
William Miller, (301) 494-4186

Ann Arundel County School District
2644 Riva Rd.
Annapolis, MD 21401
Eugene White, Sr., (301) 224-5000

Baltimore City School District
200 W. North Ave.
Baltimore, MD 21202
Howard Hartsfield, (301) 396-8700

Montgomery County Schools
850 Hungerford Drive
Rockville, MD 20850
Jess Graham, (301) 279-3000

Prince George's County Schools
P.O. Box 120
Upper Marlboro, MD 20772
Ms. Patricia Palmer, (301) 952-6000

MICHIGAN

Dearborn Public School District
4824 Lois Avenue
Dearborn, MI 48126
John Waldner, (313) 582-3010

Warren Consolidated Schools
31300 Anita Drive
Warren, MI 48093
John Hamm, (313) 977-6800

Grand Rapids School District
143 Bostwick Ave. N.E.
Grand Rapids, MI 49503
James Pitcher, (616) 456-4700

Lansing Public School District
519 W. Kalamazoo St.
Lansing, MI 48933
Dr. David Smith, (517) 374-4000

Saginaw City School District
550 Millard St.
Saginaw, MI 48607
Richard Powell, (517) 776-0200

Detroit Public School District
5057 Woodward
Detroit, MI 48202
Sterling Poole, (313) 494-1000

Livonia Public School District
15125 Farmington Rd.
Livonia, MI 48154
Eileen Urich, Purchasing (313) 523-8800

Ann Arbor Public School District
P.O. Box 1188
Ann Arbor, MI 48106
Robert Moseley, (313) 994-2234

MINNESOTA

Duluth School District
Lake Avenue & Second St.
Duluth, MN 55802
Peter Willboxon, (218) 723-4150

Rochester School District
615 7th St. NW
Rochester, MN 55902
Dr. James Sheehan, (507) 285-8571

Minneapolis School District
807 NE Broadway
Minneapolis, MN 55413
Raymond Buttschau, (612) 627-2050

Bloomington School District
8900 Portland Ave.
Bloomington, MN 55420
Jerry Vott, (612) 887-9223

St. Paul Independent School District
360 Colborne St.
St. Paul, MN 55102
Joseph Hauwiller, (612) 293-5150

MISSOURI

Kansas City School District
1211 McGee Street
Kansas City, MO 64106
Dr. Roger Gaunt, (816) 221-7565

St. Louis City School District
911 Locust Street
St. Louis, MO 63101
John Archetko, (314) 231-3720

Hazelwood School District
15955 New Haus Ferry
Florissant, MO 63031
Marvin Hahn, (314) 921-4450

NEBRASKA

Lincoln Public School District
P.O. Box 82889
Lincoln, NE 68501
James Gallagher, (402) 475-1081

NEW JERSEY

Middletown Township School District
59 Tindall Rd.
Middletown, NJ 07748
Paul Bennett, (201) 671-3850

Newark School District
2 Cedar Street
Newark, NJ 07102
Norman Jefferies, (201) 733-7333

Elizabeth School District
500 North Broad Street
Elizabeth, NJ 07207
Dr. Louis Reale, (201) 558-3000

Jersey City School District
346 Claremont Ave.
Jersey City, NJ 07305
Ms. J. Cusmano, (201) 915-6404

Hamilton Township School District
90 Park Ave.
Trenton, NJ 08690
L. Treverio, (609) 890-3717

Edison Township School District
100 Municipal Ave.
Edison, NJ 08817
John Thomas, (201) 287-4400

Trenton School District
108 N. Clinton Ave.
Trenton, NJ 08609
Thomas Mitchell, (609) 989-2400

Cherry Hill School District
P.O. Box 5015
Cherry Hill, NJ 08034
Edward Roma, (609) 429-5600

NEW MEXICO

Albuquerque School District
725 University Blvd. S.E.
Albuquerque, NM 87106
Bobby Richardson, (505) 842-3771

NEW YORK

New York City Community School District
665 W. 182 Street
New York, NY 10033
Wm. Freitard, (212) 927-7777

New York City Community School District 31
211 Daniel Low Terrace
Staten Island, NY 10301
C. Cugni, (718) 447-3300

New York City Community School District 07
501 Courtland Ave.
Bronx, NY 10451
John Lichtman, (212) 292-0481

New York City High School District Bronx
3000 E. Tremont St.
Bronx, NY 10461
Dr. Simon Duchan, (212) 892-9926

New York City Community School District 02
210 E. 33rd St.
New York, NY 10016
Maria Rehhausser, (212) 481-1640

New York City Community School District 05
433 W. 123rd St.
New York, NY 10027
Pearl Green (212) 690-5841

New York Community School District 06
665 W. 182nd St.
New York, NY 10003
Dr. Martin Miller, (212) 927-7777

New York City Community School District 28
108-55 69 Ave.
Forest Hills, NY 11375
Marilyn Eslofsky, (718) 830-3230

New York City High School District Brooklyn
1600 Avenue L
Brooklyn, NY 11203
Donald Roth, (718) 258-4826

New York City Community School District
221-10 Jamaica Ave.
Queens Village, NY 11429
J. Schondorf, (718) 740-1000

New York City Public Schools
110 Livingston Street
Brooklyn, NY 11201
Jerry Posman, (718) 935-2000

Yonkers Public School District
145 Palme Rd.
Yonkers, NY 10710
(914) 963-4567

Rochester City School District
131 W. Broad Street
Rochester, NY 14608
W. O'Connell, (716) 325-4560

Buffalo Public School District
712 City Hall
Buffalo, NY
Ed Korzelius, (716) 842-3161

Syracuse City School District
725 Hairson St.
Syracuse, NY 13210
Leslie McCormick, (315) 425-4499

New York City High School District, Queens
105-25 Horace Harding Blvd.
Corona, NY 11368
Ms. Elaine Kornbluh, (718) 592-4496

NORTH CAROLINA

Guilford County School District
120 Franklin St.
Greensboro, NC 27402
Howard Cross, (919) 271-0700

OHIO

Dayton City School District
348 W. First Street
Dayton, OH 45402
Daniel Carozza, (513) 461-3000

Youngstown City School District
P.O. Box 550
Youngstown, OH 44501
Lawrence Markasky, (216) 744-6900

Cincinnati City School District
230 E. Ninth Street
Cincinnati, OH 45202
Harold Flaherty, (513) 369-4000

Akron City School District
70 N. Broadway
Akron, OH 44308
Wm. James, (216) 434-1661

Cleveland City School District
1380 E. Sixth Street
Cleveland, OH 44114
Warren Riebe, (216) 574-8000

Columbus City School District
270 East State Street
Columbus, OH 43215
James Robison, (614) 225-2600

OKLAHOMA

Tulsa Independent School District
P.O. Box 470208
Tulsa, OK 74147
Dr. Roland Bowens, (918) 745-6800

PENNSYLVANIA

Philadelphia School District
Parkway at 21st Street
Philadelphia, PA 19103
Myron Kessler, (215) 299-7000

Pittsburgh School District
341 S. Bellefield Avenue
Pittsburgh, PA 15213
Daniel McConachie, (412) 622-3730

SOUTH CAROLINA

Berkeley County School District
P.O. Box 608
Moncks Corner, SC 29461
Mike Ratten, (803) 761-8600

TENNESSEE

Metropolitan School District
2601 Bransford Ave.
Nashville, TN 37204
L. Biggs, (615) 259-8419

Shelby County School District
160 S. Hollywood
Memphis, TN 38112
John Meeks, (901) 458-7561

TEXAS

North East Independent School District
10333 Broadway
San Antonio, TX 78217
Dr. Joseph Burchard, (512) 657-8600

Corpus Christi Independent School District
P.O. Box 110
Corpus Christi, TX 78403
Tom Robertson, (512) 888-7911

Brownsville Independent School District
1102 East Madison St.
Brownsville, TX 78520
Eduardo Hernandez, (512) 546-3101

Cypress Fairbanks School District
P.O. Box 692003
Houston, TX 77269
Norman Cunningham, (713) 469-7320

Fort Bend Independent School District
16431 Lexington Blvd.
Sugarland, TX 77487
Frank Dzierranowski, (713) 980-1300

Houston Independent School District
3830 Richmond Ave.
Houston, TX 77027
Clarence Smith, (713) 623-5011

Garland Independent School District
P.O. Box 461547
Garland, TX 75046
Ms. Lynn Rigg, (214) 494-8201

VIRGINIA

Richmond City School District
201 E. Brookland Park Blvd.
Richmond, VA 23222
Peggy Heath, (804) 780-7700

Roanoke City Public Schools
P.O. Box 13145
Roanoke, VA 24031
Richard Kelley, (703) 981-2381

WEST VIRGINIA

Kanawh County School District
200 Elizabeth St.
Charleston, WV 25311
Norman Richardson, (304) 348-7720

WASHINGTON, D.C.

District of Columbia School District
2400 Shannon Pl. NE
Washington, D.C. 20020
Charles Pollard, (202) 767-7065

District of Columbia School District
415 12th St. NW
Washington, D.C. 20004
Patsy Baker, (202) 724-4044

WISCONSIN

Madison Metropolitan District
545 W. Dayton St.
Madison, WI 53703
Chris Hanson, (608) 266-6270

Milwaukee School District
P.O. Drawer 10K
Milwaukee, WI 53201
Elroy Schneider, (414) 475-8393

INDEX